The Future of
Technology Management
and the
Business Environment

The Future of Technology Management and the Business Environment

Lessons on Innovation, Disruption, and Strategy Execution

Alfred Marcus

Publisher: Paul Boger
Editor-in-Chief: Amy Neidlinger
Executive Editor: Jeanne Levine
Development Editor: Natasha Wolmers
Cover Designer: Alan Clements
Managing Editor: Kristy Hart
Senior Project Editor: Lori Lyons
Copy Editor: Gill Editorial Services
Proofreader: Debbie Williams
Indexer: Erika Millen
Senior Compositor: Gloria Schurick
Manufacturing Buyer: Dan Uhrig

© 2016 by Pearson Education, Inc.

Old Tappen, New Jersey 07675

For information about buying this title in bulk quantities, or for special sales opportunities (which may include electronic versions; custom cover designs; and content particular to your business, training goals, marketing focus, or branding interests), please contact our corporate sales department at corpsales@pearsoned.com or (800) 382-3419.

For government sales inquiries, please contact governmentsales@pearsoned.com.

For questions about sales outside the U.S., please contact international@pearsoned.com.

Company and product names mentioned herein are the trademarks or registered trademarks of their respective owners.

Printed in the United States of America

First Printing December 2015

ISBN-10: 0-13-399613-1
ISBN-13: 978-0-13-399613-5

Pearson Education LTD.
Pearson Education Australia PTY, Limited.
Pearson Education Singapore, Pte. Ltd.
Pearson Education Asia, Ltd.
Pearson Education Canada, Ltd.
Pearson Educación de Mexico, S.A. de C.V.
Pearson Education—Japan
Pearson Education Malaysia, Pte. Ltd.

Library of Congress Control Number: 2015951698

To my wife, my two sons, David and Ariel;
to Massoud Amin, director of the Technological Leadership Institute (TLI) at the
University of Minnesota, who describes himself as "a happy geek on a mission with
expertise in complex systems, energy, defense, pioneering smart self-healing grid,
CIP security, and resilience"; and to all among us who seek peace in a time of turbulence.

Contents-at-a Glance

Contents

Acknowledgments

I would like to acknowledge my colleagues and my students. At the University of Minnesota Carlson School of Management, I have learned about innovation from Andrew Van de Ven; about strategy from Aks Zaheer, Myles Shaver, Mary Benner, Aseem Kaul, and Anne Cohen; about entrepreneurship from Shaker Zahra, Harry Sapienza, and Dan Forbes; about the environment of business from Iain Maitland, Sri Zaheer, Joel Waldfogel, Paul Vaaler, Gurneeta Singh, Jiao Luo, Russel Funk, and Sunasair Dutta; and about timing from Stu Albert. My sincere hope is that the timing of this book is right.

At the Technological Leadership Institute, which is part of College of Science and Engineering at the University of Minnesota, I have learned from the director, Massoud Amin, to whom this book is dedicated, and from Lockwood Carlson, Kirk Froggat, Steve Kelley, and Brian Isle. At the Technion in Haifa, where I teach in the spring mini-semester in the MBA program, I have learned from Eitan Naveh, Mia Erez, Dovev Lavie, Ella Meron-Spektor, Erev Ido, Avi Shtub, and Ella Glickson. The many outstanding MBA and Masters of Technology students at the University of Minnesota and the Technion have inspired me to think deeply about technology. I am also indebted to the colleagues with whom I have done research in areas related to technology, including Ari Ginsberg at NYU Stern, Joel Malen at Hitotsubashi University of Innovation Research Japan, Adam Fremeth at Ivey Business School Canada, Mazhar Islam at Tulane University, Susan K. Cohen at the Katz School of Business University of Pittsburgh, J. Alberto Aragon-Correa at University of Surrey, and Hans Rawhouser and Michael Cummings at University of Nevada Las Vegas.

I have had the good fortune of living full time in Minnesota, with its thriving established business sector, and part-time in Israel, with its aspiring entrepreneurial business sector. The great companies in both these places have provided me with many of my ideas about technology. Merav Lefkowitz, who helped me edit this book, deserves a very special thanks for the superb work she did. My wife, Judy, always inspires me with her care for my physical, psychological, and intellectual well-being, her patience, and her insights about current affairs. My son, David, who is co-editor of Dissent and teacher of history at Columbia, and my son Ariel, who is a Spotify data scientist, have brought me fresh views about technology's promise and pitfalls. The world in which they live is so different from the world in which I grew up largely because of technology. I also want to thank Jeanne Levine of Pearson for encouraging me to do this project, Natasha Wolmers of Pearson for commenting on earlier drafts, and Lori Lyons for moving the manuscript through the production process.

About the Author

Alfred A. Marcus is the Edson Spence Chair of Strategy and Technological Leadership at the University of Minnesota, Carlson School of Management and the Center for Technological Leadership. He is the author or co-author of many books, including *Innovations in Sustainability* published by Cambridge University Press; *Management Strategy*, published by McGraw Hill; *Strategic Foresight*, published by Palgrave MacMillan; and *Big Winners and Big Losers*, published by Pearson. His articles have appeared in the *Strategic Management Journal, Academy of Management Journal, Academy of Management Review, California Management Review, Business and Politics, Business and Society*, and *Organization Science*, among other places.

His Ph.D. is from Harvard, and he has undergraduate and graduate degrees from the University of Chicago. Besides teaching in the Carlson School and Technological Leadership Institute at the University of Minnesota, Professor Marcus teaches in the Industrial Engineering Department in the MBA program in the Technion in Israel. He also has taught management courses in France, Norway, Hungary, the Czech Republic, Romania, and Costa Rica.

Professor Marcus has consulted or worked with many corporations, including 3M, Corning, Excel Energy, Medtronic, General Mills, and IBM. He was involved in a multinational research project sponsored by the NSF involving companies in the United States, Finland, Israel, and India. He did a sabbatical year at the MIT Sloan School in Boston. Prior to the joining Minnesota's faculty, he taught at the University of Pittsburgh Graduate School Of Business and was a research scientist at the Battelle Human Affairs Research Centers in Seattle, Washington.

Introduction

Technology is both the cause of many of the world's problems and the best hope for their cure. All the classical economists of the late 18th and early 19th centuries, including Adam Smith, David Ricardo, and John Stuart Mill, stressed the importance of technological changes. Thomas Malthus's pessimism that runaway population growth would lead to increasing misery as the world's population expanded more rapidly than the food supply proved wrong because technological changes stayed ahead of population growth.

Prosperity is closely linked to technological advances. Technology is critical to the world's continued economic growth. It provides the knowledge to convert the factors of production into goods and services. It also gives rise to an efficient division of labor, improves productivity, and permits the accumulation of capital. In his book *The Long Wave Cycle*, the Russian economist Nikolai Kondratiev (1892–1938) maintained that economic progress took place not linearly, but in long waves, each of them lasting about half a century.[1] Each wave had periods of prosperity, recession, depression, and recovery.

In *Capitalism, Socialism, and Democracy*, the Austrian economist Joseph Schumpeter connected technological innovations to the waves of economic growth.[2] Schumpeter's argument was that technological change was a series of explosions in which one set of technologies replaced another (see Exhibit 1.1). The first period (1782–1845) was marked by major innovations in steam power and textiles; the second (1845–1892) was marked by major innovations in railroads, iron, coal, and construction; and the third period (1892–1948) was characterized by major innovations in electrical power, automobiles, chemicals, and steel.

Exhibit I.1 Waves of Innovation

1845–1892	Railroads, iron, coal, construction
1892–1948	Electrical power, automobiles, chemicals, steel
1948–1973	Aerospace, pharmaceuticals, petrochemicals, synthetic and composite materials
1973–present	Information technology, medical technology, genetics, alternative energy, artificial intelligence, the material sciences, and nanotechnology

The Next Set of Breakthroughs

From where will the next set of breakthroughs come? The American sociologist Daniel Bell has proposed, in his book *The Coming of Post-Industrial Society: A Venture in Social Forecasting*, that the period since 1973 has been one of post-industrialism,[3] in which ideas are more important than the material forces that dominated previous periods of economic growth. In this era, information technology (IT), medical technology, genetics, alternative energy, and advances in artificial intelligence, material sciences, and nano-technology are dominant forces.

The Information Revolution

The information revolution has made it possible to disseminate knowledge instanta-neously around the globe, which gives the rise to virtual communities that create and enable an expanded international economy. With massive digitization, almost limitless storage in the cloud, and ubiquitous mobility, the information revolution has trans-formed how people learn, communicate, shop, travel, and socialize. The colossal data analytic capabilities called big data now promise degrees of reliability, productivity, and system optimization that have never before been experienced in history.

Medical Technologies

Advances in medical technology are easing pain, eliminating many childhood diseases, and prolonging life. They facilitate the early detection and treatment of infectious dis-eases, the tracking of chronic diseases, the prevention of medical errors, and increased health care accuracy. The hope is that they will be able to lower health care costs as well.

Genetics

The new genetics, including the Human Genome project, provide the foundation for medical advances and for greater agricultural biotechnology that should allow the world to feed the nine to ten million people projected to inhabit the planet by 2050 using less land.

Alternative Energy

Renewable resources from the sun, wind, and plant material are starting to replace finite energy sources from coal, oil, and natural gas. Progress involving electric and other alternative vehicles has been made toward greater energy efficiency. On the horizon are smart appliances as well as a smarter electric grid.

Artificial Intelligence

With massive amounts of computational power, artificial intelligence is making deep inroads into machine learning and speech recognition. Because of biomimetic sensors, many tasks formerly carried out by human beings can be more reliably performed by computer–assisted machines.

Material Sciences and Nanotechnology

Advances in material sciences and nanotechnology have helped to produce computer memory that has greater speed. They also have generated designer alloys, ceramics, and polymers that provide for materials with super strength and other desirable properties.

Combined, and with their offshoots, these technologies offer great promise for bringing into being new economic growth and prosperity. Among other innovations, they enable wearable computers, the Internet of Things (IOT), targeted drug delivery, rapid bioassays, fuel cell cars, energy storage, advanced robotics, and 3D printing. These innovations may be the engines of growth and the sources for fulfilling employment for millions of people, or they may not be.

What This Book Is About

Their potential is what this book explores. These innovations face obstacles to their commercialization that must be managed by business firms and societies. From a commercial point of view, let alone a scientific and technical point of view, their success is not guaranteed. Their introduction involves risky decision-making.

As an unintended by-product of their introduction, these technologies can and do cause harm. Their widespread penetration, for example, does not guarantee job creation. They are likely to wipe out jobs as well as create them. They have both environmental and social costs. The servers that sustain the cloud are huge consumers of energy. Even the most well-intentioned new medical technology often has unforeseen side effects. This harm must be anticipated and prevented to the degree that it is possible without compromising society's willingness to take risks and make progress.

New technologies also offer tremendous potential for dealing with the most important societal challenges of this era. This era is characterized by cleavages between young and old, rich and poor, and scarcity and abundance. These technologies can address these issues constructively. They can play a role in easing these tensions, but they also can exacerbate them.

This book is about the foresight and strategic actions that are needed for technologies to play a positive rather than a negative role. It is about the pathways that have been taken to commercialize some of these technologies, how some of these pathways have been blocked, and how some of them have been opened. It is about the disruptions that organizations have faced as a result of technological innovations they did not expect and how they have dealt with these disruptions by altering their business strategies and executing novel strategies. This book depicts the stories of many companies and how they have confronted these issues. The purpose is to learn lessons from the experience of these companies.

The book is divided into four sections: Technology and Strategy, Managing Danger, The Environment of Technology, and Coping with Technological Disruptions. It is meant for practitioners and students, for those already well versed on the issues in the book and novices. The juxtaposition of the material found in this book is designed to generate new insights. Reflection on the material will yield takeaway lessons on innovation, disruption, and strategy execution, technology management, and the business environment for executives, practicing managers, and students. The sections in the book are best read in their entirety, but they can also be read separately. The five paired case studies in the last section of the book are ideal for executive, MBA, and undergraduate instruction in management of technology courses.

The material in this book is based on my more than thirty years of writing, teaching, and consulting in the areas of business strategy, ethics, and technology. I owe a great deal to my colleagues and to my students at the Technological Leadership Institute and Carlson School of Management at the University of Minnesota and the Technion Faculty of Industrial Engineering and Management.

Part I: Technology and Strategy

Chapter 1, "Technological Disruptions," starts with Schumpeter's idea that technology is a series of explosions and Bell's idea that the current era is one of post-industrialism. It discusses leading-edge technologies that may sustain economic growth in a post-industrial world.

Chapter 2, "Commercialization's Obstacles," goes into detail about the obstacles in commercializing leading-edge technologies. It provides stories of attempts to commercialize IT technologies, a medical technology to assist the hearing impaired, genetic technology with the aim to increase agricultural productivity, and an electric car to move the planet away from its dependence on fossil fuels. This chapter comments on the slow and arduous path to commercialization, the setbacks at many points, the uncertainty of government support, the inclination to undertake safe projects, and the need for determination, will, and persistence.

Chapter 3, "Hedging Uncertainty," is about how business organizations can manage the uncertain outcomes described in the previous chapter. It considers the use of trends, expert opinion, industry analysis, and historical analogies, and it elaborates on the value of using scenarios, the topic of one of my previous books, *Strategic Foresight: A New Look at Scenarios.*[4] It goes on to put forth a series of hedging strategies that organizations can use to deal with the uncertainty: gamble on the most probable outcome, take the robust route, delay until further clarity emerges, commit with fallbacks, and shape the future.

Part II: Managing Danger

The next part of this book deals with unanticipated consequences and the need to manage danger.

Chapter 4, "Dealing with Danger," focuses on two major industrial accidents—Bhopal and the Deepwater Horizon oil spill—and what went wrong. It highlights dilemmas in managing dangerous technologies, such as the cognitive limits of individuals, experts, and organizations. It expounds upon the issue of determining the value of a human life and extrapolating and making inferences from animal studies to humans.

Chapter 5, "Laws of Liability," focuses on major mishaps in introducing new medical technologies—Merck's Vioxx and Johnson and Johnson's DePuy all-metal hip replacement. In both instances, despite ample warning, these companies failed to inform patients about risks and danger and failed to recall the technology before patients had suffered immense damage. Both companies were sued and had to compensate the victims as well as pay large fines. Their reputations, as a consequence, suffered. This chapter examines the laws of liability in light of these two cases and traces its evolution toward harsh punitive actions and strict liability.

Part III: The Environment of Technology

Part III of the book highlights the way business organizations have responded to the challenges of the following three global divisions: those between (i) young and old, (ii) rich and poor, and (iii) energy scarcity and abundance. These fractures, among the most important features of the business environment, affect whether there will be global security, inequality, and sustainability. They provide opportunities for technologies and companies as well as presenting threats.

The topics discussed in Chapter 6 are "Old, Young, and Global Security." The rise of the elderly has led to efforts to find cures for Alzheimer's and other diseases, to reverse aging, and to improve quality of life during aging. A changing economy and changing job markets have made technology important for youth. They have given rise to a significant population of people who do not work in traditional jobs; they work from home and do freelance jobs. Conversely, the disillusion found among many young people in the world who do not have meaningful work has contributed to global violence and terror. It has stimulated companies that have developed counterterror methods that can assist in preventing the bloodshed.

Chapter 7, "Rich, Poor, and Global Inequality," discusses the technological opportunities that have been opened up at the top and at the bottom of the pyramid. Global inequality also has produced opportunities for companies. On the one hand, there are endless opportunities to develop technologies that serve the wealthy, protect their wealth, and perpetuate their standing in society. On the other hand, there are opportunities to develop technologies to uplift the poor by providing them with better housing, more drinkable water, enhanced access to health services, improved nutrition, employment, and business opportunities. At the top, hedge funds have developed sophisticated algorithms for trading that have enjoyed remarkable success but are only available to those who are already wealthy. At the bottom, on the other hand, many companies, often in collaboration with nonprofit organizations and governments, have heeded to call to introduce products and technologies that can help the poor.

Chapter 8, "Abundance, Scarcity, and Global Sustainability," considers the possibility of energy abundance brought about by advances in both finite fossil fuels and renewable energy as well as the issue of energy scarcity brought about by the failure to innovate in these areas.[5] It also considers in-between states in which the most dependable path to the future relies on either fossil fuels or renewable fuels, to the exclusion of the other. On the one hand, a review of technologies like fracking and unconventional methods of oil exploration and development demonstrates the continued promise of fossil fuels. On the other hand, major advances in energy efficiency, solar, wind, energy storage, and biofuels are also considered.

Part IV: Coping with Technological Disruptions

The final Part of the book focuses on pairs of companies operating in overlapping business segments that are confronted by technological disruptions. It discusses how they have coped and the challenges they still face in dealing with the threats to their businesses.

These chapters are presented as open-ended case studies that are meant for considering what these firms should do next. Most of these companies were pioneers in the IT revolution. They were early movers who did well with innovations they introduced or helped to introduce, like the microprocessor, the PC, Internet commerce, the sale of electronics, and the creation of content that can be viewed on the Internet. This Part includes chapters on Intel and AMD, Dell and Acer, Barnes & Noble and Amazon, Best Buy and Charles Schwab, and Disney and Time Warner.

A second wave in the IT revolution has gained momentum, threatening the business models that once made these firms very successful. This second phase is characterized by growing digitization; mobility; the commoditizing of older technologies; a move toward smartphones, tablets, and e-readers; increased reliance on the cloud; greater competition between Internet and brick and mortar sales venues; and streaming. These developments have led to the near-obsolescence of once-vibrant business segments like PCs, bookselling, electronic showrooms, movies, and cable television. Given this disruption, how should companies cope? How should they adjust their business models to new conditions they face, conditions brought about by these rapidly changing technologies?

Chapter 9, "Missing the Boat on Mobile: Intel and AMD," covers the consequences of these companies not responding to the challenge of mobile technologies. It asks the question of where they should turn to next.

Chapter 10, "From Mass Customizing to Mass Commodity: Dell and Acer," deals with the issue of the growing commoditization of PC sales, long the mainstay of these companies' business. What options do they now have?

Chapter 11, "Finding Growth and Profitability in Bookselling: Barnes & Noble and Amazon," explores the issue of declining profits and revenue in bookselling in light of the rise of digital devices like e-readers and changes in people's reading habits and bookselling practices. If these firms remain committed to bookselling, how can they innovate to stay profitable?

Chapter 12, "Escaping the Middle: Best Buy and Charles Schwab," delves into the uncomfortable positions in which Best Buy and Charles Schwab find themselves—not leaders in the high end of their businesses, a role other firms like Apple and Morgan Stanley have seized, yet also not leaders in the low end, a role they deliberately ceded to the likes of Walmart and e*Trade. How can they survive the dual threat of technological leaders above and below them?

Chapter 13, "Content for a New Age: Disney and Time Warner," deals with the consequences of the decline of cable TV channels, the most profitable divisions of Disney and Time Warner, in the face of increased preference for Internet streaming services, such as Netflix and Amazon Prime. How do these companies deal with this technological disruption?

In sum, this book takes up some of the most important problems in the future of technology management and business environment and provides important lessons on innovation, disruption, and strategy execution.

Endnotes

1. Nikolaï Kondratiev, *The Long Wave Cycle*. New York: Richardson & Snyder, 1984.

2. Joseph Schumpeter, *Capitalism, Socialism, and Democracy*. New York and London: Harper & Brothers Publishers, 1947.

3. Daniel Bell, *The Coming of Post-Industrial Society: A Venture in Social Forecasting*. New York: Basic Books, 1999.

4. Alfred Marcus, *Strategic Foresight: A New Look at Scenarios*. New York: Palgrave MacMillan, 2009.

5. Alfred Marcus, *Innovations in Sustainability: Fuel and Food*. Cambridge, UK: Cambridge University Press, 2015.

PART I

TECHNOLOGY AND STRATEGY

Technological Disruptions

Technological changes, according to Schumpeter, are like a series of explosions with innovations concentrating in specific sectors, or leading-edge industries that provide the momentum for future prosperity replacing each other in a regular, periodic way. Leading sectors propel economies forward; without them, economic growth would not be possible. According to Schumpeter, the process of technological transformation should be called "creative destruction,"[1] given that a set of superior technologies supplants inferior technologies and becomes dominant at their expense. The lagging sectors fall behind, and their time passes, while the new set of technologies surge ahead and, according to Schumpeter, spur economic renewal and revitalization.

In the world's industrial nations, a dynamic growth phase existed after the Second World War. However, by the start of 1970s, global growth slipped. The post-World War II boom in advanced industrial nations lost momentum. The need existed for a new set of advanced technologies.

The Powers of the Mind

Sociologist Daniel Bell has described the shift away from the technologies that dominated the postwar boom as post-industrialism. In this period, theoretical knowledge formed the source of innovation, while technically trained professionals became dominant and technological assessment played a leading role.

The powers of the mind gained ascendance over the brute force of things. Previously, economic activity was centered on physical labor, natural resources, and capital. Now, wealth in the form of physical resources is losing ground to wealth in the form of ideas. An example is the microchip, the key element in the emergence of information technology (IT); (see Chapter 9, "Missing the Boat on Mobile Technology: Intel and AMD"), where material costs constituted just 2 percent of production costs and most of the value came from the ideas for the design of the microchips. Other examples include medical technologies, genetics, alternative energy, artificial intelligence, material sciences, and nanotechnology. The main value is not in the materials, but in the ideas. This chapter briefly discusses the promise of these technologies, whereas the next chapter considers concrete examples of efforts to commercialize such technologies and the problems they have encountered.

Information Technology (IT)

The IT revolution has touched nearly every human endeavor. Internet usage has grown 183 percent since 2000 (see Exhibit 1.1). The number of Internet users increased tenfold from 1999 to 2013. In 2015, around 40 percent of the world's population had an Internet connection, and a wireless hotspot existed for each 150 persons.

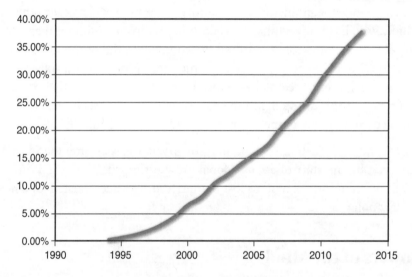

Exhibit 1.1 Growth in Percentage of People in the World Who Regularly Use the Internet

Data source: http://www.internetlivestats.com/internet-users/

The Internet changes the ways in which people socialize, relate, and do business. It has created virtual communities, via email, Facebook, LinkedIn, Twitter, and others. It has made telecommuting possible. Shopping, entertainment, and education are being done from people's homes. Opportunities exist for increased involvement in politics. Online dating is common. Interactive medicine has become common as well.

Smartphones are ubiquitous. In just one device, they integrate phones, personal data assistants, MP3 players, cameras, voice recorders, watches, calculators, and other functions. Computer use is expanding to many areas in which human intelligence previously was applied, such as driverless cars and automated medical procedures.

Thanks to enhanced computer power and performance, it has become possible to automate increasingly complex tasks. Manufacturing efficiencies are being accelerated as result of computerized controls. Although software that runs computers is not as creative as human beings, its reliability is greater and less mistake prone, which makes it preferred for routine tasks. The use of computers is growing as the programs that run them are becoming better at learning, adapting, and self-correcting.

The full promise of the IT revolution, however, has not yet been tapped. Among the trends that continue to be important are these:

- The ongoing digitization of audio, video, and film
- The spread of fiber optics that carry television, telephone, radio, and computer signals simultaneously and make rapid communications possible
- Expansion in the use of optical memory systems, such as disks, film, and barcodes
- Parallel processing, which permits many computers to be used simultaneously
- The evolution of chip technologies, which opens up the possibility for even more accelerated and powerful computers

It is not obvious which firms will take advantage of these opportunities. Their societal impact is considered in Chapter 6, "Old, Young, and Global Security," which covers the role they play in the fight against terror and in Chapter 7, "Rich, Poor, and Global Inequality," which portrays the role they play in perpetuating the world's wealth gaps.

Chapter 2, "Commercialization's Obstacles," discusses the case of Xerox, which failed to exploit technologies it had developed and missed out on the promise of the IT revolution. There are other examples that could be cited. Kodak, for instance, missed out on the digital revolution despite accumulating the technical skills to be a part of it. The inability of established businesses to take advantage of technologies they have mastered and know are coming is considered in Chapter 2.

Medical Technologies

Medical technology includes the procedures and equipment by which medical care is delivered. It has affected many medical fields. A prime example is the treatment of heart disease. Each decade from the 1970s to the present has seen successive treatment improvements:

- The 1970s introduced cardiac care units, lidocaine for irregular heartbeat, beta-blockers for lowering blood pressure, clot busters, and coronary artery bypass surgery.

- In the 1980s, there was increased use of blood-thinning agents and minimally invasive surgery.

- The 1990s saw drugs that were effective in inhibiting the formation of clots, stents to keep vessels open, and the implantation of defibrillators for irregular heartbeats.

- Since then, better tests for diagnosis are available, drug-eluting stents are in common use, and new drug strategies are centered on cholesterol-lowering statins.

Many doctors have replaced their stethoscopes with inexpensive, hand-held ultrasound scanners to detect heart problems. In the past, emergency room doctors had trouble distinguishing between bouts of heart failure and pneumonia. Now they have a blood test for B-type Natriuretic Peptide (BNP) secreted by a weakened heart muscle, which enables them to distinguish between these maladies. Although heart disease remains the leading cause of death in the U.S., overall mortality rates have fallen by almost half.

Another example of advances in technology that have changed outcomes is the treatment of preterm babies. In the 1950s, little could be done for them. However, by 1990, there were special ventilators, artificial pulmonary surfactants, and new methods of intensive care, which helped decrease mortality to a third of 1950s levels.

Surgery, too, has seen tremendous improvements. Advances have been made in surgical procedures such as angioplasty and in hip and joint replacements. Microwave scalpels equipped with lasers are replacing metal scalpels. Less invasive laparoscopic techniques have become common. Devices like MRIs and CT scanners are used commonly today. Enhanced electronic medical records systems now exist, facilitating the recording and transfer of information.

For humans with severed bones and defective hearts and lungs, bioelectricity has the potential to speed healing rates. Nerves, muscles, and glands can be stimulated to promote, repair, and restore healthy functioning, and the technique can be used as an alternative to addictive painkillers.

On the horizon are devices to provide individuals with instant health information and allow them to continuously monitor their health status. Blood sugar can be checked, sleep patterns analyzed, and people empowered with the tools to personalize their treatments and behavior on a real-time basis. Despite the advances in technology, their spread is often halted and takes longer than expected. Chapter 7 discusses the potential for finding a cure for Alzheimer's and reversing aging. The next chapter shows how hard it is to fully commercialize some of these technologies. Not all innovations are instantaneously and fully adopted, as illustrated by the story of cochlear implants.

Genetics

Genetic technology refers to efforts to understand gene expression, take advantage of genetic variation, and modify and transfer genes. Passed from one generation to another and found in all living organisms, genes are the coded instructions that organisms use to make proteins, which are the structures of all living things and which perform the functions that make life possible.

The genetic code of living organisms has been mapped for ongoing gene restructuring and remodeling. Genomics and molecular biology are laying the foundation for many advances. The integrated use of genetic diagnostics and treatment can help guide therapy. For example, diabetics who have problems making and secreting insulin can be distinguished from diabetics who react poorly to insulin and can be given custom treatments. Identifying genes and their functions can lead to the more efficient breeding of plants and animals, such as marker-assisted breeding, as the identification of desirable trait markers in genes speeds the selection process.

As scientists map the genome, they can discover and isolate disease-causing genes and identify treatments for inherited diseases like Alzheimer's and muscular dystrophy. It also gives them the ability to both predict diseases and create the treatments to fight them.

The genetic code also can be mapped to improve existing crops and create new ones. Scientists have developed seeds that resist pests and increase the nutrient content of foods, making them better for human and animal consumption. There are nearly 50,000 genes in a grain of rice. With this knowledge, scientists are trying to alter the nature of the rice so that it will be less sensitive to drought and disease. Using their knowledge of genetics, they can breed insects that attack the rice's main predators. Genetic technology has the promise to better feed the world's population.

Agricultural biotechnology may also be used to find ways to convert plant material into energy. Scientists are working on biogenetic material that can consume carbon dioxide. However, genetic technology is also controversial, and in some quarters it is met with stiff resistance that has slowed the pace of adoption. The case of Monsanto discussed in the next chapter illustrates this point. The dangers of technology and the ways societies and companies have evolved to manage these dangers are the main topic of Chapters 4 and 5.

Alternative Energy

Energy efficiency exists along with renewable energy sources like wind, solar, and bio-mass. By themselves and in combination with fuel cells, energy storage, geothermal energy, and nuclear energy, these renewal energy sources provide alternatives to fossil fuels like oil, coal, and natural gas. They address concerns spurred by fossil fuel use, such as the buildup of climate-changing gases in the atmosphere, the depletion of fossil fuel supply, and the vulnerability of nations that use fossil fuels because of security issues.[2]

There have been many advances in energy efficiency. Better software and computing technologies have improved the monitoring and control of energy use. LED lighting, which requires less energy use and is longer lasting than conventional incandescent and fluorescent lighting, has been developed. Superconductors carry and transfer electricity more efficiently and with fewer losses. They make it possible to build magnetic levitation trains and faster computer circuits that run on less energy, as well as more energy efficient advanced magnetic resonance imaging (MRI) machines.

Wind and solar power have become far less expensive than they once were. In many parts of the world, their costs are equal to, or lower than, other forms of electricity generation. Solar energy cells have been long available in pocket calculators and remote power applications. Though solar made up less than one percent of the electricity market in 2015, the International Energy Agency has projected it will be the world's most important source of energy by 2050.[3]

Lithium-ion batteries are current leaders in energy storage and are used across many applications from laptops to mobile phones to electric vehicles. With mass production, their price is likely to keep declining. Even with these advances, there have been struggles to commercialize alternative energy. In the next chapter, the effort to make energy-efficient, low-priced electric vehicles widely available is discussed, and Chapter 8 is devoted to the commercialization of renewable energy and energy efficiency technologies.

Artificial Intelligence, Material Sciences, and Nanotechnology

Working in tandem with the technologies previously mentioned are artificial intelligence, material sciences, and nanotechnology. Artificial intelligence has moved into many areas where human intelligence formerly was applied. Robots, now found in factories and homes alike, rely on a form of artificial intelligence and perform many complex, nonrepetitive tasks that humans once carried out.

In the material sciences, new materials are being constructed molecule by molecule and atom by atom using supercomputers in their design. These materials are lighter, stronger, and more resistant to heat than older materials. Many have found their way into automobiles, trucks, airplanes, and ships and made them more energy efficient. Automobiles use high-tech ceramics that are resistant to corrosion, wear, and high temperatures and make the engines leaner running. Lightweight and noncorrosive fiber-reinforced composites, which are stronger than steel, are found in buildings, bridges, and aircraft. New polymers are being created that will be used in products from garbage bags to tanks, from ball bearings and batteries to running shoes. Tailor-made enzymes for industrial use also are being produced that can assist in converting plant material into fuel. Nanotechnology holds out the promise for additional new materials (see Exhibit 1.2).

Exhibit 1.2   Applications of Nano-Technology

Information Technology	Advanced Chemicals
Photolithography, electronics, and opto-electronics	Catalysts
Quantum computing and telecommunications	Membranes and filtration
Medical	Coatings and paints
Detection, analysis, and discovery	Abrasives and lubricants
Drug delivery	Composites and structural materials
Prosthetics antimicrobial	**Aerospace and Defense**
Antiviral and antifungal agents	Weapons
Alternative Energy and Automotive	Surveillance
Fuel cells	Smart uniforms
Solar power	Life support
Rechargeable batteries (charged in under a minute)	
Power transmission	
Lighting and other forms of energy savings	
Structural materials and coatings	
Sensors	
Displays	
Catalytic converters and filters	
Fuel	
Electro-mechanical systems	

The Challenge of Commercialization

The technologies described have great promise. Already they are causing disruption. The next wave of innovation is giving birth to a post-industrial society that is less dependent on materials and force of *things* and more dependent on *ideas*. *Futurist Magazine* annually makes forecasts[4] about what is likely to take place next. Its forecasts have included innovations in IT (a more intelligent cloud), medical technology (handheld breathalyzers to diagnose disease), genetic technology (designer genes), alternative energy (cars that produce, rather than consume, power), and artificial intelligence (robot caregivers). The commercial appeal of these technologies surely is high, but they must overcome obstacles to their commercialization. The slow and arduous path of their commercialization is the subject of the next chapter.

Endnotes

1. Joseph Schumpeter, *Capitalism, Socialism, and Democracy*. New York: Kessinger Publishing, LLC, 2010.

2. Alfred Marcus, *Innovations in Sustainability: Fuel and Food*. Cambridge, UK: Cambridge University Press, 2015.

3. International Energy Agency, "How solar energy could be the largest source of electricity by mid-century." International Energy Agency. Sept. 29, 2014. http://www.iea.org/newsroomandevents/pressreleases/2014/september/how-solar-energy-could-be-the-largest-source-of-electricity-by-mid-century.html.

4. "Forecasts from The Futurist Magazine," World Future Society, 2015, Web. http://www.wfs.org/Forecasts_From_The_Futurist_Magazine.

2

Commercialization's Obstacles

Moving from the technical advances described in the previous chapter to commercialization is often rough. Invention is simply the creation of ideas in a laboratory. Innovation is ideas' wide-scale commercial adoption. Innovators, seeing the opportunities for commercial gain, must bring these two together—that is, take ideas from the laboratory and put them to wide-scale use. The ideas innovators endeavor to exploit are supposed to evolve rapidly through stages of market introduction, growth, and product maturity. However, most ideas do not pass quickly through these stages. Many show initial promise and fail. Others that take off may do so slowly.

The path to commercialization can be tortuous. This chapter illustrates this slow path with examples from the technologies introduced in Chapter 1: information technology (IT), medical technology, genetics, and alternative energy.

Fumbling the Future at Xerox: IT

Xerox fumbled the future of IT.[1] Organizations like Xerox are successful because of routines and processes that solve existing challenges and problems. They focus on solving problems in the areas in which they are familiar. It is hard for them to modify their routines because relationships with existing customers discourage them from allocating resources to the development and implementation of unfamiliar new technologies and business models. Their capabilities make it difficult for them to move in new directions.

Researchers stretching back at least far as Schumpeter have emphasized the role of entrepreneurial ventures, as opposed to incumbents, as innovators and agents of technological change.[2] Entrepreneurs do not have established routines and existing customers to satisfy, which prevents them from being committed to new technologies and gives them the flexibility to adapt according to evolving developments.

In the 1960s, Xerox's Palo Alto Research Center (PARC) had outstanding research personnel—at the time almost half of the world's top 100 computer scientists. By 1975, the company had developed the first personal computer with a mouse and graphical user interface (GUI). The interface had windows, icons, and pull-down menus. PARC scientists used the products they created in their daily work. They developed computer-generated graphics, invented laser printing, and created an Ethernet local area network (LAN). They pioneered most of what went into the PC and the systems associated with it.

However, Xerox's top management team could not see the company as a computer company. They conceptualized it as being in the office copier business. Their concern was that Xerox would not be able to transfer PARC's innovations into commercially successful products.

The culture at Xerox's New York state headquarters clashed with the culture in its West Coast research center. Years later, Xerox still was in the copying business, and even in this business, which it should have dominated, its rivals had overtaken it with more reliable, technologically superior products.

As an adolescent in Silicon Valley, Steve Jobs picked up many of PARC's ideas. Jobs commercialized many ideas originally designed by Xerox's scientists.

Medical Technology: Cochlear Implants

The commercialization of new products represents the endpoint of a lengthy process. The technologies upon which new products are based develop over long periods of time as a result of the actions of numerous private and public sector actors. It is only in the final stages of innovation, after new technologies have been sufficiently developed, that companies attract customers in sufficient numbers to be profitable. Cochlear implants provide an example that illustrates the long and windy road to commercialization.[3]

Cochlear implants were based on the idea of using electricity to bring hearing to the deaf. This technology appeared to have the potential to transform the life of the hearing impaired. In the past, only individuals with residual hearing, who had been fit with hearing aids, could be helped. Profoundly deaf people had no hope of a technological fix.

Private firms attempted to commercialize cochlear implants beginning in the late 1970s. The research underlying the development of this technology began decades earlier, but it faced many barriers to commercialization:

- Basic research was a long process conducted by scientists—in research labs throughout the world—who had little contact with commercial companies.

- These scientists had to make breakthroughs not in one, but in many different disciplines.

- The device needed a highly committed champion if it was going to become a commercial product.

- The multiple developmental paths it took were an impediment to rapid commercialization.

- Private firms involved in the cochlear implant's development did not cooperate with each other.

- Medicare reimbursement depended on endorsement from physicians' professional associations.

- FDA approval had to be obtained.

- Early adopters had to be enthusiastic about the product's benefits.

- Costs had to be driven down so that adopters could afford the product.

- Concerns about the product's safety and efficacy had to be alleviated.

- Auxiliary services to select users and support them had to be developed.

- The original companies involved in product development needed staying power.

- New companies did not have the reach to diffuse the product widely.

These impediments are not unusual in the lifetime of medical technologies and are worth examining further.

Basic Research in Diverse Labs

The idea of using electricity to bring hearing to the deaf dates back 200 years to the experiments of the Italian scientist Alessandro Volta, who first studied the effects of electrical stimulation on the ear. Physicians and researchers from around the world carried out basic research on this idea. The pioneers in the field, however, were associated with universities and teaching clinics, not commercial companies. Their concern was not commercial gain. None worked exclusively on this technology. Most of their work was dedicated to furthering basic knowledge about the science of hearing. They had little interest in bringing products to the market and making them widely available to customers.

Breakthroughs in Other Disciplines

Breakthroughs in many different disciplines had to take place before a workable cochlear implant device could be made. The extended gestation period for the technology lasted more than 40 years. Private companies, which may have had an interest in commercialization, did not fund this research; the financing came mainly from the government and universities.

A Highly Committed Champion

Researchers first reported that electrical stimulation of the auditory nerve could lead to hearing in the 1930s, but it was not until the 1950s that, in France, experiments were carried out involving these stimulations. A highly committed champion was needed for the technology. William House, the founder of the House Ear Institute in Los Angeles, took on this role. House's energy and dedication were needed to bring together innovations from many disciplines and scientists and create the first workable device. Nonetheless, it was not until 1961 that he performed the first cochlear implant operation by a clinical physician in the United States. Cochlear implants were not recognized as possessing commercial promise until an international conference on the electrical stimulation of the acoustic nerve took place in 1973.

Multiple Developmental Paths

Research in the 1970s led to a proliferation of development paths, which could take the commercialization in different directions. Implants could be extra-cochlear, meaning that the device's electrodes did not enter the cochlea (inner ear), or they could be intra-cochlear, meaning that the electrodes did enter. Implants could consist of a percutaneous plug, in which the inner ear was reached by a direct channel through the cranium, or they could be designed in a way that provided for access to the inner ear by means of magnetic couplings. Some of the early devices were single channel. Others were multichannel.

Private Firms' Failure to Cooperate

Private firms only become actively involved in the late 1970s. Companies such as 3M, Storz, Symbian, Nucleus, and Biostem pursued separate developmental paths and initiated their own proprietary research and development (R&D). Before doing the research, they had to demonstrate that the technology had commercial potential. While doing the research, they reassured funders that a payoff was likely; otherwise, cochlear implants faced elimination from corporate research budgets. Each company created its own cochlear implant program and became a competitor. Efforts to establish cooperative relations among firms did not work out because they pursued separate technological paths. Each firm had ties with different academic institutions to provide access to the basic knowledge to carry out an applied research program. The firms competed with one another in exploring the different paths to commercialization.

Professional Endorsement

Not until 1983 did the American Medical Association give cochlear implants its official endorsement. The American Speech, Language, and Hearing Association then created a special ad hoc committee that dealt with the device. The American Academy of Otolaryngology-Head and Neck Surgery only recognized the technology's potential in

1985. Without American Academy of Otolaryngology recognition, the device could not secure Medicare reimbursement.

FDA Approval

All medical products are subject to review and approval by the FDA, a process that can take from three to five years. Before clinical tests are conducted on humans, the FDA requires that they be done on animals. Based on the animal test results, the agency can decide to grant the right to carry out tests on humans. The FDA then grants a number of clinical sites the right to conduct human testing. If human tests suggest that a procedure is safe and effective and it has been shown that the device makers are engaged in good manufacturing practices, the FDA may grant premarket approval.

Cochlear implants faced a major barrier to FDA approval in 1985 when the U.S. Office of Health Technology Assessment (OHTA) found that implantation in children could result in inner-ear damage. The FDA's approval was limited to single-channel devices for categories other than children. The FDA did not approve use of the device for children and was not ready to approve the more complicated multichannel version.

Lack of Enthusiasm from the User Community

After FDA approval, the market for the device did not develop as quickly as companies pursuing commercialization had hoped. The deaf community had objections. Many in this community relied on sign language. Because of extensive involvement in schools, social activities, and other institutions, they were reluctant to change. Through much effort, they had successfully adapted to living in a world without sound. They feared entering a world of sound and the consequences this change would have on the deaf and deaf-supportive community.

High Costs

The procedure could cost users as much as $100,000. Third-party reimbursement was essential, but the Medicare coverage might not be adequate. Potential candidates had to consider the high costs in addition to the benefits. Because it was unclear that the benefits outweighed the costs to many in the deaf community, sales of cochlear implant devices did not grow quickly. Due to the high cost, the majority of the estimated 300,000 people who received the implants in the world were in developed countries.

Safety and Efficacy Concerns

Marketing of the device was hampered by concerns about safety and efficacy. Surgery was necessary for the installation of cochlear implants, which carried a risk of inner ear damage. After implantation, electrodes could not be easily replaced without further risk.

Because of these concerns, some physicians did not promote the device. The lack of physician endorsement posed a marketing dilemma for companies that sold the implants. What picture of what the device could accomplish should they portray to potential adopters?

Auxiliary Services

The firms that sold the devices had to create ancillary services. They needed assistance in identifying the people who would benefit. It was not easy to diagnose whether candidates for the procedure would benefit because they exhibited a wide range of hearing defects. After implantation, patients needed rehabilitation. They did not hear the same way as people with normal hearing, nor were they experienced with the world of hearing. Audiologists, speech and language pathologists, psychologists, and otologists had to work with patients who received implants to recognize and interpret sounds.

Withdrawal

Because of the slow development of the market, the companies originally involved with the technology withdrew. They did not perceive sufficient sales to justify their continued commitment. Although their researchers argued for continuing to work on a technology they considered promising, the original companies that laid the groundwork for the technology left the industry and took with them valuable knowledge.

New Entrants

New entrants came into the industry. As of 2013, three companies had devices approved for use in the United States. None had been original developers. These companies were an Australian firm, Cochlear Limited; a U.S. firm, Advanced Bionics; and an Austrian company, MED-E. Outside the United States, Neurelec of France and Nurotron of China sold the device.

This story is not atypical. The gestation of technologies can last for years. Companies often lose patience and abandon technologies before they achieve full commercial success.

Genetics: Agricultural Productivity

Monsanto was an established company new to the science of genetics when it decided to take the plunge into agricultural productivity.[4] Its move from commodity chemicals to agricultural productivity shows that commercialization depends on societal acceptance.

The struggle to commercialize genetically modified (GM) seeds started with Monsanto's goal of entering a higher-margin business. The company quickly met substantial opposition. Nonetheless, it persisted. Its commercialization path involved the following stages: sustainability as a corporate goal, opposition, rapid U.S. market penetration, promises of further innovations, government restrictions, increased criticism by environmentalists, and stiff competition from DuPont.

Sustainability as a Corporate Goal

The world's population was increasing and the demand for food rapidly growing. To improve yields, genetic modification of seeds seemed to be a promising solution. Gene modification allowed scientists to alter the makeup of living organisms by cutting bits of DNA from one cell and splicing them into another. The bacterium *bacillus thurungiensus* (Bt) made a poison that harmed pests but not other living things. Organic farmers had used it for decades. Rather than apply it manually, where it decomposed in sunlight and washed away in rain, it was far better to insert Bt genes into plants, thus protecting them from insects. However, Monsanto, as a chemical company, did not have the capabilities to employ the technology and had to acquire them. It decided to spin off its slow-growing chemicals businesses and acquire companies possessing ability to make genetically modified seeds. Monsanto was the first to the market with these seeds. It was making progress toward being a more sustainable company—one less involved in chemicals and more in solving the problems of society.

Opposition

Nonetheless, the Union of Concerned Scientists (UCC) was critical of the company's decision to market genetically modified seeds. This organization raised the possibility that the pests frustrated by new plant strains eventually would adapt. Once they adapted, super pests would create a hazard that would be virtually impossible to control. The UCC claimed that Monsanto's seeds promoted pesticide resistance, spread gene contamination, increased herbicide use, expanded monoculture, and fell far short of feeding the world's hungry.

GM seeds did not receive the kind of reception Monsanto hoped. The Internet quickly filled with sites like MonsantoSucks and references to MonSatan. Organizations like Greenpeace urged Monsanto to give up on biotech and embrace organic farming. Opposition put the company on the defensive and posed a barrier to commercialization.

Rapid U.S. Market Penetration

Nonetheless, by 2001 GM seeds were planted on 76 percent of the cotton acres, 74 percent of the soybean acres, and 27 percent of the corn acres in the United States. More than 30,000 U.S. products were made from genetically modified crops, including bread, pasta, meats, ice cream, candy, soy sauce, soft drinks, and cornflakes. Monsanto was rapidly penetrating the U.S. market despite the opposition. Monsanto touted the benefits of its products. For example, its genetically modified corn increased yields by 13.5 bushels on average, whereas genetically modified papaya resisted the ring rot virus that devastated the Hawaiian crop.

More Promised Progress

The company promised even more progress if it could continue unimpeded with the science. It could do the following:

- Extract genes from one species like the Brazilian nut and put them into soybeans to increase protein levels, make the soybeans more nutritional, improve their taste, and remove the saturated fats

- Introduce genes into rice to produce beta-carotene and combat vitamin A deficiency

- Incorporate vaccines for hepatitis B, diarrhea, and other diseases into bananas or sweet potatoes

- Take genes from fish swimming in icy water and inject them into strawberries so that the strawberries would be able to resist frost

- Take industrial materials like plastics and nylons from genetically modified plants

The potential benefits that might ensue from the widespread use of biotechnology were large, but Monsanto was still meeting resistance, and it had trouble focusing on which products to make first.

Government Restrictions

In Europe, arguments about the importance of genetically modified crops for feeding the world's poor had not made much impact. Many Europeans were fearful of new technology that tampered with the food supply. Putting restrictions on genetically modified crops also allowed Europeans to protect their domestic agriculture from U.S. agribusiness. In 1997, the EU recognized the consumer's right to make informed choices about genetically modified ingredients and issued a directive that required labeling on all foods containing, consisting of, or derived from genetically modified organisms. If any DNA or protein resulting from genetic modification was present, a product was subject to labeling. This ruling led to a virtual moratorium on the importation of products that contained genetically modified organisms into EU countries.

Environmentalists' Criticism

Criticism by environmentalists did not abate. They pointed to an incident in 1995 when a Brazil nut gene had been spliced together with soybeans to increase the level of the amino acids methionine and cysteine in the soybeans. The splicing together of the genes of these plants produced nutritious animal feed; however, humans allergic to Brazil nuts could die if they accidentally consumed a soybean or a soybean product with the spliced gene. Environmentalists also publicized 1999 research by a Cornell University researcher showing that eggs of the monarch butterfly could perish if exposed to Bt-modified corn pollen. The pollen destroyed three-day-old monarch larvae 44 percent of the time in a laboratory study. When it came to human consumption, environmentalists insisted on a precautionary principle—so long as risks of any kind existed, the burden was on the introducer of a new product to demonstrate complete safety. They argued that genetically modified seeds had been rushed to the market without adequate independent testing. Only minimal testing was done, or small sample sizes were used and didn't pick up negative results.

Competition from DuPont

In 1981, DuPont acquired Conoco, the world's ninth-largest petro-chemical company, at the tail end of an oil shortage to secure a steady supply of raw materials. Then in 1999, it sold Conoco in the largest initial public offering (IPO) for a U.S. company to that date. In Conoco's place, it spent $7.7 billion to buy the remaining 80 percent that it did not yet own of Pioneer Hi-Bred, the biggest seed maker and marketer in the world. Pioneer dominated the U.S. corn seed market. DuPont also financed research in the life sciences with the profits from mature businesses, such as nylon and polyester. It viewed genetic engineering as a means of using its R&D capabilities to deal with global challenges such as hunger and aging. It competed with Monsanto using similar methods of creating seeds capable of delivering greater yields in stressed environments and by selling crop protection products that were better able to control insects and improve crop quality with less environmental damage.

Nonetheless, the obstacles to the further commercialization of biotech seeds deterred both companies. By 2014, both were looking at alternative technologies, such as turbocharged selective breeding, precision agriculture, and mitigation of climate change.

Alternative Energy: The Electric Car

Still another example of the tortuous path to commercialization is the electric car.[5] This example shows how an ingenious entrepreneur, Elon Musk of Tesla, overcame barrier after barrier but still had a very long road to go.

The commercialization of the electric car was supported by the need for a vehicle that polluted less and did not rely on foreign oil. However, serious obstacles to commercialization included the car's range, the lack of charging infrastructure, and continued reliance on fossil fuels for electricity generation.

The 1990s efforts of General Motors to commercialize an electric car had been a total failure; however, Toyota's and Honda's marketing of hybrid vehicles provided evidence that commercialization might be possible. The U.S. government, interested in job creation possibilities during the Great Recession of 2007–2008, supported battery research, but the weak sales of GM's plug-in Volt were not a good sign.

A number of start-up companies made the high-risk gamble of developing electric cars, but only Tesla survived. Collaborating with its battery-manufacturing partner Panasonic, it introduced a solution to the problem of the battery's limited range. Tesla's success boosted the possibility of commercialization, yet the high costs of its vehicles continued to be an obstacle. Only a small minority of consumers could afford an electric car. Its future continued to be in question as the barriers to its commercialization remained large.

Less Pollution and Foreign Oil

Auto companies have struggled to commercialize electric vehicles for a long time. At the dawn of the auto industry, electric cars were in close competition with cars propelled by gasoline-powered engines. The gas-powered engine vehicles only pulled ahead with the elimination of the crankshaft and the mass production of gas-powered cars in Henry Ford's factories.

A renewed push for electric vehicles came in the 1990s as a result of more demanding pollution-control laws and a continued sense of energy insecurity because of reliance on oil from foreign countries that did not have the best track record as dependable supply sources. Modern research on electric vehicles had started to pick up in the 1970s during the 1973–1974 Arab oil embargo and 1979 oil price hikes associated with the Iran-Iraq war. By 1990, electric cars were seen as a potential answer to growing pollution problems and gas shortages. In cities such as Los Angeles, which were plagued by smog, these vehicles were hailed as a remedy. Other advantages of electric vehicles were that they were quieter, offered smooth drive and fast acceleration, and required less maintenance.

Range and Fossil Fuels

Yet range was a major barrier to the car's acceptance. The batteries provided a range of only about 70 miles between charges. Charging stations were not in place, and the batteries could take five to ten hours to charge. For most potential adopters, range anxiety was the largest impediment to adoption. In addition, the electricity had to be generated from existing facilities that relied on fossil fuels—coal, natural gas, and in some cases petroleum. If not fossil fuels, the electricity came from nuclear power, which some people also found objectionable.

1990s' Failure

In response to clean-air legislation enacted in states like California, which had tight laws on emissions standards, General Motors pioneered its zero-emission electric cars. The company also conducted research on a variety of other environmentally friendly, or "green," cars, including fuel-cell vehicles. However, the sales of GM's vehicles, whether because GM lacked confidence in the electric car or customers did, were dismal. By the end of the 1990s, it bought back the cars it had sold and destroyed them. This failure provided evidence that commercialization of electric vehicles probably was not feasible.

Hybrid Successes

Honda and Toyota modified the concept by adding an internal combustion engine and marketing hybrids that were part electric and part gas powered. Hybrids eliminated the range anxiety that many potential adopters had. These vehicles typically cost 20 percent more than similar sized vehicles, but the added price could be made up for in reduced gasoline costs within five years. Honda was the first to sell such a car in the United States, in 1999. Toyota's Prius hybrid, introduced in the United States in 2000, was more popular. By 2002, Honda had a hybrid version of the Civic. The hybrids that the Japanese automakers sold were successfully marketed among a small category of green, budget-conscious consumers. Both companies claimed that they made money from selling hybrids.

Weak Plug-In Sales

At the 2009 Detroit auto show, a main attraction was the Volt, a plug-in hybrid GM had decided to sell. The Volt was more expensive than the Prius or Honda Civic hybrid. It was a mid-sized family car, not a compact. GM's goal was to sell a million of these cars in the United States by 2015. This goal did not come close to being realized. It was widely reported that GM was losing large sums of money selling the Volt, despite the fact that the car obtained many accolades from car buffs and was well regarded in auto industry magazines. Even if GM met its goal, the sale of all hybrids together would amount to a very small percentage of total U.S. vehicle sales. The U.S. market was dominated by SUVs.

Battery Subsidies from the U.S. Government

The U.S. government increased its subsidization for battery research after the financial crisis of 2007 in the hope that it could stimulate industry creation and generate new jobs. Unlike the nickel hydride batteries in the Prius and Honda Civic, the lithium ion batteries GM used in the Volt were the same kind found in laptop computers and cell phones. GM bought the batteries from the Korean company LG Chem.

Yet even with U.S. government subsidies, the batteries were expensive to make. Another limitation was that they ran at high temperatures and if not monitored carefully could start a fire. For this reason, the number of batteries in a pack had to be limited. Sufficient batteries to increase range could not be stacked together, which remained an obstacle to the commercialization of electric vehicles.

A Solution from Tesla and Panasonic

Start-ups entered the electric car market, but the only one to survive and prosper was Tesla. Its high-end Roadster sports car, priced at $109,000, accelerated from 0 to 60 miles per hour in less than 4 seconds and was faster than some Ferraris. Of great importance was that the Roadster offered a solution to the range problem. Its lithium ion battery pack provided the car with a range of 245 miles. Compared to the Roadster, a Leaf, Nissan's mid-size all-electric vehicle, had a range of less than 100 miles.

Tesla overcame this longstanding barrier to the commercialization of an electric car by designing a battery pack with 7100 lithium ion cells as opposed to the 192 cells in the Leaf's battery. Together with Panasonic, its battery supplier, Tesla created a sophisticated computerized system for monitoring the batteries' temperature and cooling them should the batteries get too hot. Tesla also redesigned its car, placing the bulky battery packs under the car, where they improved the car's stability and handling. The battery packs heightened the driving experience rather than acted as a deficit. Also, the Roadster was made from super-light high-tech materials in an extremely automated factory setting to keep costs low. In addition, the car's shape was aerodynamically designed to minimize the drag. These design improvements were essential if there was any hope that the electric car could become commercially viable.

Not Yet Affordable

With the Roadster, Tesla entered the high-end automotive market. In this segment, a small slice of customers was prepared to pay a high premium to purchase an innovative vehicle. At its sale price, more than $100,000, the Roadster clearly was not for the masses, but Tesla's plan from the beginning was to take on each of the commercialization barriers it faced one by one.

The next barrier was to move down market and lower the price of the electric vehicle. Tesla's business plan, after building and selling the Roadster, was to use the money it made to build a more affordable car, and after building a more affordable car, it would use those profits to build an even more affordable car. The second model Tesla produced was called the Model S, and it sold for $69,000, competing in the same category as the Audi A6 and the BMW 5 series. The car was 10 percent faster than these vehicles and offered other attractive features that allowed it to win *Consumer Report*'s 2014 "car of the year" award. The magazine gave it the highest rating it ever gave to a car, praising it for its styling, handling, fuel efficiency, and safety. However, Tesla would still need to create an even more affordable electric car, and getting to the next level would not be easy.

A New Business Model

The batteries in a more affordable electric vehicle, depending on how many there were in a pack, could cost anywhere between $7,500 and $18,000. Could Tesla sell a mid-sized sedan for about $35,000 with batteries this expensive? To lower costs, Tesla started to build a giant battery factory in the deserts of Nevada with partner Panasonic. To ensure that there was sufficient demand for these batteries, it opened up its electric vehicle patents to all comers, including conventional automakers like GM in the hope they, too, would build this type of car in large numbers and buy the batteries.

Another way to drive down the price of the car was to sell it without the batteries. Tesla could sell the car for less than $35,000 and lease the batteries to customers. The Israeli electric car start-up Better Place had tried this model, but unfortunately it went bankrupt. One reason was that it sold a mid-sized Renault-built electric vehicle with a range of less than 100 miles. Like Better Place, Tesla was rolling out a battery charging and switching station to make driving an electric vehicle much more convenient. The infrastructure it had already installed allowed drivers to seamlessly go up and down the U.S. coasts and to drive from coast to coast. Tesla had a plan for commercialization that it stuck to and adapted, whereas Better Place lacked a consistent plan to which it adhered.

Tesla was also investing in solar power installations so that more of the energy used in electric vehicles would come from renewable sources. One by one, it was trying to knock down the barriers to electric vehicle commercialization. Yet its market share was tiny, and whether it ultimately would succeed in achieving wide-scale adoption and acceptance of this technology remained in doubt. Could the battery factory and other moves it made to overcome the barriers to commercialization be converted into business opportunities?

The Slow and Arduous Path to Commercialization

Each of the examples in this chapter shows how risky commercialization is. Commercialization does not follow a linear path. If it occurs at all, it almost always takes longer than expected. One estimate of the average time from commercialization's takeoff to sustained growth is 29 years, with a standard deviation of 15 years.[6]

These estimates apply to successful projects. What of the many that do not succeed? Although companies go to great lengths to ballyhoo commercialization successes, the failures they experience are almost always greater than their successes. Game theory may be used to explain why companies do not exploit opportunities in the first place. There can be many setbacks at many points along the road; government support, while important, is notoriously unreliable; project management is insufficient to overcome these problems; and most companies are inclined to undertake projects that are safe and to avoid the risks. Technological push and market pull have great influence. Determined, persistent innovators are necessary in trying to commercialize technologies despite the odds.

Why Xerox Missed Its Opportunity: Game Theory

Game theory can help us understand why Xerox did not successfully exploit the opportunity it had in IT.[7] The choice that a firm like Xerox faced is whether to stick with old copier technology or to switch to the new technology. The payoffs vary depending on what the other parties do. Exhibit 2.1 illustrates the payoff matrix of a hypothetical game like the one Xerox faced. For simplicity sake, the payoffs are estimated in millions of dollar (m=millions $ in the exhibit).

If both Xerox and competitors continue with old technology, they know what to expect. Xerox has the lead. The payoff for Xerox is $250m, whereas the competitors' payoff is $75m. If Xerox commercializes PC technology and its rivals do not, Xerox has additional PC revenue. It does not lose all copier revenues, but rivals gain at Xerox's expense as Xerox sets out in a new direction. An estimate of Xerox's revenues is $325m, whereas its rivals' revenues are $150m. Xerox has more revenue and the overall pie is larger, but Xerox is not as far ahead of its rivals as it has been.

Exhibit 2.1   Xerox's Commercialization Game Payoffs

Xerox's choices	Old technology (copiers)	New technology (PCs)
Xerox's rivals' choices		
Old technology (copiers)	Xerox payoff =$250m Rivals' payoff =$75m (77% market share for Xerox)	Xerox payoff = $325m Rivals' payoff= $150m (68% market share for Xerox)
New technology (PCs)	Xerox payoff =$320m Rivals' payoff =$180m (53% market share for Xerox)	Xerox payoff =$150m Rivals' payoff =$150m (50% market share for Xerox)

If Xerox's rivals innovate and commercialize the new PC technology and Xerox does not, Xerox will be able to capture some of the rivals' copier revenue. The rivals will have to go far to catch up with Xerox in PCs, and their payoff from the new technology is not likely to be as great as Xerox's would have been. If the rivals innovate and Xerox does not, then Xerox's payoff is likely to be $320m because it can capture additional copier revenue from rivals that are preoccupied with the new technology. The rivals' payoff is likely to be $180m from PCs. In this instance, Xerox's market share falls, but not as much as it would if Xerox innovated and the rivals did not. If both Xerox and rivals commercialize the new PC technology, they obtain equal market share and get $150m. When two parties make the same move at the same time, each tends to cancel out the others' gains. They neutralize each other.

If these payoff assumptions are correct, it makes more sense for Xerox to stay its course and not commercialize PC technology. Assuming that there is equal likelihood Xerox and its rivals stay put and innovate, the expected payoff for not commercializing is $285m ($250m + $320m, divided by two), whereas the expected payoff for commercializing is $237.5m ($325m + $150m, divided by two).

Payoffs are not known in advance in the real world. Companies make mistakes; they have to consider motivations, levels of awareness, and organizational politics of rivals. The bias is to be more concerned about losses than potential gains. Even if a company has identified an opportunity, as Xerox did, it may choose not to go further. As opposed to possible loss, the full magnitude of the future reward is hard to imagine. Reluctance to bet on the future generates a preference for the status quo. If a company's current position is strong, as Xerox's was, it can serve as a barrier to commercialization.

Setbacks at Many Points

After the decision to commercialize, setbacks can occur at many points. Innovators who try to commercialize a technology face the risk of failure when they try to get funding. They face it before a product reaches the market and in the early stages of production. Even after a product is on the market, obstacles can get in the way.

The examples of cochlear implants, genetically modified seeds, and the electric car show that obstacles can still exist even after products are released and on the market. For a new idea to gain widespread market acceptance, funding is needed, but the funding may not be sufficient or it may not last for the duration of a project. The funding can come from many sources, including investors, established corporations, private equity, and the government. Just as these parties extend funding, they can become discouraged and retract it.

Unexpected problems can arise at many points in time—before a product reaches the market, in the early stages of a promising commercial launch, and after product introduction. Even after prototype testing, pilot plant work, trial production, and test marketing, uncertainty runs high. The question is no longer whether a technology works, but how well under different operating conditions in the real world. Even after being introduced into the market, there were still problems with cochlear implants, genetically modified seeds, and the electric car.

Expectations that prices will fall and quality increase actually retard more rapid adoption. First adopters are tolerant of problems, but they are few in number. Other customers wait until products get better. They perceive that improvements will be made in response to experience and feedback and that the prices will go down. Why should they buy right away?

Market launch and growth in sales take place at different times, and future conditions vary. When a technology reaches the market, the conditions may no longer be ripe for those who hope to make a profit from commercialization. The general business climate can change. How could Tesla's management have anticipated the huge drop in gasoline prices that took place in 2014?

Although first movers endure the bulk of risk, they often do not fully benefit from them. It was not the original developers of cochlear implants—3M, Storz, Symbian, Nucleus, and Biostem—that benefitted, but rather late movers Cochlear Limited, Advanced Bionics, MED-E., Neurelec, and Nurotron. Often it is second and third movers that exploit a technological innovation. Those who commercialize new technologies must consider how long they will be sold once they reach the market. How dominant will their companies be in comparison to competitors and substitutes? Monsanto has to worry not only about DuPont and Syngenta, which are also selling genetically modified seeds, but also about organic farming and consumers who refuse to eat organically grown food. Tesla has to worry not only about Mercedes and Porsche, which are also developing all-electric vehicles, but also about fuel cells and other alternatives that compete for the same slice of elite customers. As the Monsanto case shows, when successful, new technologies breed imitators. Monsanto faced a formidable foe in DuPont.

The combined activity of the first movers and imitators generates a boom for a period of time, but eventually, markets for a new technology will be saturated. Over time, the PC market became weak (see Chapter 10, "From Mass Customizing to Mass Commodity: Dell and Acer"). One by one, companies that had been dominant looked for alternatives or left. Crowded markets, where supply exceeds demand and prices fall, are not attractive. Establishing a long-term market with steady stream of revenues from commercializing a new technology is not easy. There are no guarantees that this is possible.

Uncertain Government Support

Governments therefore recognize that they must support new technologies. They fund basic research because the benefits of technology extend to all of society. Without government support, technology would be underfunded because private sector companies are not in a position to capture the full benefits. There are positive externalities that extend to all of society. IT was government supported, with the Pentagon serving as the largest research backer of post-World War II U.S. government funding of IT research. Battery research obtained government support, as have alternatives to fossil fuels. It is not only the United States that funds research. Countries like Germany, Sweden, Finland, Japan, Israel, and Singapore also are leaders in research. The technology policies of the United States, the UK, France, and Russia in the postwar period were driven mainly by military needs, whereas those of Germany, Switzerland, and Japan were driven primarily by consumer needs. The primary goal of most of the Asian nations in this period was to catch up by copying the new technologies released in other countries. From 1950 to 1980, Japanese companies paid over $10 billion for more than 30,000 licensing and technology importing agreements. However, they did not just copy these technologies; rather, they looked for better ways to apply them. These firms blended technologies, making consumer-friendly, inexpensive, small, and lightweight products.

Although government support is critical, many technological innovations also suffer from the uncertainty of government support. Encouragement for renewable energy has a long history in the United States. Oil shocks and environmental concerns in the 1970s stirred the public's interest. In 1978, Congress passed Public Utility Regulatory Policies Act (PURPA), which mandated that utilities interconnect with renewable power facilities and buy the power at a price equivalent to the avoided costs. The 1992 Energy Policy Act provided a production tax credit (PTC) of 1.5 cents per kWh for renewable production, a credit that expired many times and was renewed for periods of only one and two years. Drama over extension created boom-and-bust cycles for nascent efforts to commercialize renewable energies. A similar extension of government assistance on liberal terms and then a withholding of this assistance took place in European countries after the signing of the Kyoto Protocol to limit greenhouse gas emissions. Throughout the world, government support for technological commercialization has not been reliable.

Project Management Insufficient to Overcome These Problems

The best project management techniques do not overcome these problems. The art of assigning statistical probabilities to the likelihood that commercialization will succeed is just an art. After the fact, it may be easy to analyze what happened, but it is nearly impossible to know with certainty what is to take place beforehand. Picking the winners is difficult.

Xerox did not think IT would be a winner. In retrospect, it couldn't have been more wrong. Project management techniques do not make it any easier. Sales pitches and unrealistic assessments are the reasons most projects are funded. Resource controllers, petitioned for the money, see many plans but accept few of them. If they give the go-ahead for a project, those who obtain the funding may disagree about a project's direction. Disagreement about how to proceed hurt the efforts to move ahead with commercializing cochlear implants.

Managing the disagreement is not easy. If unanticipated obstacles keep arising, the people involved start to lose patience. Exasperation builds, emotions run high, blame is assigned, some are asked to leave, and others voluntarily walk away for opportunities that appear to have better prospects.

Technological glitches take place. Many of them took place in the development of an electric car. If project goals are missed and negative cash flow persists, financial backers are sure to call for project termination. Many ventures are abandoned before they are fully commercialized.

The Inclination to Undertake Safe Projects

Because the process of commercialization is risky and takes time, most companies have compelling reasons to play it safe. In deliberating about whether to commercialize a technology or not, they have to consider the feasibility by carrying out these estimates:

- Probable development, production, and marketing costs
- The approximate timing of these costs
- Probable future income streams
- How long it will take for the income streams to manifest themselves

All these calculations are fraught with uncertainty. The only way to reduce uncertainty is to hedge the bets that are made (see the next chapter).

In all too many cases, the costs of research are underestimated and the size of markets overestimated, and new ideas are not implemented as expected. As observed in the Xerox case, sober and realistic assessments mitigate against setting out in new technological directions. Contemplation of failure often overwhelms the inclination to move forward. The bias is to stick with the status quo unless the reasons are strong and compelling and to undertake safe projects by licensing other businesses' inventions, modifying existing processes, and making minor improvements. Why commercialize a new technology when the chances of success are so slim?

Technologies Push and Markets Pull

Commercialization of new technologies is an arduous process, with failure and disappointment a frequent outcome. The technology push model starts with discoveries in basic science and engineering. From these discoveries, new goods and services come to the marketplace. However, there is also a need for a clear perception of market needs. Successful innovations must combine technical advances with market appeal. The challenge is to match technological opportunity with market need.

Within an organization, this means bringing together functions such as engineering, design, manufacturing, and marketing. R&D has an understanding of the scientific and technical challenges. Marketing has knowledge of what customers want. Frequent interaction between scientific/technical people and manufacturers is important as well. Users must have an appreciation for new technologies and must be sophisticated enough to purchase and use products that incorporate new ideas. Societal acceptance is also important. Monsanto missed this factor in its efforts to commercialize new genetic technology.

Determination, Will, and Persistence

For a technology to gain widespread commercial acceptance, the proponents of its commercialization must have persistence and the determination and will to overcome setbacks. The economist J. M. Keynes refers to this determination as "animal spirits."[8] If the decision to proceed with commercialization relied solely on rational calculation, most innovators would not bother. Keynes maintained that if animal spirits are weakened and spontaneous optimism falters, people have just rational calculations upon which to depend.

As the Xerox case shows, rational calculations are not a dependable guide. Reasonable calculation must be supplemented by animal spirits. According to Keynes, the thought of ultimate loss, which often overtakes pioneers, must be put aside "as a healthy man puts aside the expectation of death."

Endnotes

1. Douglas Smith and Robert Alexander, *Fumbling the Future: How Xerox Invented, Then Ignored, the First Personal Computer*. Lincoln, NE: iUniverse.com, Inc., 1999.

2. Charles Hill and Frank Rothaermel, "The Performance of Incumbent Firms in the Face of Radical Technological Innovation," *Academy of Management Review* 28.2 (2003): 257–274.

3. Andrew Van de Ven, Douglas Polley, Raghu Garud, and Sankaran Venkataraman, *The Innovation Journey*, New York: Oxford University Press, 1999.

4. Alfred Marcus, *Innovations in Sustainability: Fuel and Food*, Cambridge, UK: Cambridge University Press, 2015.

5. Ibid.

6. Howard Aldrich and Marlene Fiol, "Fools Rush In? The Institutional Context of Industry Creation." *Academy of Management Review* 19.4 (1994): 645–670.

7. Alfred Marcus, *Management Strategy, 2nd ed.* New York: McGraw Hill, 2011.

8. John Maynard Keynes, *The General Theory of Employment, Interest, and Money.* London: Macmillan, 1973.

3

Hedging the Uncertainty

To benefit from technological advances, an organization must carefully choose the technologies in which to invest. Early estimates of future markets for new technologies tend to be inaccurate. Achieving an advanced understanding of the costs, given changes in technology as well as the changes in the business environment, is difficult. As hard as technical success is to estimate, it is also difficult to predict market success. It is necessary to confront the uncertainty, recognize the opportunities and threats, and generate moves that can facilitate successful commercialization. The risk is great, but so too might be the reward.

There are a number ways for organizations to anticipate what can take place next. They can follow trends, rely on expert option, do industry analysis, search for analogies from the past, and construct scenarios. Once people in an organization engage in this type of thinking, they must decide what to do. Because it is impossible to predict with precision what will occur next, organizations must carefully hedge their bets so that they are prepared for different contingencies, both the best and worst possible outcomes as well as the surprises that inevitably take place.

This chapter describes and assesses frameworks that organizations can use to foresee the future and manage uncertainty.[1] These frameworks are trends, expert opinion, historical analogies, industry analysis, and scenarios. To hedge future uncertainty, this chapter provides five sets of actions organizations can take: (i) gamble on the most probable outcome, (ii) take the robust route, (iii) delay until further clarity emerges, (iv) commit with fallbacks, and (v) shape the future.[2]

Trends

Trends in one area often lead to developments in another. For example, military jet speeds presage commercial jet speeds. The number of components needed to manufacture one product can help in estimating the number needed to manufacture a similar product.

However, trends must be analyzed with caution. Simple extrapolation can be deceiving if it does not take into account the impact of one trend on another, ignores how human response can change the direction of a trend, and leaves no room for surprises and unexpected developments. Economic forecasts, for instance, are good at predicting the future based on the past so long as the future resembles the past in important ways, but often times radical breaks not predicted by economists take place. Consider the great financial crisis that started in 2007: virtually no economist predicted that it would happen, and none seemed to understand its full impact.

Trends do not necessarily predict future developments. There may be tipping points, inflections, and shifts in direction. Just because a trend is going in a particular direction does not mean it will continue that way forever. A trend can flatten out, become more pronounced, or reverse its direction in both incremental and extreme ways.

Expert Opinion

If the past does not provide a good indicator, perhaps expert opinion can be consulted. The problem is that even the most trusted experts can be fallible, as has been seen in many cases throughout history. Albert Einstein declared that nuclear energy was not possible. The analytical engine that Charles Babbage, the inventor of the computer, created was said to have no practical value by an expert panel. A committee of experts under the British Parliament's supervision found no potential in Thomas Edison's incandescent light bulb. U.S. experts in World War II declared that the intercontinental ballistic missiles could not accurately deliver their payload thousands of miles away. Another example is from the world of finance: time and again, active mutual fund managers underperform market averages. In a comprehensive study, Philip Tetlock found that experts are right less than half the time.[3] A dart-throwing chimpanzee has as much of a chance of being right as an expert.

The Rand Corporation, a think tank in Southern California, devised the Delphi method to aggregate the beliefs of experts. Each expert is asked to predict important events and to clarify why she thinks the events are likely to occur. Successive requestioning in light of the answers is meant to sharpen the results. Yet this method, too, has been found to be highly unreliable. The experts' imaginations are limited. Working together as a group, they tend to censor themselves, suppress doubts, and create the illusion of unanimity.

Tetlock argues that experts with good predictive powers must have a different style of thinking. They should not be overly attached to single explanations for events. They must not easily accept consensus opinions. They should be willing to challenge conventional wisdom and explore diverse information and analytical models and be comfortable with complexity and uncertainty.

Historical Analogies

Analogical reasoning is an approach to understanding past patterns and their relevance to contemporary challenges.[4] In analogical reasoning, known aspects of current events are compared with corresponding characteristics of historical phenomena. If the two match, then the prior cases are assumed to be good sources of evidence for understanding the contemporary phenomena.

Organizations often rely on earlier cases to understand how the actions they take might affect the future. The closer the match between aspects of the current situation and the past, the stronger the evidence that the analogy is good and the more it can be relied upon to decide how to proceed.

However, in using analogical reasoning, care must be taken to highlight relevant similarities and differences between the past and present. Examples show how difficult this is. For instance, the favorite analogy among many pragmatic analysts of foreign policy is Chamberlain's capitulation to the Nazis at Munich, which failed to bring peace, while for many idealists a favorite analogy is the imposition of harsh terms on Germany following World War I, which increased German resentment and belligerence.

The lessons of the past are complex. A singular focus on a single analogy to the exclusion of others leads to mistakes. In relying on the past, it is important to be careful about understanding the differences between what has happened, what is happening, and what is likely to happen. Analogies from the past provide useful clues about what to do, but they can be misleading, too, because the past does not fully reproduce itself in the future. Teasing lessons out of the past is not a mechanical process. Net present value calculations that rely on the past to make estimates of future returns, for instance, are only as good as the assumptions they make even if they do sensitivity analysis and experiment with a range of values. There are no guarantees that what happened previously will happen again.

Another approach, called Baysean judgment, is based on learning.[5] As the situation changes, new information comes into the picture and people continuously update their estimates based on it. The Baysean perspective offers more flexibility and room for adjustment in the face of unexpected developments and represents an improvement on the naive view that what happened earlier will occur again, but it does not entirely eliminate the uncertainty.

Industry Analysis

The five-forces-plus model is an analytical tool used in business strategy to provide insights into future opportunities and threats. According to business strategy professor Michael Porter, the five forces are suppliers, customers, competitors, new entrants, and substitutes.[6] The "plus" part of the model takes into account elements outside the industry that influence it. Typically, such external influences are technology, population and security, politics and economics, energy, and the environment. The model suggests that industries are not static. The interplay between industries and the forces outside them creates change.

This model is a useful framework for understanding industry change, but the insights obtained are not foolproof because it is not possible to have full knowledge of all elements in the model—neither the five forces themselves nor how external conditions affect them. Each force interacts with the other and with the external environment in complex ways. Many interactions are possible. Understanding all of them is impossible. Even in the unlikely event of full understanding, organizations may not know what to do with the results.

It is useful to distinguish between state, effect, and response uncertainty.[7] State uncertainty refers to imperfect knowledge of external conditions, whereas effect uncertainty refers to imperfect understanding of the impacts of these conditions on an industry. Response uncertainty is an inability to decide what to do with this information. There is no simple way to translate the insights of a five-force-plus model into a coherent plan for action. The ensuing debates within an organization about the actions it should take can be paralyzing.

Scenarios

Another way to confront future choices is to construct alternative scenarios. For example, before the Yom Kippur War, Shell Oil assessed the implications of three different energy scenarios, an exercise that forced its managers to think through what they would do should unfavorable circumstances arise. The exercise provided Shell's managers with the opportunity to better deal with these contingencies when they occurred. Shell attributed its experience with scenarios to the fact that it was in a better position than other oil companies to cope with OPEC oil price rises.

Surprises

Scenarios are important since many surprises take place:

- In the 1950s, the U.S. economy was dominant in the world. Although there were undercurrents of discontent, it was a period of social conformity. Few anticipated the political and cultural uproar of the 1960s.

- Because no remedy existed for high inflation and unemployment, in the 1970s the U.S. economy was in disarray. The challenges facing the United States included how to cope with a weak economy and high oil prices. Yet events turned around fairly quickly in the 1980s, as oil prices plummeted, the dollar gained in value relative to other currencies, and the U.S. economy picked up steam.

- The Japanese economy took off in the 1980s. By the end of the decade, the question was when Japan would have the largest GDP of any country in the world. However, with the burst of its asset bubble, the Japanese economic miracle came to a screeching halt in 1991. Meanwhile, the Soviet Union collapsed in December of that year when Gorbachev resigned.

- Throughout the 1990s, many technological advances took place in information technologies. The Chinese opened up to the world and warmly embraced a form of state capitalism previously not seen. With nearly a single world market, the future, at the turn of the millennium, looked bright. However, shortly thereafter, the tech bubble burst, and the terrorist attacks of 9/11 took place.

- Later in the decade came additional jolts, such as the subprime mortgage collapse, a sharp slide in housing prices, and global recession unparalleled since the Great Depression. The second decade of the 21st century had its own surprises, starting with the promising Arab Spring in the Middle East, which quickly degenerated into a torrent of violence. Then came the financial meltdown in Greece, civil war in the Ukraine, and Russian intervention in the war between an Iranian allied Syrian regime and ISIS.

Taking Notice of the Periphery

Human beings cannot predict such events. The goal of utilizing scenarios is not prediction but anticipating the possibilities.

How best to consider the possibilities? In their book, George Day and Paul Schoemaker advise paying attention to the periphery.[8] Most people, they argue, are blind to events that take place on the margins. When psychologists conduct experiments in which they show a film clip of teams passing a ball and ask how many times the teams have passed the ball, the subjects usually provide the right answer, but more than 90 percent of the subjects fail to notice a gorilla that walks through the scene and taunts the players. Among those who notice the gorilla, less than half get the count right. People who repeat the experiment usually get the count right and spot the gorilla, but they fail to notice other changes like a person leaving the game or a different colored curtain. This suggests that most people see beyond known knowns (the ball passing hands) and spot the unknown knowns (the taunting gorilla), but it is hard for them to recognize the unknown unknowns (players leaving the game or a change in curtain color).

Romances, Tragedies, and Comedies

A scenario calls upon the participants to consider, to the extent they are able, the unknown unknowns. Along with taking the upside of a situation seriously and not underestimating the downside, the purpose is to consider potential surprises. Classical narrative analysis calls the upside romances, the downside tragedies, and the surprises comedies. These should lead to actions to bring about the romances, avoid the tragedies, and manage the comedies (see Exhibit 3.1).

There are infinite variations from which it is possible to conceive of surprises and speculate about the unknown unknowns. Scenarios have to be regularly updated in light of additional insights and information. The process should be an ongoing one, not one carried out every couple of years.

Exhibit 3.1   Romances, Tragedies, and Comedies

Romances: Use Foresight	Tragedies: Avoid Being Blind Sighted	Comedies: Manage the Surprises
Succeed	Prevent failure	Consider the unknowns
See opportunity early	Have early warning systems	Be sensitive to uncertainty
Stay ahead of the curve	Be prepared	Monitor and test assumptions
Foreshadow weak signals	Be vigilant	Eliminate regret

The Narrative Details

- Start with the present (see Exhibit 3.2) and imagine that is disturbed by tension. The tension may come from sources other than technology—from society, politics, the economy, and conditions in the natural world. Movement toward closure may take a long time; in the meantime, there are unresolved issues and leftover tension.

- Consider who the main actors are, what their motivations are, and what actions they have taken and are likely to take next. The relations among these actors ebb and flow over time (see Exhibit 3.3). A single storyline could prevail, but more likely there will be changing stories at different intervals.

- Label the stories with phrases that can capture their underlying logic. Here are some examples: smooth sailing, unexpected turns, revival of hope, and descent into failure. They represent the reality that closure is rarely achieved. Over time what might be a romance, such as winning a war, may become a tragedy as the actual consequences of winning the war play out in unexpected ways. On the other hand, what at first seems like a tragedy turns around. In the long term, it becomes a romance.

Outcomes vacillate from period to period, if not in the five-year blocks found in Exhibit 3.3 then in some other time period. The important point is to understand that the outcome of any particular story is likely to be unstable. Nearly always unresolved, there are tensions and unintended consequences that propel stories forward into new endings.

Exhibit 3.2 Incomplete Resolution of Tension

	Characters	Motivations	Actions	Interactions
Beginning (harmony)				
Tension (disturbs equilibrium)				
Movement (toward a new equilibrium)				
Continued unresolved tensions				

Exhibit 3.3 The Ebb and Flow of Stories over Time

	Smooth Sailing	Descent to Failure	Triumph over Adversity	Revival of Hope	Unexpected Turns	Sad Tidings
1–5 years out	Romance	Romance	Tragedy	Romance	Comedy	Tragedy
5–10 years out	Romance	Comedy	Comedy	Tragedy	Tragedy	Tragedy
10–20 years out	Romance	Tragedy	Romance	Comedy	Comedy	Tragedy

Applying Scenario Logic to Technology Commercialization

The logic of a scenario can be applied to the commercialization of technologies (see Exhibit 3.4). Important questions to consider may be these: (i) whether there is sufficient technological progress for a technology to be successfully commercialized; and (ii) if there is enough social, political, and market support for commercialization to take place.

Breaking down these possibilities reveals these scenarios:

- Romance in which there is high technological advance and high social, political, and market acceptance

- Tragedy in which there is low technological advance and low social, political, and market acceptance

- Two comedies, one in which there is high technological advance and low social, political, and market acceptance and another in which there is low technological advance and high social, political, and market acceptance

Whether to continue to invest in a technology, how much to invest, and in what ways depends on how members of an organization view these four outcomes.

Exhibit 3.4   Applying Scenario Logic to Technology Commercialization

Social, Political, and Market Acceptance	High	Low
Technological Advances		
High	Romance	Comedy
Low	Comedy	Tragedy

Strategic Adjustments

An organization must take actions to deal with contingencies that scenarios reveal (see Exhibit 3.5). Positive and desirable developments should be encouraged, negative and undesirable developments prevented, and coping strategies put in place to deal with surprising and unanticipated developments. Don't assume that the best results will prevail. Be prepared for future plans to go off course.

For each set of opportunities and threats, there should be a corresponding set of actions.[9] For business organizations, these actions consist of (i) repositioning products and services, (ii) changing organizational structures, (iii) extending or contracting global operations, and (iv) introducing innovations. Repositioning means raising or lowering prices, adding or subtracting existing product or service features, or entering into related markets. Restructuring involves reconsidering the businesses in which the organization competes. Would it be best to divest or acquire others? Should there be growth or cut back in global operations? Finally, making radical or incremental changes in an organization's business model should be considered. These moves can be pursued simultaneously or in sequence; they are not mutually exclusive.

Exhibit 3.5 Taking Action to Address Contingencies

Major Contingencies: Opportunities and Threats	Actions to Address the Contingency
Positive and desirable	
Negative and undesirable	
Surprising and unanticipated	

Hedging

Hedging strategies can help deal with the moves' uncertainty. They depend on the degree to which outcomes are well described and quantitative odds can be assigned. The economist Frank Knight distinguished between uncertainty and risk based on the capacity to place objective odds on what can happen.[10] When evidence from the past is ample, the conditions are those of risk because relevant odds can be formulated about what is likely to occur. When the odds of what is likely to happen are well known, economic actors have similar information. High levels of economic gain are difficult to achieve. Competition among business firms is intense, and none of them earns great returns. When good information about the past is known and an economy is in equilibrium, there is little advantage that any single actor can achieve over any other actor.

When historical data is not ample and is hard to interpret, then the condition, according to Knight, is one of uncertainty. Only when history is an imperfect indicator of the future and there is uncertainty are some business firms able to realize superior returns. They obtain superior performance because of their ability to navigate well under these circumstances.

Corresponding to conditions of different degrees of risk and uncertainty, there are five hedging strategies organizations can pursue: (i) gamble on the most probable, (ii) take the robust route, (iii) delay until further clarity emerges, (iv) commit with fallback, and (v) try to shape the future.[11] These strategies are not mutually exclusive. They may be pursued in many different orders.

Gamble on the Most Probable Outcome

Gambling on the most probable outcome means acting on this possibility (see Exhibit 3.6). However, there may be surprises later if the world does not evolve as expected. An example of a company that made a large bet based on what it believed to be the most probable outcome was Sony in 1975 when it introduced the Betamax video cassette recorder (VCR). It thought it was offering the most innovative technology, yet years later it had to withdraw from the market because Matsushita's VHS technology was lower priced and better adapted to movie rentals.

Sony repeated this mistake in 1993, again betting wrong when it introduced the MiniDisc music player. Despite heavy investment in the technology, the MiniDisc did not gain traction and lost out to MP3 players like the iPod, which better saw the viability of flash memory.

Exhibit 3.6 Levels of Uncertainty and Hedging Strategies

Hedging Strategies	Extreme Uncertainty (qualitative outcomes cannot be described)	Moderate Uncertainty (qualitative outcomes can be described)	Moderate Risk (quantitative odds can be ascribed to the outcomes)	Low Risk (a single best forecast can be made)
Gamble on the "most probable" outcome				*
Take the robust route		*	*	
Delay until further clarity emerges	*	*		
Commit with fallbacks	*	*	*	
Shape the future	*	*		

Sometimes making bets of this kind, however, is reasonable. Extending the scope of proven business models and winning by virtue of superior execution makes sense for McDonald's or a Home Depot making investments in new stores, for example, where there is little concern about serious technological upheaval.

Take the Robust Route

Rather than bet on single future, organizations can choose robust strategies in which they know they will have no regrets regardless of what takes place. This route makes sense when quantitative odds can be ascribed or qualitative outcomes described. Often regulated utilities take this route. They bet on different technologies for generating electricity at the same time—natural gas, wind, efficiency, coal, nuclear, and solar—either by computing likely odds or knowing that these outcomes are likely to share a portion of the future.

However, only organizations with substantial slack can invest in many options. It is expensive to chase all the technological options at once. A pharmaceutical company as diverse as Pfizer may be able to cover just about all the technological bases, but a biotech start-up does not have the resources to do so. The robust route protects organizations from harm, but it is also likely to dilute their returns.

Delay Until Further Clarity Emerges

Delaying taking action until the situation becomes clearer, following developments, and waiting for a better moment to act may be the most appropriate strategy when there is moderate or extreme uncertainty. If there is little threat from the competition, organizations may decide to wait and see. They may postpone making final commitments until more information is available.

The risk is that while they wait for the situation to become clearer, they may lose market opportunities to the competition, and when they decide to fully put their stake in the ground, it is too late. Such was the case not only with Xerox, but also with Kodak, whose adjustment to digitization was far too slow. By the time it acted in response to this change in technology, competitors had entered the space, and it could not dislodge them. U.S. automakers also waited too long to respond when they delayed investing in small vehicles in the 1970s. They lost ground and fell permanently behind Japanese automakers in small passenger cars.

Postponing may mean being permanently shut out from an important market or, conversely, may be beneficial. Delay may ultimately work to Boeing's benefit in its decision not to pursue a superjumbo jet option. Airbus made this advance a high priority, whereas Boeing chose to wait and see. Boeing's view of the future was that larger aircraft would not necessarily dominate. It was too early to tell. Boeing was confident, though, that if the situation changed it would be an effective late mover.

Commit with Fallbacks

Committing with fallbacks makes sense under a number of contingencies. Intel, which started as a producer of computer chips for the memory market, had a fallback position in microprocessors. (See Chapter 9, "Missing the Boat on Mobile Technology: Intel and AMD.") This fallback allowed it to make a successful transition when the market for computer chips collapsed. Major petroleum companies once had fallback positions in renewable energy. Johnson and Johnson (J&J) does not make irreversible commitments to specific technologies without significant fallbacks. It maintains limited commitments in a number of areas via alliances, joint ventures, and partial equity ownership. It works in diverse technological areas, some combining drugs and devices and some involving prevention as well as treatment. It monitors the environment for signals as to when it should exercise these options or abandon them.

There are problems, however, in choosing what should be an organization's main commitment and what should be its fallbacks. Also, there are problems in deciding how many fallbacks are needed. Fallbacks should fit into a broader pattern and not be isolated initiatives. They should be easy enough to adopt should an organization decide to shift its focus and change. They should not be prohibitively costly to give up if there is a decision to abandon them.

Shape the Future

Should the situation be one of extreme or moderate uncertainty, it might become more possible to shape the future. Use organizational resources and capabilities to build a strong and supportive ecosystem for entirely new endeavors. Form coalitions and partnerships to bring the future into being. Companies like Uber, Spotify, LinkedIn, Amazon, FedEx, and Southwest Airlines used innovative business models and technologies to shape the future.

When technological change is rapid and discontinuous and the future is hard to forecast, it may be possible to create close ties with customers, build brand loyalty, and lock up supply and distribution before competitors. Shaping the future is a high-risk and high-return strategy. For incumbents with well-established businesses, this route may not appear to be worth it.

Conclusion

The takeaway is that technological change is not smooth. Positive and negative developments are hard to predict. Given that the future is uncertain, hedging strategies are among the most critical choices organizations make. Hedges can be put in place to protect organizations against different possible futures.

Endnotes

1. Alfred Marcus, *Strategic Foresight: A New Look at Scenarios*, New York: Palgrave Macmillan, 2009.

2. Hugh Courtney, *20/20 Foresight: Crafting Strategy in an Uncertain World*, Boston: Harvard Business School Press, 2001. Michael Raynor, *The Strategy Paradox*, New York: Doubleday, 2007.

3. Philip Tetlock, *Expert Political Judgment: How Good Is It? How Can We Know?* Princeton, NJ: Princeton University Press, 2006.

4. Alfred Marcus and Zach Sheaffer, "Analogical Reasoning and Complexity, *Journal of Homeland Security and Emergency Management* 6.1 (2009).

5. John Paulos, "The Mathematics of Changing Your Mind," *New York Times*, 5 Aug. 2011: n. page. http://www.nytimes.com/2011/08/07/books/review/the-theory-that-would-not-die-by-sharon-bertsch-mcgrayne-book-review.html?_r=0.

6. Michael Porter, *Competitive Strategy: Techniques for Analyzing Industries and Competitors*, New York: The Free Press, 1998.

7. Frances Milliken, "Three Types of Perceived Uncertainty about The Environment: State, Effect, and Response Uncertainty." *Academy of Management Review* 12.1 (1987): 133–143.

8. George Day and Paul Schoemaker, *Peripheral Vision: Detecting the Weak Signals That Will Make or Break Your Company*, Boston: Harvard Business School Press Publication, 2006.

9. Alfred Marcus, *Management Strategy*, 2nd ed. New York: McGraw Hill, 2011.

10. Frank Knight, *Risk, Uncertainty, and Profit*, New York: Houghton Mifflin, 1921.

11. Courtney, *20/20 Foresight: Crafting Strategy in an Uncertain World*.

PART II

MANAGING DANGER

4

Dealing with Danger

echnologies are not exclusively beneficial; they can also generate dangers that must be anticipated and prevented. However, sometimes companies mismanage these dangers and cause irreparable harm. This chapter describes tragic instances of the irreparable harm that companies have caused, such as the Bhopal chemical plant explosion and the Deepwater Horizon Oil Spill. The companies involved, Union Carbide and BP, missed what in retrospect were obvious warnings that could have stopped these tragic events from occurring. This chapter discusses dilemmas in managing dangerous technologies—the cognitive limits of individuals, experts, and organizations in trying to rationally manage them, the issue of how much a life is worth, and the problem of making inferences from animal studies to humans.

Bhopal: What Went Wrong

The 1984 accident in Bhopal, India, killed more than 3,000 people and injured hundreds of thousands more.[1] At the time, Union Carbide was manufacturing a highly toxic chemical in a part of India that had primitive infrastructure. It experienced an uncontrolled emission of poisonous gas that trapped thousands of victims. None of the backup systems designed to control a leak of this nature worked as planned. The company suffered from many organizational shortcomings and had ignored warnings that the plant was troubled and had potential for a catastrophe.

Highly Toxic Chemicals

The Union Carbide plant in Bhopal, India, was originally built in the 1960s in open fields within two miles of a local commercial and transportation center. At the time of start-up, it was used to mix chemical components that had been manufactured overseas and shipped to India to be made into final pesticide formulations that would be marketed. The plant did not pose much of a threat to neighboring residential areas. However, by 1978 Union Carbide, under pressure from the Indian government to manufacture the precursors to the pesticide in India, as opposed to abroad, built and began operating the facilities necessary to manufacture highly toxic compounds domestically.

Although some local authorities objected to the plant's location, state and national government officials overruled them. The plant was an important part of the local economy. Among the pesticide components manufactured at the plant was the highly toxic and unstable methyl isocyanate (MIC) used to make the active ingredient in the pesticide Sevin. It was manufactured in batches and stored in three large refrigerated concrete tanks within a few yards of each other just below the surface of the soil.

Weak Infrastructure

Bhopal was the capital of one of the least industrialized states in India. Beginning in the 1950s, the government actively encouraged industrial development in the region, but it did not engage in a comprehensive planning effort. As a consequence, the infrastructure of services like roads, utilities, and communications services was poor. By the 1980s, stagnation in agricultural production in the country's rural areas drove thousands of people to cities like Bhopal to look for work. Bhopal's population increased sixfold between 1961 and 1981, almost three times the average for the country as a whole. A severe housing shortage forced migrants to build shantytowns wherever there was open space. Areas near industrial plants where work might be found were the migrants' favorite choices. Right outside the walls of Union Carbide's Bhopal plant could be found crowded squatters' dwellings.

An Uncontrolled Explosion

At 11:00 p.m. on the evening of December 2, 1984, everything seemed normal at the Bhopal plant. However, half an hour later, a worker noticed an MIC leak near the vent gas scrubber. The workers planned to fix the leak after the 12:15 a.m. tea break, but by the time the break was over at 12:40 a.m., it was too late. The pressure in one of the tanks shot up and quickly exceeded its upper limits. The thick concrete tank cracked open and unleashed poisonous gases. A white cloud of MIC smoke shot out of the vent gas tower attached to the tank and settled over the vicinity. Each tank was equipped with pressure and temperature gauges, a high-temperature alarm, a level indicator, and high- and low-level alarms. Additionally, there was several safety systems designed to handle accidental leaks. They included a vent gas scrubber, which neutralized toxic gases with a caustic soda solution; a flare tower, which could burn off the gases; a refrigeration system to keep the chemical at low, stable temperatures; and a set of water-spray pipes, which could control escaping gases or extinguish fires.

Nonfunctioning Backups

Within a few minutes, the fire brigade began to spray a curtain of water in the air to knock down the cloud of gas. The tower from which the gas was escaping was 120 feet high, however, and the water only reached about 100 feet in the air. The system of water spray pipes was too low to help. The vent gas scrubber, designed for an emergency of this nature, did not function. The scrubber had been under maintenance and had not been charged with a caustic soda solution. Even if the scrubber had been operational, it would have been ineffective because the temperature of the escaping gas was hotter than the system was designed to handle. The plant operators were afraid to turn on the flare tower for fear of igniting the large cloud of gas that enveloped the plant. It, too, was being repaired and was missing a four-foot section. Likewise, the coolant in the refrigeration system had been drained weeks before to be used in another part of the plant and was, therefore, useless in fighting the poisonous fume. Finally, routing the escaping gas into an empty MIC storage tank was not possible because, contrary to established safety procedures, there were no empty tanks available.

Trapped Victims

As the gas began to escape, the warning alarm sounded for just a few minutes before it was shut off. As the workers fled the plant in panic by foot, the four buses parked near the entrance, which were intended to be used for emergency evacuations of plant workers and nearby residents, were left sitting. In the shantytowns and neighborhoods outside the plant, chaos reigned. The gas seeped into the rooms of the sleeping population, suffocating hundreds in their sleep and driving others into a panicked run through the narrow streets where they inhaled more gas. Blinded by the cornea-clouding effect of the gas, lungs on fire, thousands died or were injured. Long after, the accident victims suffered from breathlessness, coughing, lung diseases, eye disorders, abdominal pain and vomiting, menstrual disorders, and psychological trauma. Many women had to contend with reproductive illnesses.

Organizational Shortcomings

In the weeks and months after the accident, a horde of reporters, Indian government officials, and Union Carbide technical experts analyzed the causes. Union Carbide contended that the accident was the result of sabotage by an unhappy employee. Whatever the proximate cause of the accident, it was clear that the magnitude of deaths and injuries were the result of more than an act of sabotage. The safety policies and procedures that were intended to prevent such an accident were not followed, and the reasons were rooted in the deteriorating financial condition of the Bhopal plant.

The Bhopal plant was an unprofitable unit in an unimportant division. The plant had lost money for three years in a row. As profits fell and budgets were cut, maintenance was deferred, employees were laid off, and training programs were scaled back. Morale was low, and many employees left voluntarily. Safety training was inadequate, and workers did not know how to deal with emergencies. They knew little about the toxic effects of MIC. Formal control of the plant had been turned over to an Indian subsidiary because of Indian law, but Union Carbide's top management in Connecticut was still in charge of making important day-to-day decisions. Based on the receipt of monthly reports, the Connecticut management team continued to make financial, maintenance, and personnel decisions, while Indian personnel took care of safety inspections. The unpreparedness of the emergency infrastructure of the local government exacerbated the problem. The accident was not the result of technical malfunctions in equipment but stemmed from human errors and organizational shortcomings.

Warnings Ignored

There had been many small accidents in the past, yet the Department of Labor of the state where the accident occurred was grossly understaffed. It had only 15 inspectors for more than 8,000 industrial plants. Trained as mechanical engineers, most inspectors had little understanding of the hazards of a chemical plant. When a journalist from the Bhopal area wrote a series of articles in 1982 detailing the death of an employee that was caused by a chemical leak at the plant and warned of the possibility of a catastrophe, neither the plant management nor the government took action, even after the journalist wrote a letter to the chief minister of the state to warn him of the danger. A top government bureaucrat who requested that the plant be moved to another location because of the threat it posed to neighboring slum residents was transferred to another post.

The Price of the Accident

The plant was closed, 650 high-paying jobs were lost, and 1,500 other jobs were lost. Union Carbide was hit hard. Besides the $3 billion lawsuit filed against the company by the Indian government on behalf of the victims, the company's reputation came under attack. Activist groups undertook a variety of campaigns against the company. The company's stock dropped, its debt rating was reduced, and its shareholders sued it for not warning them about the risks. Ultimately, it could no longer operate as a separate company, and the remaining assets were sold to Dow Chemical.

Union Carbide could have avoided this accident if it had taken the precautions needed to run the plant in a safe way. It should have designed the plant differently, made certain that safety equipment was running, not let financial considerations get in the way, and trained the workers in how to prevent an accident. The company should have heeded the warnings of journalists and government officials that an accident could happen.

The Deepwater Horizon Oil Spill: What Went Wrong

BP made similar mistakes in the Deepwater Horizon oil spill.[2] The company had publicly announced it was moving away from petroleum while it was trying to expand its processing of Canadian tar sands. It had previous operational problems, leaks, and explosions at other facilities, even before the massive Deepwater Horizon oil spill, but it did not learn from them.

Beyond Petroleum

BP was the first major oil company to acknowledge the risks of global warming. In 1996, BP left the Global Climate Coalition, an organization that opposed actions to reduce greenhouse gas emissions, and joined the Business Environmental Leadership Council, which supported the Kyoto Accord. It tried to foster a new culture. It attempted to hire management with strong environmental beliefs and to be a cleaner and more progressive oil company, one with extensive pollution-prevention efforts.

In 1998, the company purchased Amoco, and in 2000 it created a new slogan: "Better people, better products, beyond petroleum." It invested in wind, solar, biofuels, gas-fired power generation, and hydrogen. It aimed to expand its solar subsidiary fourfold by 2007 and spent billions to develop renewable energy. The American Petroleum Institute treated it as a traitor and said that the company had "left the church."

Tar Sands Processing

BP stumbled with its decision to expand capacity to process oil derived from Canadian tar sands at its Whiting, Indiana, plant, an expansion it undertook six years after its rebranding effort began. BP's plan was to invest $3.8 billion to expand the facility, including $1.4 billion for environmental improvements. At first, Indiana Governor Mitch Daniels welcomed the initiative because of the positive economic impact on the state. Indiana's Department of Environmental Management (IDEM) and the EPA were on board to approve a water permit for the facility after BP notified county and city officials, received comments, and subjected its permit to multiple peer and other reviews. But the *Chicago Tribune* published an article titled "BP Gets Break on Dumping in Lake," which led to protests, organized boycotts, more investigative news articles, and a petition campaign opposing the permit.

Explosion in Texas City and Oil Leaks in Alaska

At the same time that the controversy was taking place in Indiana, BP was receiving bad press from a 2005 explosion at its Texas City facility, which claimed the lives of 15 workers and injured more than 170 people. This industrial accident was the worst in the United States in a decade. The explosion raised the scrutiny of investigators because of the many possible, suspected legal violations. Investigators did find that the firm's refineries in Texas, which it had inherited from Amoco, were seriously mismanaged. Employees were not openly reporting accidents or safety concerns because of a company culture that relied on fear and intimidation to keep sensitive matters quiet.

In 2006, the public became aware of a large oil leak in its Alaska pipeline. Up to 267,000 gallons of oil had been allowed to escape into Alaska's North Slope tundra. The steel-workers' union stated that for years it had been warning the company about such an accident, but its voice had been systematically ignored. In 2007, BP announced plea bargains over the tragedy in Texas City and the Alaska pipeline leak and admitted to legal violations. Its CEO was forced to resign.

The Spill

In 2010, the Macondo 252 well site in the middle of the Gulf of Mexico ruptured. BP had contracted with Transocean to drill this well below 5,000 feet of seawater and down into 13,000 feet of seabed. It licensed the Deepwater Horizon rig from Halliburton. The rig went up in flames, killing 11 crewmembers and seriously injuring 17, and the companies blamed each other. Many technical barriers had been breached, including the cement at the bottom of the well, the mud in the well and in the riser, and the blowout preventer. The Deepwater Horizon was the largest marine oil spill in the history of the petroleum industry, Following the explosion and sinking of the oil rig, the sea-floor oil gusher continued for 87 days. The total discharge was 4.9 million barrels of oil, and reports indicated the well site still had not completely stopped leaking. A massive effort had to be undertaken to protect beaches, wetlands, and estuaries. There was extensive damage to marine and wildlife habitats and fishing and tourism industries. Dolphins and other marine life died in record numbers, and tuna and other fish developed deformities of the heart and organs.

The Many Mistakes

Many investigations explored the causes of the spill and identified them to be technical and procedural failures and poor management oversight. BP, Transocean, and Halliburton blamed each other. The U.S. government's 2011 report mostly faulted BP for defective cement on the well, but also rig operator Transocean and contractor Halliburton. BP and its partners were blamed for cost-cutting, insufficient safety systems, and the neglect of systemic root causes that could lead to a reoccurrence without significant reform in their practices. The day before the accident, the crew had pumped cement to the bottom of the borehole, a standard procedure that should have stopped the oil from leaking. It conducted checks to determine that the well had been properly sealed, but eight safety systems failed:

1. The cement at the bottom of the borehole did not seal.

2. The two mechanical valves designed to stop the flow of oil and gas failed.

3. The crew misinterpreted pressure tests to determine whether the well had been sealed.

4. The crew did not spot the leak early enough.

5. A second valve called the blowout preventer used by the crew did not work properly and failed to stop the flow of oil.

6. The flow of oil ignited when it overwhelmed a separator that was meant to divert the mud and gas away from the rig and vent it safely through pipes on the side.

7. The gas alarm detection system should have triggered the closure of ventilation fans to prevent ignition.

8. The blowout preventer's safety mechanisms did not shut the valves automatically because of a defective switch, and the battery did not have power.

In 2012, BP and the United States Department of Justice settled federal criminal charges, with BP pleading guilty to 11 counts of manslaughter, two misdemeanors, and a felony for lying to Congress. BP agreed to four years of government monitoring of its safety practices and ethics and accepted a record-setting $4.525 billion fine and other payments. In 2014, a U.S. District Court judge ruled that the company was primarily responsible for the spill because of its gross negligence and reckless conduct. Additional penalties as high as $18 billion had serious repercussions for BP's future. The company's expansion plans were reduced, and its ability to compete with other large multinational oil companies like Exxon Mobil and Shell became limited.

Inherently Dangerous Technologies

Sociologist Charles Perrow has argued that the operation of toxic chemical plants in developing countries and the search for oil deep under water in the world's oceans are inherently dangerous technologies that even under the best conditions are difficult to manage.[3] They have the capacity to take the lives of many people at once and do irreparable harm to people and the environment. Perrow claims that these types of technologies are prone to normal accidents. No matter how effective the management practices are, they are likely to fail. Better operator training, safer designs, more quality control, and more effective regulation cannot entirely eliminate the threat because the technologies involve not only catastrophic risks, but also complexity and tight coupling. Reactions occur quickly, systems are interrelated, and they cannot be isolated from one another.

Complexity means that the technologies have many components (parts, procedures, and operators) that interact in unexpected ways. Failure can take place in more than one component at a time. (For example, a fire starts and the fire alarm remains silent.) Given the interaction of multiple failures, the causes of failure may be incomprehensible for a critical period of time to operators. During this critical period, the operators may not be able to figure out what has gone wrong and what to do. The problem of not knowing what to do may be overcome if slack—the time and resources needed to figure out what has happened and how to fix it—is available. However, the systems are subject to tight coupling and do not have sufficient slack. They work fast, their parts cannot be isolated from each other, and they cannot be quickly or easily shut off. Many of the interactions that take place are not directly observable by operators, so it is hard for them to know what is really going on.

Because of complexity, tight coupling, and catastrophic potential, managing the danger of these technologies, according to Perrow, is impossible (see Exhibit 4.1).[4] Complexity and tight coupling call for contradictory management actions. Complexity requires preparation for unexpected contingencies. Therefore, it is necessary for those who manage these technologies to take independent, creative action. In contrast, tight coupling means actions have to be carefully monitored and controlled. Therefore, those managing these technologies cannot afford to make mistakes and take independent action. This contradiction makes it hard to safely manage these technologies.

Exhibit 4.1 Problems in Managing Inherently Dangerous Technologies

	Catastrophic Potential	Inconsistent Management Principles
COMPLEXITY	Many Components ■ Unexpected interactions ■ Causes of failure incomprehensible for critical period	Prepare for Unexpected ■ Operators have to be prepared to take independent, creative initiative
TIGHT COUPLING	Systems Interconnected ■ Work fast ■ Parts can't be isolated ■ Systems can't be easily or quickly shut off	Can't Afford Mistakes ■ Operators have to be carefully monitored and controlled

Perrow stated:

> In the past, designers could learn from the collapse of a medieval cathedral under construction, or the explosion of boilers or steamboats, or the collision of railroad trains on a single tract. But we seem to be unable to learn from chemical plant explosions or nuclear plant accidents.[5]

Learning, according to Perrow, plateaus. The learning curve is flat, and societies do not get better at managing dangerous technologies.

Dilemmas in Managing Dangerous Technologies

Organizations frequently face troubling dilemmas with regard to dangerous technologies. Rational assessment means estimating the magnitude of the risk (see Exhibit 4.2) and then considering what can be done to mitigate it.[6] However, the risk that a technology will cause harm is a statistical likelihood. Ranging from local phenomena to global hazards, technological risks are not reliably known. The decisions that organizations make depend on answers to questions that cannot be definitively answered. Identifying every failure mode in a technology is not possible, nor is it practical to test technologies under every conceivable circumstance. Computer simulations only go so far in subjecting technologies to real-world conditions. The decisions that organizations make about technologies affect future as well as present generations. The norms for making decisions when the scientific information is ambiguous are not well established. Limitations of time and money and incomplete knowledge mean that there are questions that cannot be answered with certainty.

Exhibit 4.2   The Basics of Rational Risk Assessment

1.	**The Magnitude of Risk**
	■ Nature, potency, distribution of hazard
	■ Number of people exposed
	■ Means by which exposed
	■ Adverse health effects at different exposure levels
2.	**Management of the Risk**
	■ Action based on public health, environmental goals, legislation, legal precedent, values, and financial and social considerations

Conditions of perfect knowledge would permit fully rational decisions, but those conditions cannot be realized. Under conditions of perfect ignorance, on the other hand, choices are random. Between these extremes lie dilemmas. Some evidence is available, but, despite good efforts to dispel it, uncertainty still exists. Testing and experience can reduce uncertainties, but residual uncertainty cannot be eliminated entirely, and subjective judgment plays a role. Judgment is critical, but there are cognitive limits at the level of the individual, as expressed by experts, and at the level of the group. There are also intractable problems of quantification, such as the value of a life worth, and questions of scientific evidence, such as how appropriate it is to extrapolate animal studies to human beings.

Individual Cognitive Limits

Psychologists have taught that humans confronted with decisions under uncertainty make fundamental mistakes.[7] They tend to consider themselves immune to hazards, which others readily acknowledge. They have difficulties imagining events of low probability with severe consequences like 9/11 or a nuclear power plant meltdown. In addition, psychologists have found that people are less tolerant about the risks of involuntary activities as opposed to those that arise from voluntary actions like riding a motorcycle or driving a car. If they have good information and are given choices, they are willing to take risks that they otherwise might avoid. According to psychologists, people fear events that have a low probability of occurring but have severe consequences, like a plane crashing, more than events of high probability with small consequences, like falling when riding a bicycle.

In addition, psychologists have found that people tend to underestimate error and unreliability inherent in small samples of data.[8] They have unreasonable expectations and undue confidence about the replicability of early results, and they judge probability based on the ease of retrieving information from memory. These biases mean that people get set in their judgments and are reluctant to revise despite what the subsequent evidence suggests. In line with this finding is that people tend to rely on saliency as well as recency in making their evaluations. Direct experience and reporting bias their judgments.

Experts' Cognitive Limits

Experts like economists and engineers are supposedly trained to rely on computational tools, theories, specific observations, and their experience to estimate risk.[9] However, they tend to assign the same weights to hazards that take many lives at once as they do to hazards that take many lives one at a time. They lump voluntary and involuntary hazards together and underestimate possible pathways to disaster. They have been known to be slow to detect chronic, cumulative health, safety, and environmental effects. Experts try to overcome the indeterminateness of their knowledge by attempting to simplify tasks: They narrow the range of data they take into account and put limits on the amount of information they obtain.[10]

Organizations' Cognitive Limits

Although an individual may choose to subject himself to a risk in which there is high likelihood of danger, the decisions of organizations impact large numbers of people whose choices are limited. It is unclear if they would voluntarily accept the same risks as an individual. Confrontation between individuals of opposing positions in an organization is desirable because it puts forth varied positions, but adversary procedures do not necessarily resolve issues of uncertainty. Collectively shared attitudes and conceptions can lead to greater realism, but also to biases.

In collective decision-making bodies, there may develop an illusion of invulnerability and the suppression of doubt as a result of group consensus, insulation of the group from external criticism, and a dominant individual expressing her views to the exclusion of others. Groups often do not make sound use of the knowledge they already possess. Negligence or failure to attend to what is known is a source of failure.

Negligence about what was known played a role in the Bhopal and BP oil spill tragedies. Warnings were ignored. Often, information overload incapacitates decision makers from distinguishing true signals from the noise. Someone in the organization must have the power to take action based on the warnings that have been given. Power and not merely knowledge is necessary to correct errors.[11]

How Much a Life Is Worth

Even if organizations can estimate the risk, there is the issue of quantification.[12] Quantifying the value of a human life is one of the most difficult problems in the rational assessment of risk. Although disturbing, it may be necessary to attempt to answer the basic question: how much is a life worth? The legal system provides a simple answer: the net present value of a person's expected lifetime earnings. Obviously, this is problematic inasmuch as women are valued less than men in terms of earnings, minorities are valued less than the majority, old people are valued less than the young, and people without employment and without the prospect of working have, according to this system, no worth at all.

An alternative is to use a "willingness to pay" criteria. It is possible to ask questions on surveys, for instance, about how much someone is willing to pay for lifesaving procedures, such as to have a heart attack ambulance in her neighborhood to reduce the number of deaths, or how much a person would be willing to pay to join a group of 10,000, one of whom will be chosen at random for execution. Or how much would a person be willing to pay to buy back bullets in Russian roulette?

The problem is that these situations are artificial. Some economists derive the value of a human life on the more objective basis of how much people are willing to pay for homes in areas with little pollution. In different cultures, life may be valued differently. U.S. juries, for instance, award much larger sums in cases of wrongful death. In India, where the Bhopal incident took place, the typical award has been much less.

Inferences from Animal Studies to Humans

For chemical as well as pharmaceutical and medical product companies, risk assessment may require extrapolation from animal to human data.[13] Consistently positive results in two sexes of animals and in several strains and species as well as higher incidence at higher doses tend to constitute the best evidence. However, such consistent observations may not be available. Typically, a given percentage of animals shows results, a smaller percentage in the control group has less results, and it is necessary to decide if the difference is statistically significant or attributable to chance. One group of animals is usually given the highest dose that can be tolerated, a second group may be exposed at half that amount, and a control group may not be exposed at all. The highest amount that can be tolerated is used for a number of reasons. First, if a small amount is used, it may not induce sufficient results in a small group of experimental animals to be statistically significant. Second, individuals are not exposed to a single substance in the real world, but to numerous substances, which may act concurrently with each other. Problems of safety therefore plague chemical, pharmaceutical, and medical product companies when they try to introduce new products. In the next chapter, two instances of these problems in the pharmaceutical and medical products industries are traced: first Merck's introduction of Vioxx and then J&J's introduction of an alternative hip therapy. In both instances, serious mistakes were made, and the companies were subject to high levels of liability.

Conclusion

This chapter discussed dilemmas in managing dangerous technologies—the cognitive limits of individuals, experts, and organizations in trying to rationally manage them, the issue of how much a life is worth, and the problem of making inferences from animal studies to humans. The next chapter turns to issues that can arise in the commercialization of technologies that are designed to reduce pain and prolong life. Care must be taken in the introduction of these technologies so that the laws of liability, which are discussed in the next chapter, are not breached.

Endnotes

1. For the sources of this case, see Alfred Marcus and Sheryl Kaiser, *Managing Beyond Compliance: The Ethical and Legal Dimensions of Corporate Responsibility,* Garfield Heights, OH: North Coast Publishers, 2006. Paul Shrivastava, *Bhopal: Anatomy of a Crisis*, Cambridge, MA: Ballinger Publishing Co., 1987. David E. Whiteside, "Note on the Export of Pesticides from the United States to Developing Countries," Cambridge, MA: Harvard Business Publishing, 1983: 127. Stuart Diamond, "The Disaster in Bhopal: Workers Recall Horror." *New York Times.* Jan. 30, 1985: A6. Alfred Marcus and Robert Goodman, "Corporate Adjustments to Catastrophe: A Study of Investor Reaction to Bhopal." *Industrial Crisis Quarterly* 3 (1989): 213–234. Sanjoy Hazarika, "Indian Journalist Offered Warning." *New York Times.* Dec. 11, 1984: A5. "Slumdwellers Unaware of Dangers." *New York Times.* Jan. 31, 1985: A8.

2. For the sources of this case, see Alfred Marcus and Andrew Van de Ven, "Managing Shifting Goal Consensus and Task Ambiguity in Making the Shift to Sustainability," *Leading Sustainable Change*. Eds. Rebecca Henderson, Ranjay Gulati, and Michael Tushman. Oxford: Oxford University Press, 2015. 298–323. G. Augustine, "Whiting Refinery: Beyond Petroleum (A) BP and the Whiting Refinery: Beyond Petroleum (B)," case 1-428-727 and mini-case 1-428-736. Ann Arbor, MI: Erb Institute University of Michigan, 2008. J. Huyn, J. Kaplan, S. Katpally, B. Pierce, and B. Pierson, "BP: Beyond Petroleum?" Ann Arbor, MI: Erb Institute University of Michigan, 2008.

3. Charles Perrow, *Normal Accidents*, New York: Basic Books, 1984.

4. Ibid.

5. Perrow, *Normal Accidents*, p. 12.

6. Alfred Marcus, "Risk, Uncertainty, and Scientific Judgment," *Minerva* 2 (1988), pp. 138–152. Alvin Weinberg, "Science and Trans-Science," *Minerva* 10 (April 1972), pp. 209–222.

7. Daniel Kahneman, *Thinking Fast and Thinking Slow,* New York: Farrar, Strauss and Giroux, 2011.

8. Ibid.

9. Marcus, "Risk, Uncertainty, and Scientific Judgment."

10. Ibid.

11. Ibid.

12. L. B. Lave, *How Safe Is Safe Enough? Setting Safety Goals,* formal publication no. 96, Center for the Study of American Business, Washington University, January 1990.

13. Marcus, "Risk, Uncertainty, and Scientific Judgment."

5

Laws of Liability

This chapter discusses the introduction of the painkiller Vioxx by Merck and the introduction of an alternative hip replacement by Johnson & Johnson (J&J). Both companies had impeccable reputations, but they did not handle these products' dangers to patients well. These cases led to large liabilities that were avoidable had the two firms taken the early warnings seriously. The chapter concludes with a primer on liability law. Liability law is meant to compensate victims for the harm companies cause in introducing new technologies and to deter companies from irresponsibly putting innocent people at risk by not warning them of foreseeable dangers.

Vioxx: What Went Wrong?

On September 30, 2004, Merck had to pull its $2.5 billion blockbuster painkiller drug, Vioxx, from the market.[1] Vioxx was a prescription COX-2 selective, non-steroidal anti-inflammatory drug (NSAID) prescribed for osteoarthritis, acute pain in adults, and menstrual symptoms. The discovery that the drug could cause heart damage to humans was a severe blow to the pharmaceutical company. Merck clearly did not want to take it off the market because the drug represented 10 percent of its 2003 revenue. Margins were high, and years of research and millions of dollars had gone into the research and development (R&D) that had brought the drug to the market. Once FDA approved, Merck was able to advertise and sell Vioxx as a painkiller.

Despite Merck's positive reputation and its search for a blockbuster drug like Vioxx without gastrointestinal complications, it ignored early warnings and vigorously marketed the drug without being certain of its full safety. It failed to communicate the risks to patients, and after the FDA required that it make the risks known, it withheld evidence that showed the connection between Vioxx and coronary diseases. After more criticism, Merck finally recalled the drug voluntarily but faced thousands of suits for liability. In the end, it even faced criminal charges.

Merck's Positive Reputation

That the Vioxx incident happened at Merck came as a surprise. It is an indication of what can happen at any company, no matter how strong or positive its reputation. Merck manufactures, develops, discovers, and markets many medicines in various therapeutic categories. The company's values, published on its website, include the following:

> We are responsible to our customers, to Merck employees, to the environments we inhabit, and to the societies we serve worldwide.[2]

To work for Merck, employees must sign and accept this statement. The company has a charitable organization that brings medicine to people in underprivileged areas. It has been named one of *Fortune* 500's top companies several times.

The Search for a Blockbuster Drug Without Gastrointestinal Complications

Merck needed a blockbuster drug to compensate for other drugs that were about to lose patent protection and because so many of its drug development efforts had not been productive. The company began studying COX-2 drugs in the 1980s, hoping to discover a painkiller without gastrointestinal complications. Painkillers, such as Vioxx, and over-the-counter anti-inflammatory drugs, like Advil and Naproxen, are used to relieve many kinds of pain from backaches to osteoarthritis. The company's studies of COX-2 drugs suggested that they produced the same benefits as other pain relievers without the negative gastrointestinal effects. Vioxx, which was put through several rounds of tests, looked to be of great potential for pain relief without the risk of ulcers.

Early Warnings

Although the FDA sensed early on that Vioxx caused cardiovascular problems based on some of the clinical studies, removing the product from the market was difficult. Nearly 25 million Americans had taken the drug when Merck recalled it. However, as far back as 1984, Garret Fitzgerald at the University of Pennsylvania, in work published in *The New England Journal of Medicine*, showed that the COX enzyme in Vioxx, by preventing arterial blood clot formation, could harm people with damaged blood vessels. Merck understood these concerns, but in the studies leading up to Vioxx's FDA approval, it excluded patients with a history of cardiovascular disease.

After 10 years of effort, the FDA approved Vioxx for sale in 1999. In its first year on the market, Merck spent over $160 million, more than any other drug company that year, on advertising and promoting the drug's benefits, and in its first seven months on the market, doctors wrote five million prescriptions for Vioxx. However, in 2000, Merck's research chief, Ed Scolnick, continued to warn of the cardiovascular complications.

A study, designed to demonstrate Vioxx's gastrointestinal benefits, was ongoing. Among the subjects of this study, unlike previous Merck studies, 4 percent had a history of prior cardiovascular disease. The Vioxx users in the study had two to five times the rate of cardiovascular problems of subjects who used the generic drug Naproxen.

Failure to Communicate

Although Merck knew of the problem, it did not communicate Vioxx's ill effects in its marketing material. It reasoned that the study had been done without a placebo. Therefore, it was impossible to know whether Vioxx caused the negative results or they showed up because Naproxen had cardiovascular benefits. However, in 2001, another study appeared that cast additional doubt on Vioxx. The Cleveland Clinic's Dr. Eric Topol published a study in *The Journal of the American Medical Association* that showed increased rates of heart attacks and strokes connected to Vioxx. The information that something could be wrong with Vioxx started to leak to the public. A Merck employee provided *The Wall Street Journal* with internal emails. In one, a Merck employee said that the company excluded all heart patients from its Vioxx studies so that cardiovascular problems would not surface. In another, a different Merck employee discussed how the company designed its studies to minimize unflattering comparisons with other drugs. This email acknowledged it would have been hard to hide the unfavorable comparisons.

The FDA's Required Warning

The FDA responded to the controversy. An advisory panel recommended that the agency require Merck to put a warning label on Vioxx. The agency told Merck to stop misleading doctors about the cardiovascular effects of Vioxx. In a letter to Merck, the FDA accused the company of minimizing the cardiovascular findings and misrepresenting Vioxx's safety in its marketing of the drug.

The requirement that Merck put a warning label on Vioxx, however, was delayed until 2002. Under pressure from Merck, the label provided information about Vioxx's benefits first. The potential heart and stroke problems were only mentioned much later in the warning. Merck, alarmed, canceled a planned 2002 study to test whether patients with acute coronary syndrome who were given an anti-inflammatory drug like Vioxx would benefit. It did not want to carry out Vioxx-related studies that involved subjects with coronary disease. In 2003, it suspended a study it initiated to determine if Vioxx could be used for the prevention and treatment of colon polyps and colorectal and prostate cancer because initial results of the study showed a high rate of cardiovascular deaths.

More Criticism

Vioxx was the blockbuster Merck needed. The drug brought in $2.5 billion in revenue in 2003. One billion dollars of this revenue came from Medicaid. However, Medicaid advocates started to criticize Merck. They wondered what outcomes patients with cardiovascular disease were getting from Vioxx. In addition, *The Lancet*, a British medical journal, published a study in 2004 based on data from 25,000 patients and 18 clinical studies that showed that patients taking Vioxx exhibited 2.3 times the cardiovascular risks of patients taking competitor drugs or placebos.[3] The FDA, too, released the results of an incomplete study.

David Graham carried out an epidemiological study for the FDA and made public his unpublished data.[4] His claim was that using pain relievers other than Vioxx would have prevented 27,000 heart attacks and sudden cardiac deaths in the United States. Publicly, Merck stood behind the efficacy and safety of Vioxx. However, employees leaked other documents to *The Wall Street Journal*. One in particular caught people's attention. It was called the "Vioxx Dodge Ball" and instructed sales representatives not to directly answer questions that physicians posed about Vioxx's safety.

Voluntary Recall

In the fall of 2004, Merck decided to act. Before the FDA could force a recall, the company voluntarily recalled the painkiller. The company's CEO made the announcement. Merck maintained that it only knew of the full extent of the danger after the publication of the article in *The Lancet* and that as soon as it made the discovery, it initiated its recall. Merck also maintained that the FDA had permitted it to continue marketing Vioxx with a warning label, but that it was taking the responsible route and withdrawing the drug voluntarily. After Merck took this step, its stock price fell drastically. However, over time it recovered, and Merck did not suffer lasting financial damage.

In the fall 2004, Senator Charles Grassley started a congressional investigation of Vioxx. He maintained that Merck was not the only blameworthy organization, but that the FDA had to accept some of the responsibility as well because it knew of the questionable results long before it acted. The FDA countered that drugs like Vioxx often appear to be safe at first and are only proven unsafe later on, after many additional studies. At the hearings, Grassley questioned the FDA's independence. He revealed potential conflict of interest in that 10 out of 32 of the expert committee members chosen by the FDA to evaluate Vioxx had ties to the industry, had consulted for Merck, or owned stock in other pharmaceutical companies.

Thousands of Suits

Starting in 2005, lawyers started to file thousands of lawsuits against Merck on behalf of plaintiffs who claimed injury. In some of the cases, perfectly healthy people who did not have a history of weight problems, did not smoke, and had no past heart disease problems died from heart attack or stroke after taking Vioxx for nine months or more. Merck's legal liabilities were estimated to exceed $18 billion in 2005. Physicians leveled charges against Merck for spending millions of dollars on advertising. They felt pressured into prescribing Vioxx when ordinary over-the-counter drugs like Advil and Ibuprofen would have been safer, cheaper, and just as effective. An *Archives of Internal Medicine* study showed that nearly three-quarters of the people who took Vioxx did so unnecessarily. They could have relied on simpler over-the-counter medication. In 2007, Merck agreed to pay $4.85 billion to settle 27,000 lawsuits and signed a corporate integrity agreement promising to monitor its future promotional activity and report back to the government regularly.

Criminal Charges

In 2011, Merck pleaded guilty to a criminal charge of selling Vioxx and agreed to pay $950 million in fines to the Department of Justice. Tony West, assistant attorney general of the Justice department's civil division, made the claim that Merck had subverted FDA rules that were meant to keep medicines safe and that it had undermined the ability of healthcare providers to make good decisions on behalf of their patients.

Johnson & Johnson's Hip Replacement: What Went Wrong?

Merck was not the only example of a company with a positive reputation that put patients at risk with a technological innovation. Johnson & Johnson (J&J), the world's largest seller of healthcare products, had created such brands as Band-Aid, Tylenol, Listerine, Lubriderm, Rogaine, Bengay, and Baby Powder. However, by the end of the first decade of the 21st century, it faced numerous lawsuits over an apparently innovative hip replacement technology that had injured thousands.[5]

J&J had consumer healthcare, medical device and diagnostic, and pharmaceutical divisions and 250 subsidiaries, including three that were of particular interest regarding health and safety issues in this time period: DePuy, Ethicon, and McNeill. DePuy made hip implants that left patients with metal poisoning and other complications, Ethicon made transvaginal mesh implants that led to serious complications and required multiple revision surgeries, and McNeill had serious product quality issues. Because of lawsuits stemming from these problems, J&J, like Merck, had to pay billions of dollars in damages. What went wrong in the DePuy case with a company that had been viewed as a paragon of social responsibility was acquisition of this subsidiary, infatuation with a new technology, failure to warn patients of design problems with a technology, an FDA investigation, voluntary recall, suits, and massive reimbursement to patients who had been harmed.

A Paragon of Social Responsibility

Johnson & Johnson's credo stated that its *first* responsibility was to doctors, nurses, patients, children, mothers, and families who used its products and services.[6] Its next responsibility was to employees, communities, the environment, and natural resources. Stockholders were its last responsibility, and it claimed that it only owed them a fair return of their investment. In 1982, J&J showed that it lived up to the principles in its credo when, despite concerns about the shareholder reaction, it initiated a rapid recall of 31 million bottles of Tylenol after seven people died from ingesting cyanide-laced pills.[7] However, the same J&J that recalled Tylenol in 1982 was forced against its will to withdraw 288 million items from the market, including liquid Tylenol, Motrin, Zyrtec, and Benadryl, because of quality-control problems at J&J plants in Pennsylvania and Puerto Rico in the 21st century. J&J again had to withdraw 500,000 bottles of infant Tylenol in 2012 reluctantly and against its will.

The Acquisition of DePuy

The most outstanding example of the problems that J&J faced relate to the hip implants sold by its DePuy subsidiary. J&J acquired DePuy, a commercial orthopedic manufacturer and device maker, in 1998. In 2010, this subsidiary of the company was the world's top manufacturer of hip replacements. With the Pinnacle Hip Replacement System, which was introduced in 2000, the Articular Surface Replacement (ASR) system that DePuy sold internationally in 2003, and the ASR XL Acetabular System that DePuy sold both internationally and in the United States in 2005, DePuy was a pioneer and technological leader in introducing a metal-on-metal design in hip replacement.

All-Metal Replacements

Orthopedic surgeons believed that all-metal replacement hips like DePuy's ASR system would last longer than traditional replacement devices made of plastic and metal. By 2010 DePuy's Pinnacle systems had been installed in as many as 40,000 U.S. patients, and up to 37,000 U.S. patients used its ASR products. Outside the United States, another 56,000 patients relied on Pinnacle systems and ASR products. Starting in 2003, DePuy sold the products outside the United States as an alternative to a replacement procedure called resurfacing. Two years later, the company adopted the resurfacing component for standard hip replacements in the United States. The problem was that the metal ball and cup components in these products often rubbed together, causing friction and releasing metal debris and particles into the user's bloodstream, which in turn caused tissue damage and crippling injuries. The implants also often loosened, and patients suffered joint dislocation that required additional surgeries.

Design Problems

These design problems came to light in Australia and England shortly after the first sales were made in those countries. According to internal DePuy documents revealed at subsequent trials, a consultant to the company warned the head of DePuy's orthopedic unit, Andrew Ekdahl, who oversaw the hip's introduction, that there was a serious design flaw with the implants. However, for years DePuy insisted to surgeons who complained when the device failed that their implanting techniques, not the device itself, were responsible.

FDA Investigations

The all-metal system was once highly popular with surgeons, but by 2011 the metal devices were rarely used because of high failure rates. After reports of complications from consumers and physicians, the FDA was about to take action, and J&J agreed to a recall. This technology had been designed to improve the quality of life of thousands of patients, but instead it left many of them with serious permanent injuries. Because of the many problems patients encountered, the FDA investigated the ASR and Pinnacle devices. The FDA told DePuy that it would reject its approval of resurfacing technology in the United States because of the high concentrations of metal ions that were reported to have been released in European patients' bodies. When the FDA asked DePuy for more safety data, the company panicked. It decided it would have to phase out of the ASR, but it first chose to sell its inventories of the devices without telling physicians or patients about the problems. In the foreign countries in which it continued to sell this technology, J&J did not reveal the FDA's regulatory decision.

A Voluntary Recall

In 2010 the company discontinued the Pinnacle line of implants and decided to voluntarily recall all hip replacements. Its claim was that it acted as soon as it had definitive information on the dangers and that it voluntarily recalled the product immediately after obtaining data from the National Joint Registry of England and Wales that showed the devices were failing prematurely and at a higher rate than competing implants. It also promised to pay the medical costs of replacement procedures.

However, during patient lawsuits, another picture emerged of what J&J knew, when it discovered this information, and what it did with it. Internal company documents showed that DePuy officials knew long before the recall that the product's design was flawed and that it failed at prematurely high rates. In testimony, a DePuy engineer admitted that by 2008 company officials were fully aware of reports by an English surgeon that found that the resurfacing version of the ASR technology released high levels of metallic ions, especially in female patients. At that time, company officials understood that the product was defective and that it would have to be redesigned. Orthopedic databases to which the company subscribed showed that most artificial hips had a lifetime of 15 years or more before they had to be replaced. However, by 2008, these databases showed that ASR metal systems failed patients at high rates after just a few years. Indeed, internal DePuy documents brought to light by lawyers during trials against the company estimated a 40-percent failure rate for most patients in five years, a rate that was eight times higher than for other hip devices.

Suits Against the Company

Because DePuy had not warned its patients of these risks, the company confronted as many as 12,000 legal claims against it in the United States alone. The estimate was that in two-thirds of these cases patients would have to have additional surgeries to remove and replace their original implants. In addition to those who had already undergone painful and costly procedures to replace their implants, the projections were that thousands more would have their hip replacements fail in coming years. Based on the number of patients who already had undergone device replacements, DePuy estimated that 37 percent of patients who used the all-metal system would need to have it replaced within five years.

A British implant registry updated its projected failure rates for ASR patients in 2011. The devices were failing in one-third of cases. DePuy publicly challenged this estimate, but other global medical organizations projected even higher failure rates. DePuy settled three hip-related lawsuits in the summer of 2012 for $200,000 each. A 2013 court verdict then ordered the company to pay plaintiffs $8.3 million in damages. The company took a $3 billion special charge related to the medical and legal costs of the metal-on-metal technology. Later in the year, it agreed to pay $2.5 billion to settle more than 7,500 state and federal lawsuits affecting more than 8,000 people who had to have their all-metal artificial hips removed and replaced with another device.

The Reimbursement Plan

Under the reimbursement plan to these people, the typical patient obtained $250,000, before legal fees, for pain and suffering. However, it was uncertain if this deal would satisfy a sufficient number of the claimants. The proposed settlement, submitted to a federal judge in Toledo, Ohio, had to have the support of 94 percent of eligible claimants to go forward. Some claimants could do much better if they held out for better terms. Under the terms of the settlement, some patients were entitled to only small payouts, whereas other patients' payments would be lowered based on how long the patient had the implant. The payment to a patient who had a device for five to six years fell to $225,000, and if the patient had a device for six to seven years, the payment went down to $200,000. However, patients could qualify for a special pool, based on the severity of their injuries, and obtain more money. About 10 percent of the claimants were eligible. For example, some patients in the special pool had replacements on both hips. The average basic award of $250,000 was affected by a variety of factors. Plaintiffs who smoked, were overweight, or were older also had their payments reduced. In 2014, J&J had to increase the money it reserved for the damages.

The takeaway here, like in the Vioxx case, is that organizations introducing new technologies cannot ignore early warning signs of dangers. They must address these dangers with prompt action or face dire consequences. They need to monitor new technology introduced into the market and be prepared for a quick withdrawal should surprises take place, regardless of the short-term financial considerations.

The Laws of Liability

From a legal point of view, what type of due diligence is needed?[8] According to classic legal doctrine, companies have to act as a reasonable person would under the same circumstances. If they do not conform to this standard, they are at fault and have to compensate the victims. The compensation can be very large. In the Union Carbide, BP, Merck, and J&J cases, the liability amounted to billions of dollars. Modern legal theory does not require proof of fault. The doctrine that prevails is strict liability, but strict liability does not mean that a company is without a defense. The company must show that the technologies it brings to market have no design or manufacturing defect, that it has provided adequate warnings, and that users have voluntarily assumed the risk. The latter can be demonstrated by showing that the company has provided users with enough information to make an independent judgment.

Evolution of the Law

How has the law of damages evolved in the United States? In legal terminology, this branch of law is called torts. Derived from French and Latin roots and meaning "to twist," tort law deals with private harm or injury. When a person is harmed, the plaintiff (the person claiming to have been harmed) may bring an action against the defendant (the person alleged to have caused the harm). The purpose is to restore the situation to the condition before the harm was caused and, inasmuch as possible, to compensate the plaintiff for the damage that was done.

Tort law also has a deterrent effect. If a company knows that a victim must be compensated, there is less of a chance that a perpetrator will commit an act that is known to cause harm. Insofar as tort law aims to restore a situation to its prior condition, its purpose is to promote a sense of justice in society. The deterrent effect of plaintiff suits in instances like Bhopal, BP, Vioxx, and J&J's hip replacement can be quite large, but corporations often seem able to absorb these charges and go on as if nothing has happened.

Classic Tort Law

According to the classic tort law, a plaintiff has to prove breach of duty, actual damages, and causation, and a defendant can argue contributory negligence and assumption of risk. Even if the harm is unintentional, the defendant owes the plaintiff the duty of care that a reasonable person would show under the circumstances. When the courts find fault with the actions of both parties, they are not faced with an either/or situation. In some states, they have the right to apportion blame on a percentage basis.

This rule reduces the plaintiff's burden to prove that the defendant is at fault. By applying a standard of comparative negligence, states can reduce the award the defendant owes the plaintiff by the percentage for which the plaintiff is responsible. The exact apportioning of responsibility between defendant and plaintiff is one of the most controversial aspects of tort law. Therefore, some states have adopted no-fault, which simplifies the process by eliminating costly and lengthy court procedures. It also guarantees that the victim receives some compensation, regardless of who is at fault.

Assumption of Risk

Assumption of risk means defendants can claim that the plaintiff was aware of the risks but decided to pursue the activity anyway. The protection offered by this claim has grown in importance as U.S. society becomes more litigious. For organizations introducing new technologies, this point of law is important. Sharing what is known about the risks with those who might be affected is critically important. The plaintiff's awareness of risk need not be conscious and explicit, but the defendant's argument is strengthened if a consciousness of the risks involved is specific. Therefore, there are many instances of risk-sharing when it comes to technologies. For instance, patients in hospitals are almost always required to sign papers acknowledging their awareness of risks before any type of complex surgery is performed. This sharing of what was known was absent in the Bhopal, BP, Vioxx, and J&J hip replacement cases.

Punitive Action

When the plaintiff has been warned, the courts are far less likely to take punitive action against the defendant. A plaintiff can still recover even after admitting awareness of risk, but the awards will be limited to compensation for tangible medical costs and lost earnings rather than intangible emotional distress or pain and suffering, which means that awards will be substantially lower. Withholding of relevant information led to punitive action in the Bhopal, BP, Vioxx, and J&J hip replacement cases.

Strict Liability

The classic theory of torts puts the burden of proof on the plaintiff to prove that the defendant is at fault. However, with the move toward strict liability, modern tort theory means that the plaintiff no longer has to prove fault. Strict liability theory derives from the treatment the courts give to inherently dangerous activities. For example, if a person owns wild animals, such as snakes or leopards, and those animals injure someone, the owner is responsible regardless of the care exercised. Likewise, a company that uses explosives is responsible for harm even if it observes safety rules. Strict liability was attached to the Bhopal, BP, Vioxx, and J&J hip replacement cases because in each instance the activity or product was inherently dangerous. According to strict liability, responsibility exists without the sense of moral opprobrium that applies under the classic approach.

The Justification for Strict Liability

What is the justification for strict liability? Why should a defendant have to pay when the harm inflicted is unintentional and the defendant's actions are reasonable and appropriate under the circumstances? It is necessary to recognize that someone will have to bear the costs of damages, whether the victim, the injurer, or society at large through its governmental institutions. Modern tort law has decided to make the defendant or the defendant's insurance company mainly responsible. Tracing the evolution of the doctrine of strict liability shows three periods:[9]

- Recovery from damages was mainly governed under contract law in the first period, which lasted until the beginning of World War I.

- The classic theory of torts developed during the second period, which lasted from World War I to the mid-1960s.

- A strict liability standard emerged during the third period, which has been in effect since the mid-1960s.

Under contract law, if a manufacturer of a technology caused a product defect, the consumer had no right to recovery if the consumer's transaction was with the retailer, not the manufacturer. Privity of contract meant that a plaintiff could sue only when she had a legally binding contract with the defendant.

Legal analysts, however, subsequently viewed the privity of contract requirement as prejudicial to consumers, who lacked the knowledge, expertise, and power of the manufacturers of technologies. The *MacPherson v. Buick Motor Co.* decision of 1916 ended the privity of contract requirement in product liability cases. A buyer typically purchases a car from a dealer, not a manufacturer. Regardless of contractual obligations, the courts hold manufacturers responsible.

After this decision, product liability became a subset of tort law rather than contract law. Under this doctrine, a buyer has to prove that the manufacturer of a technology did not provide reasonable safety features or adequate warnings. A famous decision issued in 1947 by Judge Learned Hand in *United States v. Carroll Towing Co.* defined reasonable precaution as the expected injury exceeded the costs of precaution, and the defendant failed to take action. In the Bhopal, BP, Vioxx, and J&J hip replacement cases, this was the situation—the expected injuries exceeded the costs of precaution, and the defendants failed to take action.

Further Movement from a Fault-Based System

Further movement away from a fault-based system can be seen in a case against Coca-Cola Bottling Co. decided by Justice Traynor of the California Supreme Court in 1944. In this case, a Coca-Cola bottle exploded in the hands of a waitress. The courts decided against Coca-Cola Bottling with three main points being part of the decision:

- It is cheaper for society to have a strict liability standard. A plaintiff has to prove only damage and causation, not fault; the burden of proof—and the time and expense of legal proceedings—is reduced. The plaintiff did not have to show that Coca-Cola was responsible for the bottle exploding. Although more trials may take place, the ease of execution of tort cases should reduce total costs to society.

- It is less expensive for the producer to bear the cost of the damage than it is for the victim. The cost of a single accident can be devastating for the victim, who is often uninsured and unprepared. On the other hand, the costs of an accident may be trivial to the producer, who should have the foresight to acquire insurance. Also, liability costs can be passed on to consumers in the form of higher prices, which are probably only a few pennies for each product sold. The option of spreading the risk, available to the producers, is unavailable to customers.

- The producer's intimate knowledge of the product and capability to change the situation dwarfs the consumer's knowledge and the customer's ability to change the situation. The consumer buys technically sophisticated goods that pass through a long and complex chain from factory to retailer. The consumer is unlikely to know where in the chain of design, production, and distribution a defect can occur. Therefore, if the consumer is seriously injured, the manufacturer is responsible.

These three points were incorporated into the 1965 Second Restatement of Torts by the American Law Institute.[10] Thus, strict liability became the norm and, in effect, replaced the slogan "Let the buyer beware (caveat emptor)" with "Seller beware." A seller is held strictly liable even if it exercises all possible care in the preparation and sale. Clearly, Bhopal, BP, Vioxx, and J&J did not exercise all possible care.

Refinements of the Laws of Liability

The Second Restatement of Torts has since undergone a number of refinements that have made it more like the classic law of torts. First, the need to show product defect so that a manufacturer can be held liable pushes strict liability toward classic tort law. A defect can occur in the design or manufacture of the product or by virtue of a failure to warn. These defects existed in the Bhopal, BP, Vioxx, and J&J cases. Determining whether a defect has occurred, especially in product design, is similar to determining whether fault has taken place under the classic theory. The concept of reasonable behavior under the circumstances, often formulated as a state of the art defense, plays an important role.

A second element pushing strict liability toward classic tort law is the continued consideration of contributory negligence. Most courts would hold that a manufacturer cannot be held liable if the consumer blatantly misuses the product.

A third way in which strict liability is similar to the classic doctrine is that it retains the concept of assumption of risk. Defendants can claim that the plaintiff was aware of the risks but decided to pursue the activity anyway. Thus, warning labels and disclaimers are needed. Had Union Carbide, BP, Merck, and J&J adhered to these principles, they would have coped much better with technological danger.

Conclusion

This chapter has discussed what went wrong when Merck introduced the painkiller Vioxx and J&J introduced alternative all-metal hip replacements. Given the positive reputations of both companies, it was a surprise that they ignored early warnings because of commercial concerns, failed to communicate openly with customers, and suffered from huge damage payments even after they voluntarily recalled these products from the market. The large fines and liabilities, which the firms suffered, were avoidable had they taken the early warnings seriously. The chapter concludes with a primer on liability law. The laws of liability require that firms take warnings seriously and that they communicate openly and honestly with customers. Otherwise they may be subject to large punitive action claims against them.

Endnotes

1. Mike Adams, "Scandal to Bury Vioxx Heart Attacks, Risks, Intimidate Scientists, and Keep Public in the Dark," *Newstarget.com*. March 27, 2005. Theresa Agovino, "Pre-Trial Hearing Begins for Vioxx Case," *Associated Press*. March 10, 2005. Mathew Arnold, "Public Address," *Medical Marketing and Media, CPS Communications*. Feb 2004. Theresa Agovino, "Merck Faces Huge Financial and Credibility Fallout Over Vioxx Lawsuits," *Associated Press*. Nov. 4, 2004. Richard Alonzo-Zaldivar, "The Nation: Early Vioxx Alarms Alleged," *Los Angeles Times*. Nov. 19, 2004. Alex Berensen, Gardiner Harris, Barry Meirer, and Andy Pollack, "Despite Warnings, Drug Giant Took Long Path to Vioxx Recall," *New York Times*. Nov. 14, 2004. Robert Burton, "How Merck Stacked the Vioxx Deck," *Salon*. March 31, 2005. "FDA Public Health Advisory: Safety of Vioxx," *FDA.gov*. Sept. 30, 2004. Barnaby Feder, "Merck's Actions on Vioxx Face New Scrutiny," *New York Times*. Feb. 15, 2005. Gardiner Harris, "Study Says Drug's Dangers Were Apparent Years Ago," *New York Times*. Nov. 5, 2004. Sepp Hasslberger, "Vioxx, Celebrex, Bextra: COX2 Inhibitors Unsafe Warns FDA Panel," *News Media Explorer*. Feb. 28, 2005. Lily Henning, "Awash in Vioxx Suits, Merck Recruits Big-Time Help," *Fulton County Daily Report*. Dec. 8, 2004. Katharine Greider, "Vioxx: Downfall of a Superdrug" *AARP Bulletin Online*. November 2004. Denise Kersten, "After Vioxx, The FDA Faces Public Demands for More Information About Dangerous Medications," *Government Executive* 37.4 (March 15, 2005). Anna Wilde Mathew and Barbara Martinez, "E-Mails Suggest Merck Knew Vioxx's Dangers at Early Stage," *The Wall Street Journal*. Nov. 2, 2004. Rita Rubina, "How Did the Vioxx Debacle Happen?" *USA Today*. Oct. 12, 2004.

2. Merck website: http://www.merck.com/index.html.

3. Richard Alonzo-Zaldivar, "The Nation: Early Vioxx Alarms Alleged," *Los Angeles Times*. Nov. 19, 2004. Alex Berensen, Gardiner Harris, Barry Meirer, and Andy Pollack, "Despite Warnings, Drug Giant Took Long Path to Vioxx Recall," *New York Times*. Nov. 14, 2004.

4. Ibid.

5. Alex Nussbaum, David Voreacos, and Greg Farrell, "Johnson & Johnson's Quality Catastrophe," *Bloomberg Business Week*. March 31, 2011. http://www.bloomberg.com/bw/magazine/content/11_15/b4223064555570.htm. Jonathan Rockoff and Jon Kamp, "J&J Latest Recall: Hip-Repair Implants," *Wall Street Journal*. Aug. 27, 2010. http://www.wsj.com/articles/SB10001424052748703959704575453492107751662. Jonathan Rockoff and Dionne Searcey, "Hip Joints Set Off New Rush to Court," *Wall Street Journal*. July 8, 2011. http://www.wsj.com/articles/SB10001424052702303365804576432051261804910. Jonathan Rockoff,

"When J&J Learned of Implant Problems," *The Wall Street Journal.* Jan 23, 2013. http://www.wsj.com/articles/SB10001424127887323940004578258503673382 928. Barry Meier, "Hip Maker Discussed Failures," *New York Times.* Feb. 21, 2012. http://www.nytimes.com/2012/02/22/business/flawed-depuy-hip-implant-had-early-fda-notice.html?_r=0>. Barry Meier, "Maker Hid Data About Design Flaw in Hip Implant, Records Show," *New York Times.* Jan. 25, 2013. http://www.nytimes.com/2013/01/26/business/johnson-johnson-hid-flaw-in-artificial-hip-documents-show.html. Barry Meier, "In Medicine, New Isn't Always Improved," *New York Times.* June 25, 2011. http://www.nytimes.com/2011/06/26/health/26innovate.html.

6. http://www.jnj.com/about-jnj/jnj-credo?sitelink=The&J&J&Credo&utm_source=Google&utm_medium=cpc&utm_campaign=J&J&Love&utm_term=j%26j%20credo&utm_content=J%26J+-+Heritage+-+E|mkwid|sI3rPB9w4_dc|pcrid|53649332174.

7. Judith Rehak, "Tylenol Made a Hero of Johnson & Johnson: The Recall That Started Them All," *New York Times.* March 23, 2002. http://www.nytimes.com/2002/03/23/your-money/23iht-mjj_ed3_.html.

8. Robert Cooter and Thomas Ulen, *Law and Economics*, Boston: Pearson Addison Wesley, 2007.

9. Ibid.

10. *Restatement of the Law Second, Torts*, Philadelphia: American Law Institute, 1965. https://www.ali.org/publications/show/torts/.

PART III

THE ENVIRONMENT OF TECHNOLOGY

6

Old, Young, and Global Security

The world today faces aging societies in Europe, Japan, China, and the United States and youthful societies in much of the Mideast, Africa, and parts of Latin America. Too many of these young people cannot find productive employment. In many countries, youth unemployment rates remain uncomfortably high. When the opportunities for a normal life are diminished, young people often choose a path of violence.[1]

A wealth of historical studies shows that cycles of violence have coincided with periods when young people composed unusually large proportions of the population.[2] Demography plays a leading role in global security because young people have never been evenly distributed in the population, whether today or in the past.[3] Young people also have been the "protagonists of protest, instability, reform, and revolution."[4] They provided recruits to fascist movements in the 1920s and demonstrations and protests in the 1960s.[5]

Technology influences the extent to which the transition from generation to generation is peaceful. This chapter describes the challenges posed by demographic transition, starting with aging and concluding with issues of youth. Technologies can be used to ameliorate these quandaries. This chapter features some of them, including innovations to help find a cure for Alzheimer's and extend life for the elderly and innovations for countering and exposing terrorism to reduce violence and bring about a more peaceful world.

The Rise of the Elderly

For most of human history, people older than 65 years old comprised no more than 3 to 4 percent of the global population.[6] However, in 2015, in developed countries they constituted 15 percent of the population. They are likely to become a quarter of the world's population by 2050, more than two billion people. With the exception of sub-Saharan Africa, the median age in all countries is increasing. In Germany, Italy, and Spain, the elderly are expected to comprise more than 35 percent of the population, and in Japan, Korea, and Singapore, more than 40 percent. Life expectancy in the world in 1950 was 48 years old. By 2010 it approached 70 years, and by 2050 it is expected to reach 75 years. To the extent population growth occurs in the world, it is likely to happen among people over 65 (see Exhibit 6.1).

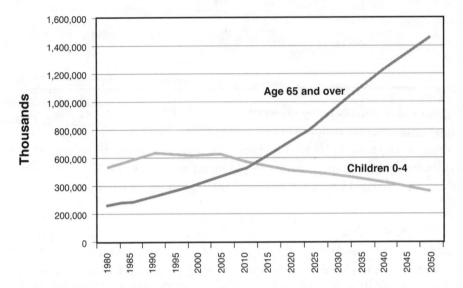

Exhibit 6.1 Anticipated world population in 2050: children 0–4 years of age and people over 65 years of age

United Nations Population Division

Declining Fertility

Throughout the world, fertility has been declining.[7] In 1950, the average woman had 5.0 children. In 2015 she had 2.5, and this number is likely to decline to below 2.0 by 2050. In developed countries, the number was less than 1.5 babies per woman. These sub-replacement fertility rates have spread to every corner of the globe. The United Nations assumes that fertility rates will continue to decline and that world fertility rates the world over will converge on 1.85 children per woman by 2050; at this point in time, the world's population will start to decline (see Exhibit 6.2).

Fertility rates have been declining for many reasons, including the rising status of women in society, more education, and increased participation by women in the workforce. Declining fertility is a result of the widespread availability of birth control and the weakening of traditional religious and cultural values. Another reason is economic—the

money needed to raise a child has skyrocketed. In the United States, if a college education is included, estimates of the average cost of raising a single, middle-class child may
surpass a million dollars.[8]

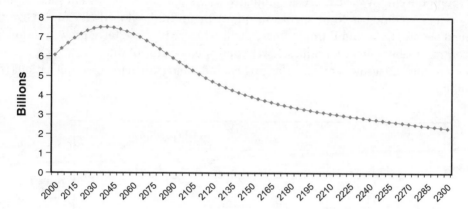

Exhibit 6.2 A Projection of World Population in the Year 2300

United Nations Population Division

In most of southern and central Europe and newly industrialized East Asian countries,
fertility rates are below replacement levels in 2015. When fertility rates fall below 2.1
children per woman, the population of a country does not replace itself. It loses population in the next generation. The fertility rate in Singapore of 1.2 children per woman was
among the lowest in the world. In Northern and Western Europe, fertility rates are just
slightly higher. If an average woman has 1.4 babies, the population of a country declines
by 50 percent in a half decade.[9] Because of low fertility, Japan's population is expected to
fall by a quarter to 95 million by 2050. Nigeria continues to be one of the only countries
in the world where fertility rates are rising. In 2015, it is slated to be the fourth most
populous country in the world, but many developing countries in North Africa and the
Middle East have declining fertility (see Exhibit 6.3).

Exhibit 6.3 Fertility Rates in North African and Middle Eastern Nations, 2009

Country	Lifetime Births Per Woman
Iran	1.72
Tunisia	1.74
Algeria	1.89
Lebanon	1.90
Turkey	1.92

Economic Impacts

Rapid aging is bringing about changes in the world economy. As people age, their productivity goes down. There also are fewer young people to support each older person. Although the elderly have more accumulated assets than other groups in society, more of society's income has to be spent to support them. In developed economies like the United States, Japan, and Europe, where the workforce is aging, GDP growth is slowing in contrast to emerging economies, fewer young people are entering the work force, and labor productivity growth rates are lagging behind their growth in emerging nations (see Exhibit 6.4).

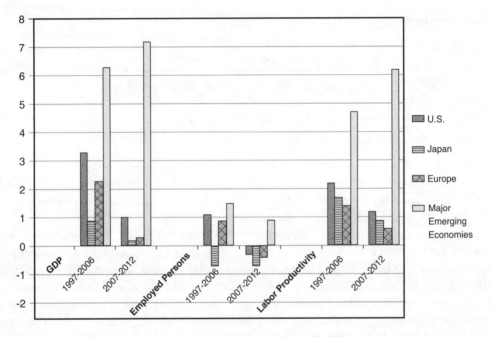

Exhibit 6.4 Average Percentage Changes in GDP, Employed Persons, and Labor Productivity 1997–2013

Based on 2014 Conference Board Data

The EU projects that by 2025 there will be fewer than three employed persons for each retired person.[10] In 2015 in Spain, about 9 percent of the country's GDP went toward entitlements for the aged, whereas education spending was less than 5 percent of GDP. Money spent on pensions and healthcare for retirees reduces the amount of money available to educate the young for productive employment. Many countries already have skilled labor shortages because of an aging workforce All nations in the world therefore covet talented immigrants. The demand for workers with skills has grown, and the competition to attract them is intense. However, because of rampant unemployment and the lack of effective integration of immigrant populations, many nations are experiencing civil discord. The long-term implication of these changes is that the balance of economic power among nations is shifting. China, because of the one child per family policy it had, continues to age. By 2050, it is expected that the median age in China will be 49. In contrast, India remains a relatively young society, and by 2050 it almost certainly will have more people than China.

Technology to Assist the Elderly

Caring for the elderly is a burden on society. The elderly are more likely to suffer from cardiovascular, respiratory, musculoskeletal, neurological, and mental diseases and cancers, which are responsible for approximate a quarter of the world's healthcare spending.[11] Various technologies, however, can ease the burden of age-related disorders like Alzheimer's, dementia, stroke, chronic obstructive pulmonary disease, and vision impairment. For technology companies, like GE, Philips, and Google, aging presents a business opportunity. Pharmaceutical companies have shifted their research and development (R&D) from diseases that afflict children to those that affect the elderly, too.

Technologies that cater to the elderly are in high demand. Sales for home health monitoring devices have more than doubled from their 2010 levels.[12] Auto companies are preparing to meet the needs of this market. For an increasingly older population, they are adding such features to their vehicles as infrared night vision, lane departure warnings, blind spot detectors, and automatic parking.

A Cure for Alzheimer's

Finding a cure for Alzheimer's has attracted the attention of many companies. Although the cause of this disease remains unknown, the race has been on for the next-generation of drugs to treat it. The market opportunity for a company that makes a technological breakthrough is large, but the risk is, too. Decades of research have not resulted in new treatments. The drugs currently available for treating Alzheimer's, like Pfizer's Aricep, Forest Laboratories' Namenda, and Novartis' Exelon, were approved decades ago. Their combined sales in 2015 exceeded $6 billion annually, while estimates of the potential market for an effective treatment are in the range of $20 billion per year.[13] Finding treatments that work has not been easy. Much research has gone into the buildup of plaque in the brain, while a host of other treatments are still being investigated.

Blocking Plaque

Blocking the production of plaque in the brain is one approach to Alzheimer's disease. The problem with this approach is that plaque may, in fact, be a consequence of Alzheimer's and not its cause. There have been many failures in attempts to find a treatment that relies on this approach. A joint venture that Pfizer, Johnson & Johnson, and

Elan inaugurated to test a plaque inhibitor called bapineuzumab, for example, failed in 2013.[14] These three companies suffered losses of nearly $1 billion and decided to abandon their further Alzheimer's research for the time being.

Similarly, in 2013, Eli Lilly and Merck were in the late testing stage for an anti-plaque inhibitor called solanezumab. In the initial tests for this drug, it reduced cognitive decline by as much as 34 percent in some patients. However, later tests in 2015 had to be stopped because patients began to exhibit liver problems. A small Massachusetts company with a promising drug also closed down its research efforts in 2015 because the drug it was testing to block plaque had safety problems. Biogen reported good early results with the amyloid (plaque) antibody aducanumab in 2015.[15] Patients reacted positively to the drug when the company conducted cognitive tests and brain imaging. This news buoyed Biogen stock, even though the company had done nothing more than early testing. The sample sizes in its tests were small, and there was some indication of brain swelling in patients who carried the gene APOE4, which confers Alzheimer's highest genetic risk. In large, well-controlled tests, aducanumab, like other drugs, could still fail.

In 2015, the Alzheimer's Association International Conference showcased a BACE inhibitor from Merck that blocked amyloid production.[16] This drug had been in development for more than 10 years. It reduced amyloid in patients' spinal fluid by more than 80 percent. However, the drug may only work for people who have not yet shown symptoms of the disease. Plaque buildup in the brain probably starts 15–20 years before the onset of symptoms. For those already showing signs of the disease, there were question about whether the drug would work. It may be effective only if taken very early in the disease's onset, but it remained unclear how early and for which people it was likely to be most effective.

Other Treatments

Despite the disappointments, scientists continued to work on the problem. More than 80 other treatments for Alzheimer's existed. For example, at the 2015 Alzheimer's Association International Conference, the Italian firm Chiesi Pharmaceuticals reported that an anti-inflammatory drug it developed showed promise in clinical trials.[17] Researchers had long noticed that the brains of people with Alzheimer's were inflamed and believed that anti-inflammatory drugs, like Chiesi Pharmaceuticals', could be an effective treatment. Patients who took the firm's anti-inflammatory drug for 16 months showed cognitive improvement of one-fifth to one-third in comparison to their prior cognitive functioning. Other approaches showed promise and attracted attention but failed to live up to expectations.

Finding a cure for Alzheimer's remains a major challenge. Without a cure, millions of elderly people require expensive care that puts a large strain on society.

Reversing Aging

If it were possible to reverse aging, the burden of caring for the elderly would decrease. Thus, there has been an intense search for methods that may achieve this goal. Many apparent breakthroughs have been announced, but no definitive cure has emerged. In 2013, for example, Harvard scientists reported that they had found a compound that could make old cells young again. Cells age because they lack enough oxygen. Without enough oxygen, the mitochondria in the cells are not as efficient in converting glucose into energy, and the cells become sluggish and are prone to inflammation and muscle degeneration, eventually ceasing to function. Dr. David Sinclair, the head of the Harvard team, reported in an article in the journal *Cell* that a compound called NAD (nicotinamide adenine dinucleotide) found in young cells has the potential to revitalize old ones.[18] Just one week after scientists gave this compound to older mice, their cells started to resemble the cells of mice one-third their age. The compound appeared to reverse aging, and the hope was that if the levels of NAD are increased in humans, it would have a similar effect.

Commercializing NAD

The problems with commercializing a drug like NAD, however, are many. The route to making it available to humans is through the FDA, but FDA testing takes years. Moreover, the FDA views aging as too general a condition to allow scientists to specifically target it. A start-up called Elysium Health, founded by MIT biologist Leonard Guarente, has tried to get around this problem. It converts compounds like NAD that lengthen the lives of mice in the laboratory into over-the-counter vitamin pills. Vitamins and supplements can be sold over the counter without FDA approval if their ingredients are known to be safe and their backers do not make explicit health claims.

Elysium's first product, a pill called Basis, does not guarantee it will help people stay young. Rather, the claim that the company makes is a minimal one: the pill may be effective in improving a person's health and wellness. Scientists have shown in labs that they can reliably extend the life of laboratory mice through caloric restriction, a process that seems to be mediated by molecules called sirtuins, which need NAD to work. NAD levels fall with age, so by taking the pill as a supplement, a person can increase the amount in the body. Whether aging actually will be reversed, however, remains uncertain.

Biologist Guarente, Elysium's founder, previously had been involved with Sirtris Pharmaceuticals, a biotechnology company that studied resveratrol, another anti-aging compound, which is found in red wine and therefore received vast media coverage. It was said to be responsible for the "French paradox"—that is, the tendency of the French to eat many fatty foods, like foie gras and cheese, without showing signs of heart impairment, apparently because of the large quantities of red wine they drink. The media coverage stimulated high levels of resveratrol sales, and GlaxoSmithKline bought Sirtris, believing that it had acquired a blockbuster drug. However, resveratrol failed the human trials the company carried out under FDA supervision.

To avoid the FDA, Elysium, therefore, is trying to market NAD as a dietary supplement. The company has carried out preliminary testing to ensure that the product is safe and to see if it is effective; it aims to do follow-up surveys and post-marketing studies. The supplement is only available through the company's website, costing $60 for a 30-day supply or $50 per month for an ongoing subscription. The potential for this supplement in the $30 billion supplements market is high, with this market growing at more than 7 percent a year. Daniel Fabricant, a former director of the FDA's division of dietary supplements, sits on Elysium's board. The company also counts five Nobel Prize winners among its advisers, including neuroscientist Eric Kandel, biologist Thomas Südhof, origin-of-life theorist Jack Szostak, and the 2013 laureate in chemistry Martin Karplus. Elysium plans to gradually add other compounds that show in academic studies to extend the lifespan of animals to its product line. Whether this route will yield an effective anti-aging agent is yet to be determined.

Rapamycin

Another compound with anti-aging properties is rapamycin.[19] Derived from a rare bacterium streptomyces hygroscopicus, it has been heralded as a drug with substantial promise. Suren Sehgal first isolated it in 1971 in a soil sample at Ayerst Laboratorie, a pharmaceutical company in Montreal, Canada. He conducted tests and analyzed the drug for many years. Purifying it and naming it rapamycin, he initially thought its main use would be as a cream for athlete's foot and other fungal conditions. Wyeth bought Ayerst in 1987, and Sehgal continued to analyze the drug. He discovered that it suppressed the immune system and could be used to prevent transplant rejections. After 1999 FDA approval, the drug was commonly used for this purpose. It helped save millions of transplant patients' lives and earned Wyeth millions of dollars.

It is not possible to patent rapamycin because it is a biological agent, but derivatives of the compound can be patented. The derivatives are routinely used as anti-cancer drugs and coatings on cardiac stents. They also show promise in delaying the onset of age-related diseases such as cancer and heart disease and may be helpful in fighting Alzheimer's. The evidence that they can delay aging's onset is based on a rigorously designed National Institutes of Health (NIH) funded clinical study in 2009 that showed that rapamycin derivatives enabled male mice to extend their lives by 9 percent and female mice by 14 percent; for humans these results are expected to mean life extension of 30 percent. Therefore, Novartis has taken steps to position rapamycin it as an anti-aging drug.

The mechanism by which the drug works is also just starting to be understood. A rapamycin molecule inhibits a key cellular pathway regulating growth and metabolism by tapping into the body's systems for dealing with reduced nutrition. By these means, it reduces age-related bone loss, reverses cardiac maturity, and reduces chronic inflammation. In mice, rapamycin shows signs of reversing Alzheimer's. If further studies verify that there are benefits in humans and there are no significant adverse side effects, rapamycin could become the ultimate preventive medicine for chronic diseases that kill people later in life.

However, because rapamycin suppresses the immune system, and the immune systems of older patients are already diminished, it may be dangerous. This barrier is the largest hurdle of using it to slow aging. A rapamycin derivative called everolimus has been shown to enhance aspects of the immune response, boosting the efficacy of a flu vaccinations in elderly patients, but only when administered in limited doses. Additional research is needed before the full potential of rapamycin is known.

Other Anti-Aging Agents

Identifying the pathways and proteins associated with aging is yielding other promising anti-aging targets. By tweaking these pathways, researchers may be able to find other treatments for age-related diseases. The odds are that there is no single magic bullet. Another anti-aging drug under investigation is metformin. Millions of diabetics already take it, and it has a long history. In a federally funded clinical trial, it exhibited the ability to extend the lives of mice. A large retrospective analysis found that diabetics who take the drug have a 15 percent lower mortality rate than non-diabetic patients who do not take it. Bimagrumab is another example of a drug under investigation, which has the potential to reverse muscle loss among the elderly. The FDA has called the drug a possible breakthrough. Late clinical trials have started for a rare condition called sporadic inclusion body myositis, but bimagrumab could have wider use in the treatment of muscle wasting and frailty among the elderly. Other than Alzheimer's, these conditions are the main reasons for depression and incapacitation among the elderly. Also being considered are drugs that could restore cartilage in aging joints and a radical gene therapy that could reverse the loss of cells needed for hearing.

As previously mentioned, a problem for all companies doing research in this area is that the FDA does not approve drugs for aging because it views aging as a condition and not a disease. Another problem is the exceptionally high safety standards the FDA has set for preventive drugs taken by healthy persons. According to FDA guidelines, the side effects of such drugs have to be near zero. Nonetheless, many companies persist in studying aging and are trying to arrive at a cure for this generic condition. Calico, for example, a research venture founded by Google, has a $750 million partnership with AbbVie to do work in this area.[20] With the right technologies in place, the experience of aging could be very different, not to mention that a healthier and more vigorous elderly population would be a great benefit to the generations coming after it.

Among the Young: Hope and Disillusion

The U.S. National Intelligence Council Among identified two different orientations among young people (ages of approximately 16–32) in the period immediately following the 9/11 attacks on the World Trade Center.[21] It characterized one group of young people as being optimistic and entrepreneurial. It believes in freedom of choice and competition, and its proclivities are materialistic, although members of this group may be aware of materialism's costs, such as increased pollution. More so than their parents, this group of youth is willing to live for the moment and to take on added debt. It is affected by advertising, the media, and popular entertainment and culture. This group seeks affluence, although it may be concerned that this affluence will not be widely shared. It favors the opening up of societies and the introduction of cosmopolitan ideas.

According to the U.S. National Intelligence Council post=9/11 assessment, another group of young people, also educated and relatively advantaged and well off, is equally serious, intent, and motivated, but it is also resentful and disillusioned. This group suffers from a feeling of hopelessness. Its members tend to believe that they have no future and that there is little hope that things can get better. Their strong collective identity finds focus in religious ties and ethnicity.

The first group of young people typically can be found in the rising sectors of such Asian countries as India and China and Latin American countries like Brazil, Chile, and Mexico, but they are located throughout the world wherever there is hope that self-improvement is possible and that societies can advance based on individual initiative. Like the first group, many in the second group live in countries once occupied by colonial powers. However, their disappointment at having lost national or religious power and glory remains strong. They revisit collective memories of injustice, and to regain lost glory and dignity, many reach the conclusion that there is no other way to redress wrongs that have been inflicted upon the groups to which they belong other than violence.

According to the U.S. National Intelligence Council post-9/11 assessment, the rise of the former group has manifested itself in the rapid increase in the economic growth rates of China and India, and they're catching up to the wealth and lifestyles in the United States and Europe. By the year 2050, people in these countries are likely to be living at levels much closer to those in the United States. India has many advantages over its neighbor. It is a democracy, is less heavily dependent on manufacturing, and is developing a large base of sophisticated knowledge workers. China is aging because of its one-child-per-family policy. Because of its dependence on heavy manufacturing, it faces natural resource and environmental constraints to its growth.

There are no guarantees that the catch-up of China and India with the United States will be smooth. The growth rates of both countries may be slower than anticipated, and U.S. growth rates may be faster. The future of GDP growth rates in these nations and elsewhere in the world is hard to predict.

Young people outside the entrepreneurial and optimistic group are more often found in the Middle East and in Africa. However, they are located throughout the world, including nations in Asia like Sri Lanka, the Philippines, and Indonesia and in Latin American in nations like Ecuador, Bolivia, and Venezuela. They are also found in the developed economies of the United States, Western Europe, and Japan, to which some have migrated and where some were born. Often, they have contempt for western values and are disgusted by its individualism, materialism, loose morals, free speech and freethinking, and self-indulgence. Many in this group are Muslim, but certainly not all. Nearly every religion has bred people with this worldview. The high birth rates of people who adhere to traditional religions tend to increase the number of young people who belong to this group. The lack of employment opportunities is another factor. Many people who have adopted this point of view are concentrated in areas of the world already subject to high levels of violence, where the prospect of more violence is great.

Meaningful Work

As indicated, a key element in the disaffection of the second group of youth, the disillusioned one, is the lack of meaningful work. Technology has been a major factor in influencing whether productive jobs can be found. Many experts imagine a future in which robots and digital agents displace workers, causing further breakdown in the social order.[22]

Technology in the Internet era increases demand for educated and talented people and allows them to advance quickly, but it leaves many other young people, especially those who lack access to the newest tools and skills, far behind. Can technology create ample jobs to support an influx of enough young people into the labor force? Technology raises productivity and makes societies wealthier, but it also reduces the need for many types of work. The prospects for many types of jobs are bleak as automation progresses from manufacturing to clerical and retail jobs.

Robots and advanced automation are commonplace in manufacturing. Far fewer people work in this area of the economy than previously. Industrial robots, for example, are able to weld and paint auto body parts without significant human intervention and have transformed automotive assembly. The Kiva robot similarly is transforming logistics. Created by Kiva Systems, a start-up founded in 2002 and acquired by Amazon in 2012, Kiva robots move across large warehouses, grabbing hold of ordered goods and quickly packaging them for delivery. They move ceaselessly and respond instantaneously to electronic orders. Warehouses are able to process up to four times as many orders as similar warehouses that are run by humans. The net impact is hard to pinpoint because greater productivity is not solely about doing the same work with fewer people. It is also about growing businesses for new markets. The outcome of Kiva's automation may not only be putting people out of work, but as it lowers shipping costs, it could also facilitate the growth of e-commerce start-ups.

Blue-collar and service jobs are not the only ones that have been altered. Professional jobs in law, education, financial services, and medicine also have been changed. Countless routine white-collar tasks have been automated to some degree, and artificial intelligence, big data analytics, and digital processes have made important inroads. Tasks previously done by humans are being assigned algorithms. IBM, for example, is trying to move what it calls super-smart computing into the work life of high-status professionals. For instance, it has developed medical applications in which technology assists in diagnosing, evaluating, and prescribing treatments for cancer patients. The applications rely on advanced natural-language processing and analytic capabilities to move through massive amounts of data and guide an individual's diagnosis and treatment. IBM claims that although the technology lacks intuition and judgment and is not entirely as good as humans in dealing with uncertainty, it is more reliable. For the average person, and for the system as a whole, reliability trumps the creativity that an experienced professional can bring to a problem.

Applying this type of technology to other services is less controversial than applying it to medicine. The next frontier is the military. Not only are machines defusing bombs and pilots being replaced by drones, but robots are also being prepared for deployment alongside regular combat soldiers. And often, technologies developed for the military are then given civilian use, such as the iRobot vacuum cleaner and Facebook's face recognition software.

For many young people, the result of these trends is unemployment as well as underemployment; they are likely to always hold part-time jobs yet never find jobs that fully reflect their education. Already many college-educated young men and women are not able to obtain full-time jobs in the fields of their choosing. They have to rely, instead, on temporary or entry-level jobs in other areas. This phenomenon exists in the United States, in Western Europe, and in many developing countries where it is combined with state failure and the breakdown of law and order.

Violent societies tend to be those with the highest numbers of young people who are idle and have little chance of productive employment. Iraq and Afghanistan are good examples of this phenomenon. In comparison to the United States, they have huge youth bulges (see Exhibit 6.5) and significant unemployment. In Iraq, the unemployment rate has been more than 30 percent since 2010, and in Afghanistan it has been about 20 percent in this time period. These countries also ranked first and second in number of terrorist incidents in 2014.[23] In that year, 6,362 people were killed and 14,947 injured in 2,492 terrorist attacks in Iraq, and 3,111 were killed and 3,721 people injured in 1,148 terrorist attacks in Afghanistan.

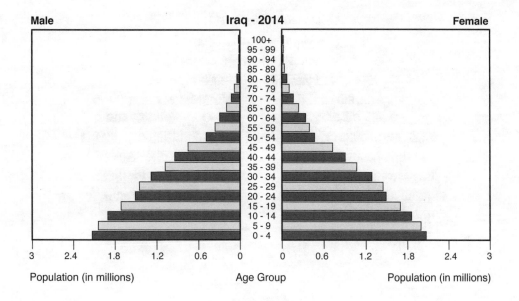

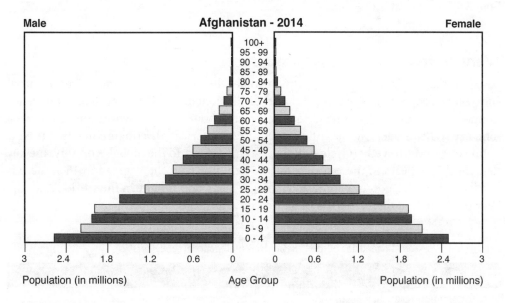

Exhibit 6.5 A Comparison of Population Pyramids in Iraq, Afghanistan, and the United States in 2014 http://www.indexmundi.com/iraq/age_structure.html

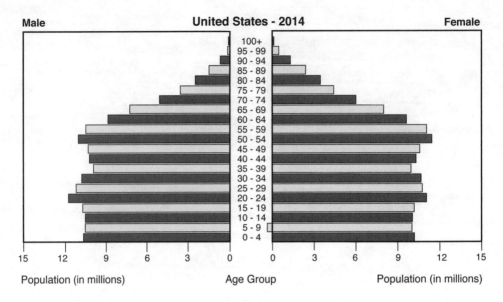

Exhibit 6.5 Continued

What Next

Based on the distinction between young people who are optimistic and entrepreneurial and young people who are resentful and disillusioned, the U.S. National Intelligence Council (NIC) after 9/11 created four scenarios about how the world might evolve: a romance (called Davos), a romantic comedy (Pax Americana), a tragic comedy (the New Caliphate), and a tragedy (Cycle of Fear).[24] With respect to the global economy, the key element that appears in these scenarios (see Exhibit 6.6) is the degree to which there is free flow of capital, goods, people, technology, ideas, and money in the world. With the freer movement of these, there is more potential for peace and prosperity.

Exhibit 6.6 Post-9/11 Scenarios of the U.S. Central Intelligence Agency

Davos World	Pax Americana
Robust economic growth, globalization, particularly China and India	U.S. central pivot
Gains in economic freedom	Addresses wide range global issues
Democratization, gains in political freedom	Global order comes from high military expenditures and foreign assistance

Davos World	Pax Americana
Rising global migration rising	Military spending grows less in rest of world, thus increasing U.S. preponderance
Technological advances	
Increases in productivity	
New Caliphate	**Cycle of Fear**
Mega-movement in world	Spread of weapons of mass destruction to countries and non-state actors
Large numbers Muslims give up on traditional states	Disruption of globalization
Puts brake on globalization, disrupts relationships with West	Decreasing liberalization of domestic economies
But not all Islam united	Less economic freedom
Division and conflict	Less political freedom
Conflicts in Islamic world and between it and outside	Substantial drops in migration
Population migrations from among skilled and highly educated	Increase of diseases such as SARS or Avian Flu
High military spending	Losses in productivity

Pax Americana rests on different assumptions than Davos. In the Pax Americana scenario, the United States plays the role of the world's policeman, keeping global order to preserve prosperity. Military spending grows, and regard for the United States in the rest of the world diminishes. The New Caliphate is what takes place if the United States is not a successful global peacekeeper. The Middle East and other areas of global instability collapse. As they fall apart, the most advanced and ambitious elements in their population leave, creating a void, which makes it hard for these societies to rebuild. A Cycle of Fear can unfold if epidemics and weapons of mass destruction are added to the mix. With regard to these scenarios, there are many wildcards, and their management is critical to the outcomes (see Exhibit 6.7).

Exhibit 6.7   Post-9/11 Wildcard Questions Critical to the Outcomes

TREND	Wildcard Questions that Influence Trends' Outcome
Globalization largely irreversible, but less Western	EU an ex-superpower?? Lagging economies?? Asian countries set "rules"??
Total war unlikely	But ability to manage many flashpoints??
U.S. power	Other countries challenge?? U.S. loses technology and scientific leadership??
Aging populations	Adapt?? Retiree benefits?? Migrants integrated??
World economy substantially larger	Gaps between "haves" and "have-nots"??? Backsliding of fragile democracies?? Managing of containing financial crises??
Political Islam potent force	Growth of jihadist ideology?? Constant conflict?? State unity?
WMD capabilities	More nuclear powers?? Terrorists have biological, chemical, radiological, nuclear weapons??
Instability Middle East, Asia, Africa	Precipitating events?? Overthrow of regimes??
Growing power of non-state actors	Willingness and ability to be accommodated by state system??

Diminishing Youth Bulges

Another wildcard is what happens when youth bulges start to diminish. Youth bulges are currently slowing down, and in some cases they are shrinking. Fertility rates in the Middle East have dropped more than 48 percent overall (see Exhibit 6.8). In countries like Iran and Lebanon, which have seen a decline in their birth rates, an abundant cohort of 15-to-24-year-olds has been followed by a sparse cohort of 0-to-14-year-olds (see Exhibit 6.9). However, not all Middle East nations' fertility rates have fallen, notably in Syria and the Palestinian territory of the West Bank (see Exhibit 6.10). Nevertheless, as the youth bulges in these societies tend to recede, it leads to the possibility that the anger, hostility, and willingness to act out among the 15-to-24-year-olds who exhibit the most strife will subside.

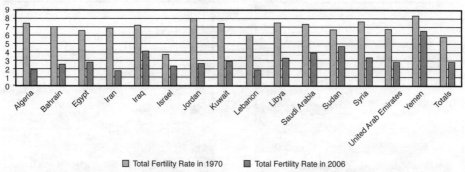

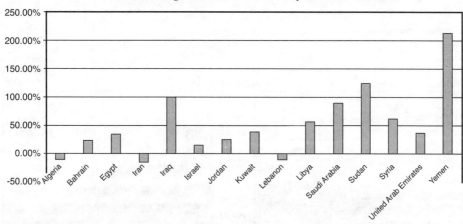

Exhibit 6.8 Population Bust—Declining Number of Children per Women in Mideast Nations

Numbers taken from the CIA Website

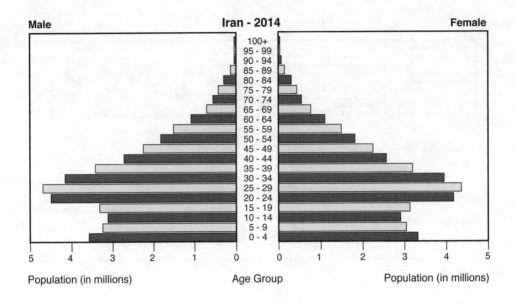

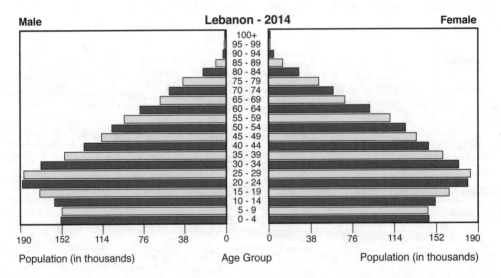

Exhibit 6.9 Youth Buusts in Iran and Lebanon, 2014

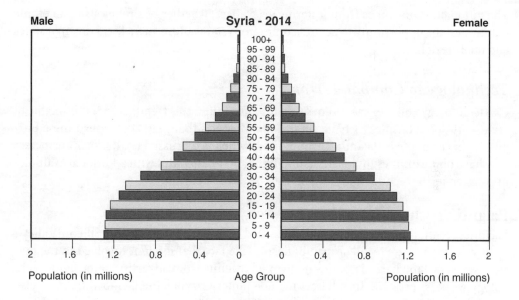

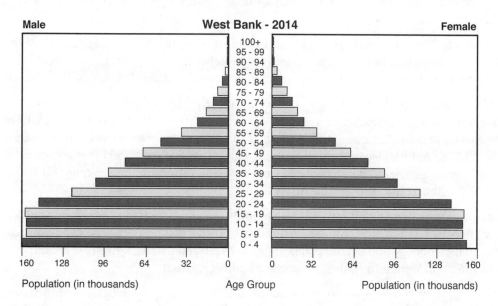

Exhibit 6.10 Youth Bulges in Syria and the West Bank, 2014

When youth surges quiet and are followed by population busts, will there be less violence? The empirical evidence suggests that this positive result is likely to take a long time to unfold.[25] A series of factors will continue to provide the motivation, rationalization, and opportunity for violence. The motivation comes from rising expectations.

The rationalization comes from festering grievances, whether of a religious or an ethnic nature, and the opportunity to act out comes from state failure and a breakdown of states and the rule of law.

Technology to Combat Terror

Can technology come to the rescue? Can it help contain this trend, even if it is unable to reverse it? Some businesses have created technologies that help accomplish these purposes. One example is Palantir Technologies, which is discussed next. Other businesses may have opportunities in this domain. The chapter concludes with additional examples of counter-terror technologies that need to be developed.

Palantir Technologies

Palantir Technologies is not a publicly traded company.[26] It is one of Silicon Valley's most valuable private tech companies despite the fact that it is not involved in the new trends of social media and obtains none of its revenue from advertising. Its digital technology work is secretive. Its advisers include James Carville, the Democratic strategist, Condoleezza Rice, the former secretary of state, and George J. Tenet, the former CIA director.

Created in 2004 after getting $2 million from In-Q-Tel, the venture capital arm of the U.S. CIA, Palantir's software has exposed terror networks. It also has helped to calculate safe driving routes through the discordant passageways of Baghdad.

Palantir has more than $1 billion in revenue, mostly from organizations interested in adaptations of its intelligence software. Since 2009, its contracts from the CIA have totaled more than $215 million. The company has moved from secretive data-mining for the CIA, NSA, FBI, Department of Defense, Homeland Security, and other government intelligence agencies to doing contract work for corporations in the banking, insurance, retail, healthcare, oil, and gas industries.

Palantir sells software that mines large amounts of data. Its software lets clients quickly see links in relationships and understand patterns in phone numbers, bank records, friend lists, photos, and license plates. It has been alleged that its software was central to the work that went into finding Osama bin Laden's hideout.

The company converts messy information into visual maps, histograms, and charts that can help solve global issues like fraud and human trafficking as well as terrorism. The software finds connections between fingerprints on artillery shell fragments, location data, anonymous tips, and social media. It is used to help Marines in Afghanistan predict insurgent attacks and detect roadside bombs and by the Mexican government to catch drug cartel members. Yet this same software is employed by banks to uncover cyber fraud, money laundering, and employee theft and to sort out distressed mortgages.

Pharmaceutical firms have used the software to analyze new drugs. However, the software has come under scrutiny from privacy advocates.

As of 2015, Palantir still was not yet profitable, although investors had provided it with almost $900 million. Its implied valuation was between $9 billion and $15 billion, making it the world's third most-valuable venture capitalist-backed company, behind Uber and Xiaomi. Its aim, according to Alex Karp, the company's cofounder and chief executive, who founded the company with law school classmates Stephen Cohen, Joe Lonsdale, Nathan Gettings, and Peter Thiel, is to use the software it developed to improve the world. Thiel, a Silicon Valley entrepreneur and PayPal founder, conceived of the company in 2003 after eBay acquired PayPal. After 9/11, Thiel was interested in finding a way to make the United States safer without sacrificing people's freedoms. Also, PayPal had lost large amounts of money in stolen credit card numbers but had figured out how to spot fraudulent activity so it could be investigated. Thiel believed that this approach could be applied to national security and to solving other problems.

Other Counterterrorism Technologies

A host of counterterrorism technologies might be developed.[27] They include the following:

- **Network-centric operations**—By means of network-centric operations, it should be possible to improve the operational effectiveness of law enforcement officials and emergency responders. Through sensors, the law enforcement and emergency responders can have improved shared awareness. They can engage in quicker self-synchronized operations carried out more efficiently and with greater security and safety. The technologies for better integration are available but need to be tailored and applied to this task. These include the passing of high volumes of secure digital data through integrated and diverse databases that link cable, fiber-optic, wireless, and satellite communication systems, among others.

- **Biometrics**—Biometrics measure the unique physical or behavioral characteristic of individuals. They include iris recognition, hand geometry, fingerprint recognition, face recognition, and voice recognition. They are more reliable and harder to forget, lose, have stolen, or falsified than ID cards, personal identification numbers, and passwords.

- **Nonlethal weapons**—Nonlethal weapons can be used to minimize collateral damage to civilians. They provide military and law enforcement with options to aggressively fight terror without endangering innocent bystanders. They include methods to control crowds and prevent vehicles, vessels, or aircraft from entering an area and disabling and neutralizing this type of transportation when necessary. Nonlethal weapons include acoustics systems, chemicals, electromagnetic and electrical systems, entanglement and mechanical systems, optical devices, and nonpenetrating projectiles. They involve malodorants, high-powered micro-waves, and lasers.

- **Explosives-detection technology**—Explosives-detection technology can be used at security checkpoints and baggage and cargo screening areas to better detect the trace amounts of explosives on and inside bags as well as casts, prosthetics, wheelchairs and other places where explosives can be hidden. Some devices are large and work like MRI machines at hospitals, but other screening systems are tiny and can detect potential liquid or gel threats in a passenger's property.

- **Aircraft protection**—There is a need to provide further protection to aircraft. A number of additional countermeasures can be employed by military and the civilian aviation authorities to provide further layers of protection. An especially important area of need is for this protection to be extended for large, slow-moving aircraft that can be hit by shoulder-fired missiles. Attacks on helicopters by rocket-propelled grenades (RPGs) and small arms fire can be stopped by improving threat detection devices and by using coatings.

Conclusion

This chapter has examined the major division in global society between old and young and emphasized the role that technologies can play in extending and improving the quality of life for the elderly and protecting the world from terror, which is often the result of youth disillusionment and unemployment. The next chapter examines another major division—between rich and poor—and the role that technology plays there, too.

Endnotes

1. Alfred Marcus, Mazhar Islam, and John Moloney, "Youth Bulges, Busts, and Doing Business in Violence-Prone Nations," *Business and Politics* 10:3 (2008).

2. Hassan Hakimian, "From Demographic Transition to Fertility Boom and Bust: Iran in the 1980s and 1990s." *Development and Change* 37:3 (2006): 571–597.

3. Rand Institute, *Long-Term Global Demographic Trends: Reshaping the Geopolitical Landscape*, Santa Monica, CA: Rand Corporation, 2001. Print.; Brian Nichiporuk, Julie DaVanzo, Laurent Murawiec, Stephan De Spiegeleire, and David M. Adamson. *Demography and Security: Proceedings of a Workshop, Paris, France, November 2000.* Santa Monica, CA: RAND Corporation, 2001. Web. http://www.rand.org/pubs/conf_proceedings/CF169: also see Colin Kahl, *States, Scarcity, and Civil Strife in the Developing World.* Princeton: Princeton University Press, 2006.

4. Sam Huntington, *The Clash of Civilizations and the Remaking of World Order.* New York: Touchstone, 1996, 117.

5. Louis Feuer, *The Conflict of Generations.* New York: Basic Books, 1969.

6. *World Population Ageing 2013.* New York: The United Nations, 2013.

7. Phillip Longman, *The Empty Cradle: How Falling Birthrates Threaten World Prosperity and What to Do About It.* New York: New American Books, 2004.

8. Ibid.

9. Ibid.

10. Eurostat. "Labour Force Survey Statistics—Transition from Work to Retirement." *Eurostat: Statistics Explained.* European Commission, 2015. http://ec.europa.eu/ eurostat/statistics-explained/index.php/Labour_force_survey_statistics_- _transition_from_work_to_retirement.

11. United Nations Department of Economic and Social Affairs, Population Division. *World Population Ageing 2013.* New York: United Nations, 2013.

12. Eric Wicklund, "New Analysis Sees Growth in Home Health Monitoring Market—with the Patient as the Customer." *Mhealth News.* April 18, 2012. http:// www.mhealthnews.com/news/new-analysis-sees-growth-home-health-monitoring-market-%E2%80%93-patient-customer.

13. Lynne Taylor, "Alzheimer's Drug Market Set to Triple By 2022," *PharmaTimes.* Oct. 31, 2003. http://www.pharmatimes.com/Article/13-10-31/Alzheimer_s_ drug_market_set_to_triple_by_2022.aspx.

14. Nathan Sadeghi-Nejad, "The Lessons of Failure: What We Can Learn from Bapineuzumab's Blowup," *Forbes.* Aug 7, 2012. http://www.forbes.com/sites/ natesadeghi/2012/08/07/the-lessons-of-failure-what-we-can-learn-from-bapineuzumabs-blowup/.

15. John Carroll, "In a Setback, Biogen's Mid-Range Dose of Aducanumab Flops in Alzheimer's Study," *FierceBiotech.* July 22, 2015. http://www.fiercebiotech. com/story/setback-biogens-mid-range-dose-aducanumab-flops-alzheimers-study/2015-07-22.

16. "Merck BACE Inhibitor Clears a Safety Hurdle, Gets New Trial." *Alzforum.* Dec. 19, 2013. http://www.alzforum.org/news/research-news/merck-bace-inhibitor-clears-safety-hurdle-gets-new-trial.

17. Brenda Goodman, "2 New Alzheimer's Drugs Show Promise in Early Studies." *Health Day.* July 14, 2013. http://consumer.healthday.com/cognitive-health-information-26/alzheimer-s-news-20/2-new-alzheimer-s-drugs-show-promise-in-early-studies-678248.html.

18. Alice Park, "Reversing Aging: Not as Crazy as You Think," *Time*. Dec. 19, 2013. http://healthland.time.com/2013/12/19/reversing-aging-not-as-crazy-as-you-think/.

19. Bill Gifford, "Does a Real Anti-Aging Pill Already Exist?" *Bloomberg Business*. Feb. 12, 2015. http://www.bloomberg.com/news/features/2015-02-12/does-a-real-anti-aging-pill-already-exist-.

20. Sarah Buhr, "AncestryDNA and Google's Calico Team Up To Study Genetic Longevity." *TechCrunch*. July 22, 2015. http://techcrunch.com/2015/07/21/ancestrydna-and-googles-calico-team-up-to-study-genetic-longevity/.

21. See U.S. National Intelligence Council, *Global Trends 2020*. Washington: Central Intelligence Agency, 2004. http://www.dni.gov/files/documents/Global%20Trends_Mapping%20the%20Global%20Future%202020%20Project.pdf.

22. Guy Wright, "Will a Robot Replace You by 2025?" *Tech Guru Daily*. Aug. 9, 2014. http://www.tgdaily.com/social/123796-will-a-robot-replace-you-by-2025.

23. Institute for Economics and Peace. *Global Terrorism Index 2014*. Institute for Economics and Peace. University of Maryland, 2015.

24. U.S. National Intelligence Council, *Global Trends 2020*.

25. Marcus, Islam, and Moloney provide empirical evidence that the violence does not subside with the onset of youth busts.

26. Quentin Hardy, "Unlocking Secrets, if Not Its Own Value." *New York Times*. May 31, 2014. http://www.nytimes.com/2014/06/01/business/unlocking-secrets-if-not-its-own-value.html?_r=0; Andy Greenberg and Ryan Mac, "How a 'Deviant' Philosopher Built Palantir, A CIA-Funded Data-Mining Juggernaut," *Forbes*. Sept. 2, 2013. http://www.forbes.com/sites/andygreenberg/2013/08/14/agent-of-intelligence-how-a-deviant-philosopher-built-palantir-a-cia-funded-data-mining-juggernaut/.

27. For technologies that can fight terror, see the following websites: http://www.nato.int/docu/review/2004/issue3/english/military.html.

http://www.heritage.org/research/lecture/the-future-of-anti-terrorism-technologies.

http://science.howstuffworks.com/5-innovations-war-on-terrorism.htm#page=5.

http://science.howstuffworks.com/5-innovations-war-on-terrorism.htm.

http://radar.oreilly.com/2008/03.

7

Rich, Poor, and Global Inequality

he gap between the top of the wealth pyramid and the bottom is large. As this chapter will show, there are technological challenges and opportunities at both levels.

This chapter starts by reviewing the state of affairs with respect to income and wealth distribution, using the United States as an example. It describes a technology designed especially for the wealthy, which gives them the potential to enhance and perpetuate their wealth, and which the poor are restricted from using in the United States. This chapter also discusses technologies and technological solutions whose purpose is to reach the bottom of the pyramid and eliminate poverty. However, the conditions under which they actually accomplish this goal appear to be somewhat limited. This chapter considers these limitations as well as the promise of these technologies.

Trends

Forbes magazine annually records the number of billionaires in the world.[1] In 2014, it identified 1,645 billionaires worldwide, more than double the number in 2009, with a combined $6.4 trillion in wealth, up from $4.4 trillion in 2008. To be among the wealthiest *half* of the world's population, a person needed just $3,650 in assets in 2014, to be in the *top 10 percent* required $77,000, and to be in the *top 1 percent* required close to $800,000.[2] The wealthiest 10 percent owned 87 percent of the world's assets, the top 1 percent owned close to 50 percent, and the bottom half of the population owned less than 1 percent.[3] Within nations, the wealth gap is increasing, but between nations it is declining, as middle classes have emerged in China and India and household income in the United States and other wealthy nations has stagnated.

Within Country Gaps

According to the commonly used Gini index, zero means everyone in a society has the same income (perfect equality), whereas one means a single person in the society has all the income.[4] Whereas more than half of the world's high-income countries have relatively low inequality, two-thirds of the world's upper-middle-income countries have high or very high inequality based on their Gini indexes.[5] This difference may indicate that countries' income gaps rise before they fall. A country has to be rich for it to have a low Gini index. Lower inequality tends to be found in clusters of the richest countries in Europe. Yet inequality has grown in many of these countries, including Germany, France, Sweden, Denmark, the Netherlands, Austria, Finland, Luxembourg, and the Czech Republic. Many high-inequality countries are found in South America and southern Africa. In a number of these countries, including Colombia, Honduras, Rwanda, South Africa, and Thailand, income inequality has gone up. However, other countries with high income inequality, such as Bolivia, Brazil, Chile, Guatemala, Lesotho, Mexico Nicaragua, Panama, Paraguay, and Swaziland, have managed to reduce the gap between rich and poor.

More than 70 percent of the world's population lives in countries with rising levels of inequality, including China, India, Russia, and the United States. Despite China's economic progress, inequality has grown because of the disparity between its urban and rural populations.[6] Third to the United States and Japan in income inequality, China claims more of the top 10 percent of global wealth holders than any other country. Inequality is not as high in China as in India[7] because China has fewer people at each of the extremes of the income distribution.

Between-Country Gaps

Inequality within countries remains high and is getting higher, although *between* countries inequality has started to diminish.[8] This type of inequality, which grew rapidly in the 1980s and 1990s, started to fall after 2000. According to the World Bank,

- To be a high-income country, the per capita gross national income of a country in 2009 U.S. dollars must be greater than $12,276. By this standard, Poland as well as the United States and Canada are rich countries.

- To be an upper-middle-income country, the per capita gross national income of a country in 2009 U.S. dollars must be between $3,976 and $12,275. China, Russia, and Brazil fall into this category.

- To be a low-middle-income country, the per capita gross national income of a country in 2009 U.S. dollars has to be between $1,006 and $3,975. Guatemala, India, and Nigeria belong here.

- To be a very low-income country, the per capita gross national income of a country in 2009 U.S. dollars has to be $1,005 or less. Bangladesh, Cambodia, and Kenya fall into this category.

In constant 2005 dollars, the average income in the top (high-income) countries was $33,232 per year, in the next tier it was $8,731, in the following tier it was $3,287, and in the lowest tier it was $1,099.

More than half of the world's total population lived in high- and middle-income countries in 2010. These countries also saw higher percentages of their schoolchildren enrolled in secondary education, had higher life expectancy at birth, and experienced lower infant mortality.

The income gap between rich and poor countries has fallen primarily because of a rise in incomes in China and India.[9] In 1950, the combined output of China, India, and Brazil accounted for only 10 percent of the world's output, whereas Canada, France, Germany, Italy, the UK, and the United States accounted for about half. In 2015, the combined output of these two groups of countries was about equal. From 2000 to 2010, average per-capita incomes grew by just 0.5 percent per year in high-income countries, whereas they increased by 3.7 percent per year in low-income countries.[10]

Another way to show the decline in the income gap between rich and poor countries is to analyze it relative to changes in the world's Gini index.[11] Between 1982 and 1994, the Gini index signaled growing inequality, mainly as a result of poor economic performance in Latin American, Africa, and Soviet bloc countries. However, after 2000, it exhibited declines, mainly due to better economic performance in China and India. Without these two countries, the global Gini index showed an overall increase in income inequality since 1982.

The U.S. Wealth Gap

The U.S. Gini index has been increasing since 1982, indicating rising inequality.[12] Since the 1990s, 80 percent of U.S. households have experienced income stagnation, whereas the incomes of those with the most means have soared.[13] Ninety-five percent of all income gains in the United States from 2009 and 2012 were experienced by the top 1 percent of the population.

In theory, some income inequality is desirable because it provides incentives for hard work and innovation. Above a certain point, however, inequality can impair growth if it lowers spending and restricts people from pursuing the educational opportunities that would enable them to gain better opportunities and improve their standing. For young people, the 2007–2008 recession was especially devastating. Entry-level jobs created after the financial crisis were not of the same caliber as those created after previous recessions, and the reduced wages for those young people who could find work were hard to bear.

Before adjusting for taxes and income transfers, U.S. income inequality has been the highest in the world among developed countries. After adjusting for taxes and transfers, the U.S. was in tenth place among the 31 countries listed by the Pew Research Center in 2010. Taxes and transfers make a big difference in the distribution of income in the United States. In 2010, they raised the lowest quintile of earners from a 2.3-percent share of national income to a 9.3-percent share (see Exhibit 7.1), and they lowered the highest quintile of earners from having a 57.9-percent share to a 47.2-percent share.

Exhibit 7.1   The Impact of Transfers and Taxes on the Distribution of U.S. Income, 2010

Adjustments to Income	Quintiles of Income				
	Lowest	Second	Middle	Fourth	Highest
Market Income	2.3	7.4	13.0	21.0	57.9
Social Security and Medicare	36.2	22.1	16.7	11.7	11.4
Other Transfers	47.0	22.8	13.3	8.8	6.2
Federal Taxes	0.0	2.8	9.2	18.4	69.3
Income After Taxes and Transfers	9.3	11.0	14.3	19.8	47.2

The portion of total U.S. output that the richest 1 percent of earners obtained more than doubled between 1970 and 2008.[14] In 1928, the top 1 percent earned 24 percent of all income; in 1944, these individuals earned 11 percent (see Exhibit 7.2). By 2012, the top 1 percent was earning 23 percent of the nation's income, about the same as they did in 1928.

Based on levels of inequality, the 1929–2007 period divides into four stages:[15]

1. The Great Compression from 1929–1947 when real wages for industrial workers grew by 67 percent, whereas real income of the richest 1 percent fell by 17 percent.

2. The Postwar Boom from 1947–1973 when growth was widely shared—real wages for industrial workers rose 81 percent, whereas the income of the richest 1 percent of the population increased by 38 percent.

3. Stagflation from 1973–1980 when all groups lost ground, with real wages for industrial workers declining by 3 percent, and the income of the richest 1 percent dropping by 4 percent

4. A so-called New Gilded Age from 1980–2007 when incomes for the richest 1 percent soared by 197 percent, whereas incomes for other groups fell.

Capital's share of income—whether in the form of corporate profits, dividends, rents, or sales of property—grew after steadily falling since before World War I. Corporate profits increased, whereas wages, including those for highly educated people, did not grow. Since the early 1970s, real wages for most U.S. workers have hardly gone up, but those for the top 1 percent of earners have increased substantially.

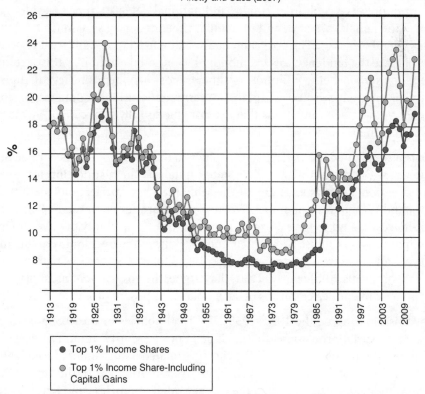

Top Income Shares. United States. 1913-2012

Sources: The World Top Incomes Database. http://topincomes.g-mond.parisschoolofeconomics.eu/
Piketty and Saez (2007)

- Top 1% Income Shares
- Top 1% Income Share-Including Capital Gains

Exhibit 7.2 Earnings of Top 1 Percent in the United States Compared to Total U.S. Income

Source: Facundo Alvaredo, Tony Atkinson, Thomas Piketty, and Emmanuel Saez, *The World Top Incomes Database*
http://topincomes.parisschoolofeconomics.eu/#Database

The Rise of Neoliberalism

The post-1980 stages in U.S. inequality have been accompanied by a rise in a neoliberal philosophy not only in the U.S. but in many countries in the world. Increased inequality is a reflection of policies such as deregulation and supply-side economics, which reduce marginal tax rates to encourage investment. Inequality also has been a result of stagnant minimum wage rates, a decline in unions, and a rise in factors that have favored the wealthy like the increased importance of higher education. An outcome of neoliberal policies of lowering marginal tax rates is that governments worldwide have been attempting to control budget deficits, making it harder for them to redistribute wealth through transfers, which are the most direct ways to reduce inequality.

Neoliberal philosophy regards individual freedom as the highest value and places its trust in the market, which values and promotes individual freedom. It accepts, however, the need for government intervention in some areas. In particular, there is the need for government to preserve civil order (police and national defense), to act as rule-maker and umpire (the judicial system), and to maintain the monetary system (in the United States, the Federal Reserve). The government also has a need to use antitrust regulation to counterbalance the tendency toward monopoly and to take action against externalities, the classic example being pollution. Although most neoliberals believe that people should care for themselves, some accept that government must take some responsibility for caring for vulnerable populations that are not able to fully take care of themselves, such as children and the elderly.

Neoliberalism supplanted the welfare state capitalism that took hold in the United States during the Great Depression. For welfare state capitalists, the justification for governmental intervention stems from many of the same market imperfections identified by neoliberals, and it includes uncompetitive factor and product markets. Welfare state capitalists, however, tend to have a broader view of the responsibility of government to provide for public goods, to use fiscal and monetary policy to correct for instability in the business cycle, and to redress inequality. According to their view, the free market system does not necessarily distribute fairly. Thus, they argue, the government must play a role adjusting in these inequities by means of such policies as progressive taxes and welfare.

Guided by this philosophy, the 1933–1938 New Deal policies of the U.S. government built a system of social protections that included Social Security, minimum wage, fair labor standards, public jobs, and public works. It regulated banks and imposed high tax rates on income derived from capital ownership. After World War II, the United States was relatively undamaged compared to the carnage other countries experienced. Facing limited international competition, it was able to spread the benefits of a welfare economy through a redistributive tax system, high unionization, large-scale expansion of higher education, and business regulation. After 1980, this system came under attack, and many of its aspects were cut back or eliminated. Marginal income tax rates and capital gains taxes were reduced. The result was erosion in support for families, schools, and communities and increased separation of people by classes. In the United States, a prosperous, educated class tends to live apart in enclaves that are geographically removed from the rest of the population, which, in turn, struggles with high rates of crime, substance abuse, insecure employment, and family dissolution.[16]

Technology at the Top of the Pyramid

With regard to technology, the top of the income pyramid in the United States, and elsewhere in the world, has access to technologies that are unavailable to those below them in the income pyramid. For instance, the wealth management industry has created sophisticated tools to enhance and preserve the wealth of individuals with high net worth (those with more than $5 million in assets) and ultra-high-net-worth (those with more than $30 million in assets). These tools are examined next.

Sophisticated Models

Quantitative traders have developed sophisticated models to try to offset portfolio risk. The models exploit market anomalies using algorithmically driven programs trading in multiple securities that can make trades extremely quickly. Traders monitor large numbers of indicators electronically and are able to initiate instantaneous transactions in response to small price and trading pattern variations. The time-series and cross-sectional information on which they rely to analyze asset classes and stocks is too vast for human traders unassisted by computers to effectively access. Based on analysis of this data, traders create rules to predict future price movements that are incorporated into algorithms that react to small patterns they detect and automatically initiate trades in a rapid and reliable manner.

As computing power has developed, so, too, has the use of these advanced techniques. To predict price movements, the models mathematically combine many variables, including prior price momentum, price/earnings ratios, inflation rates, changes in unemployment rates, returns on the S&P 500, and indexes of the U.S. dollar, corporate bonds, and commodity prices. The models employ interaction terms and, when appropriate, use quadratic as well as linear reasoning. Before rules are introduced for predicting future performance, tests are run to determine if the models are good at predicting the past. The models are not without risks because they depend on historical data. Unprecedented events can happen, as took place at the onset of the 2007–2008 financial crisis, when many quantitative funds suffered large losses.

These tools that help keep clients informed, enable them to carry out transactions and generate meaningful intelligence for investment decisions. In turn, the ability to harness tools to assist these people provides those with specialized skills in global financial markets the opportunity to earn large fortunes. People who are recruited for these jobs in the finance industry do not just come from business and financial backgrounds. Increasingly, they are extremely talented mathematicians, physicists, statisticians, and engineers who can achieve greater compensation in the financial sector than in other professions, including those in for which they have been trained. If they succeed in generating high and consistent returns, their firms benefit from a boost in reputation and increased investment. They also are compensated very well for their performance.

What Hedge Funds Do

A hedge fund is a descriptive term for a pooled investment that does not have to be registered with the U.S. Securities and Exchange Commission.[17] It does not necessarily have to be involved in the buying and selling of financial instruments, although this is what most hedge funds do. It has less regulation and more flexibility than investments like mutual funds.

Each hedge fund tends to have different investments in which it specializes. It can specialize in the buying and selling of hotels, for example, or fine art or stuffed animals. Only some funds use sophisticated quantitative technologies. Many continue to rely on human judgment or a combination of judgment, experience, and quantitative methods. Both quantitative and nonquantitative analysts access similar data from government, industry, and other sources. The main difference is the greater rigor the quantitative methods employ in analyzing this data.

Hedge funds first attracted wide-scale notice in the 1980s, with funds managed by Julian Robertson, Michael Steinhardt, and George Soros. Soros became famous for a 1992 bet made by his Quantum Investment Fund against the British pound when it was driven into the European Exchange Rate Mechanism at too high a rate. Quantum earned $1 billion on this bet.

Hedge funds charge both management fees and performance fees, with the performance fees a defining feature because they align the fund managers' interests closely with those of investors and motivate them to generate high returns. Mutual funds charge only a management fee. They do not have the added performance incentive. Hedge funds also generally engage in a wider range of investment and trading activities than do mutual funds. They may employ high-risk strategies using large amounts of borrowed money. They invest in a broad range of assets that mutual funds typically avoid, such as foreign exchange, commodities, and real estate.

Trades of the quantitative funds usually are carried out by computers using algorithms that remove human judgment.[18] Exhibit 7.3 provides examples of the investment strategies of some hedge funds—strategies not restricted to the quantitative funds. Yet, large hedge funds, in terms of the dollar amount of assets managed, have been the main adopters of these quantitative technologies. They trade in multiple asset classes and hedge against international equity movements. With multi-asset-class algorithms, they have squeezed out inefficiencies in many financial markets. Managers of other types of funds and financial institutions have increasingly embraced these methods as well.

Exhibit 7.3 Hedge Fund Trading Strategies

Strategy	Definition
Global Macro	Focus is on macroeconomic environment, often concentrating on currencies or major interest-rates moves.
Emerging Markets	Investments are in the debt or equity of emerging markets typically characterized by lack of transparency and liquidity, in addition to an inability to find viable derivatives contracts for hedging.
Equity Market Neutral	Trades are in pairs of shares—buying one and selling another—to be neutral to changes in the market that may involve trading in single stocks as well as pitting indexes or Exchange-Traded Funds (ETFs) against each other and against other indexes.
Fixed Income Arbitrage	Focus is on anomalies among related bonds, often with high leverage.
Event-Driven	Trades are based on anticipated corporate events, such as expected merger, take-over activity, or bankruptcy filings.

Only for the Already Wealthy

By law, most hedge funds can be offered only to investors who are already wealthy.[19] The computer models, algorithms, and trading strategies that hedge funds use cannot be employed by average investors because hedge funds require a minimum investment of several million dollars. Legally, only accredited investors can invest with hedge funds because the government wants to protect average investors from the risks involved. An exception is made for 35 nonaccredited investors. The legal threshold defined by law for the ability to invest in a hedge fund is annual income greater than $200,000 and net worth above $1 million for an individual, excluding the individual's primary residence. An investor also must have a net worth of more than $1 million, owned alone or jointly with a spouse, must have earned either $200,000 annually in the past two years or $300,000 with a spouse, and must have a reasonable expectation of earning the same amount in the future. For institutions, such as pensions, endowments, and trusts, the primary qualification is having at least $5 million in assets.

Most hedge funds, however, have even stricter standards than these and set their own levels for qualified purchasers. Typically, they are looking for individuals with at least $5 million in investable assets and trusts and endowments and pension funds with at least $25 million in investable assets. Unlike mutual funds, hedge funds can reject investors without cause or reason. It is hard for the average investor to know about hedge funds because by law they are not allowed to advertise their services. The purpose of these restrictions is to protect them from taking on inordinate risk, but the unintended consequences are that hedge funds are an exclusive club for the super wealthy.

Renaissance Technologies

Renaissance Technologies (RenTech) is a good example of a hedge fund that has benefited from the migration of high-level talent to the financial sector. Jim Simons, a math genius with several breakthrough theories to his credit, shifted to financial services mid-career and became one of the world's richest individuals after founding a hedge fund called Renaissance Technologies in 1982. The company mostly hires people like Simons, individuals with math, science, and engineering backgrounds.

Simons obtained an undergrad degree from MIT in 1958 and his Ph.D in math from Berkeley in 1962 at the age of 23. Prior to being appointed chair of the math department at Stony Brook University in 1968, he was a researcher in the communications division of the Institute for Defense Analyses and a professor of mathematics at MIT and Harvard. The American Mathematical Society awarded him the Oswald Veblen Prize in Geometry in 1976 for ground-breaking work on geometric invariants that resulted in the Chern-Simons theory, which is widely applied in string theory. In 1978, he decided to turn his formidable intellect to the financial markets, and he established his first hedge fund several years later.

Although Simons continued to be the company's chair, he retired from RenTech in 2010 and turned over the firm's day-to-day leadership to Bob Mercer and Peter Brown, both of whom had PhDs in computer science and had done code-breaking research for the Defense Department before Renaissance Technologies hired them in 1993. Renaissance Technologies has less than 300 employees. Most of them are mathematicians, physicists, computer scientists, and astronomers or have military backgrounds, including expertise in software code breaking, like Mercer and Brown. The company specializes in quantitative analysis. It uses complex software to exploit market inefficiencies with the goal of predicting price movements and taking advantage of small, brief market anomalies and inefficiencies by large-scale trading. Its traders rapidly buy and sell global commodities and futures contracts as well as equities, currencies, and mortgage derivatives. The company is diversified with thousands of investment positions at any point in time. It continually reevaluates and revises the holdings in its portfolio. Traders regularly adjust positions and generate returns by actively looking for investments that yield results quickly.

From 1988 up to the Great Financial Crisis of 2007–2008, the average annual returns to investors in Renaissance Technologies' flagship Medallion fund were 38 percent.[20] With the exception of the years during and immediately following the crisis, the funds associated with Renaissance Technologies achieved outstanding returns. The returns were achieved after a management fee of 5 percent and a performance fee, which Renaissance Technologies takes, of 44 percent, among the highest fees charged by any hedge fund. During this streak, the fund lost money in only one year, 1989.

The Medallion Fund, a part of Rentech, which primarily focuses on commodities and futures trading, was closed to outside investment in 1993. In 1999 and 2005, the company started funds that rely on the computer models and trading strategies of Medallion and opened them to new investors. Given that the models and strategies that Renaissance Technologies uses depend on historical patterns, these funds did not do well in 2007–2008, and many investors withdrew their assets. However, the company made a comeback later when it tweaked its sophisticated algorithms to take into account new realities, and its funds again substantially outperformed other companies in the hedge fund industry, which did not beat the standard stock indexes in this period.

Most hedge funds charge management fees of 2 percent and take at least 20 percent of the gains they make. However, successful hedge funds with strong track records, like Renaissance Technologies, as seen, can raise these amounts. They mandate greater initial investments and charge higher fees, which is another reason they are outside the average investor's reach.

Technology at the Bottom of the Pyramid

Hedge fund technologies, when they work, benefit people at the top of the pyramid. Turning to the bottom of the pyramid, there also are technologies that have the potential to uplift the poor.[21] There are up to four billion poor, defined as those living on $2 to $3 a day (1990 purchasing power), who are underserved by the private sector and in need of new products to provide for their needs. Attending to the poor at the bottom of the pyramid offers businesses, which are eager to generate growth and struggling to create it in well-saturated existing markets, the opportunity to expand into new markets.

Although the opportunity is great, the challenges in reaching this market are substantial. The market for serving the poor is not homogenous, and it does not have well-developed infrastructure. Those at the bottom of the pyramid are found in many different circumstances. They live in both rural and urban settings. In India, most are rural, and their access to markets and Western-style purchasing environments is limited. In Latin America, they are predominately urban. They are packed into dangerous slums of large cities. Different types of technology are needed to serve the varied segments of the poor. The solutions to the problems of the poor must be delivered at an affordable price, but with this much variety, it is nearly impossible to reach the economies of scale in terms of production and distribution that would enable reduced costs.

Nonetheless, the needs of the poor for the products and services that people higher up in the income pyramid take for granted are great. These needs include communication, health, clean water, energy, food, hygiene, and jobs. To meet these needs, it is not always possible to just copy or strip down the technologies used in developed nations or wealthier markets; rather, adaptation is needed. To reduce costs and get these products and services to the poor, significant innovation in product design, supply chain management, inventory control, delivery, and post-delivery maintenance is necessary. If mass production is not possible when people are scattered and carrying out their crafts in separate locations, then virtual, as opposed to actual production, scaling must be introduced to bring costs down and provide jobs. Information technology, if deployed in innovative ways, can be a useful way to bridge this gap.

For businesses, the benefits of moving in the direction of making cheap, high-quality products and services available to the poor are not only to generate growth and profits, but also to answer the critiques of stakeholders who question the purpose of businesses. Another side benefit of serving the poor is the chance to experiment with new concepts which may not otherwise be taken seriously. It may be possible to transfer innovations that are introduced to serve the poor to more mainstream markets. An example is a small fuel-efficient nano-car. If it can be made inexpensive and even less energy consuming, it could eventually be adopted in cramped urban settings by drivers of all economic classes.

Telecommunications

The earliest achievements in the quest to better serve the poor with technology took place in telecommunications. By 2010, more than four billion people in the world had mobile phones and were connected through some type of wireless vendor. Supplied by established companies like Nokia, Motorola, Samsung, and LM Ericsson, many new firms came into existence to provide these services, such as Mobile Tel Networks in South Africa, Cel Tel in Sub-Saharan Africa, and Bharti-Airtel, Globe, and Philippines in India. In India, the adoption of new telecommunication services was rapid. From 2008 to 2009, the country added more than 10 million new subscribers per month. Having a cell phone allowed people to do their work more efficiently. For example, if they sold goods, they could more easily find out about current prices, and if they bought goods, they could more easily order them. They were less reliant on slow and unreliable postal services. Cell phones also gave them the capacity to quickly get medical information and entertainment.

An innovative project to make cell phone services widely available to the poor took place in rural Bangladesh in the 1990s. The micro-credit provider Grameen branched out using its business model of working with women entrepreneurs in rural villages where the per capita income was less than $500 a year. Married women were trusted with loans to start businesses since they were nearly certain to pay back the loans because of the social pressures. The new telecom branch of Grameen loaned women the equivalent of $175 and gave them training, a cell phone, and a solar charger. The women sold cell phone usage on a per-call basis. The pilot started in 950 villages. The women doubled their income. Farmers used the service to find out about crop prices and to order goods. With the extra income the women earned, they were able to provide for their children's education and healthcare, and they managed to scale the social ladder in their communities. Grameen

Telecom was a profitable business. It took the next step and offered rural Internet services via kiosks using a similar business model.

As a result of international debt, Morocco had to shift from state-based planning to a freer market. The state-run telecom monopoly ceased to exist in 1999, and three companies vigorously competed to provide telecom services. The upshot was that the number of mobile phone subscribers grew from 2.6 million in 2000 to more than 20 million in 2008. Penetration in the population exceeded 65 percent. Diffusion to low-income and semi-skilled laborers was rapid and the impacts significant. It increased coordination and expanded worker productivity. The incomes of regular phone users grew by 56 percent. Many took advantage of the phones to create or expand small businesses. Each additional phone in use generated eight new jobs based on an expansion of the users' social networks. The phones enlarged the radius in which the users were able to operate. It allowed them to rapidly mobilize temporary workers for jobs. Workers were able to find employment more rapidly. The phones were used to follow up leads with customers and cement ties with suppliers. Older means of connectivity (bicycles, mopeds, and public transportation) and of people (in storefronts, worksites, mosques, soccer fields, and cafés) became more valuable because calling lowered the cost of interacting and enabled people to put together productive undertakings.

Potable Water

The lack of clean, drinkable water damages the health and productivity of more than a billion people globally. Proctor & Gamble (P&G) collaborated with the Centers for Disease Control and Prevention (CDC) on a $10 million project to make a powder-based packet to purify water at 10 cents per 10 liters. The company anticipated that the product would be well received in the rural villages and urban slums of India. However, the product failed to take off for a number of reasons, including the taste, which was bland, and because the P&G sales personnel who marketed the water were not natives of the villages or urban neighborhoods where the water was needed. In 2004, P&G decided to change the undertaking into a philanthropic venture and donated the product to nongovernmental organizations (NGOs) and government programs and refocused on distributing the product in Sub-Saharan Africa where local vendors earned a commission and sold the product at a low price. These changes turned this initiative into a success.

In Mexico, governments had dealt with water quality issues by building large centralized water treatment plants and erecting far-reaching distribution systems. Most of the water that flowed through these systems was for toilets, laundry, bathing, and lawns and gardens and not for human consumption. The systems were not in good repair and had rusty pipes, leaks, and contamination. Rather than fixing them, the World Resources Institute (WRI), a nonprofit organization, introduced point-of-use water treatment for human consumption in parts of Mexico where the government was not willing to make investments in public infrastructure. It engaged entrepreneurs in the local community in which the entrepreneurs sold innovative fruit drink concentrates mixed with the water, a partnership program with local businesses that WRI hoped to spread elsewhere in the world where it was needed.

Health Services

A 2005 joint venture of the nonprofit Acumen Fund and the Indian public sector corporation HLI Lifecare LifeSpring resulted in the creation of a chain of small, 20-bed maternity hospitals in low-income Indian neighborhoods to provide a safe environment in which women could give birth. The hospitals were basic operations to keep their costs low. They had no air conditioning and did not provide meals. The narrow specialization of the hospitals was on healthy births. Because all complications were referred to other hospitals, they did not require sophisticated staffs of nurses and doctors. The prices charged were 65 to 85 percent less than other options. To attract women to the hospitals, LifeSpring sent representatives to visit pregnant women and gave them discount vouchers, which it then asked the women to distribute to other pregnant women.

The need to keep costs low is evident in another healthcare example. Indian engineers who worked for GE Healthcare developed an electrocardiogram (ECG) machine that was uniquely customized for rural India where there was no electricity, few trained doctors, and widespread poverty. Used by paramedics, it was battery operated, light so that it could be carried around, robust so that it would not break easily, and capable of printing ECG results on the spot to enable quick identification of problems. The machine was priced at $800 in contrast to the typical price of more than $10,000 for an ECG machine in the United States.

Nutrition and Crop Protection

Solae, a division of DuPont, made soy protein for food products that it marketed to the poor using community representatives. It introduced Solae's soy powder food supplement into poor rural villages in India in the years between 2006 and 2008. In communities in which it found the need, it selected 20 women as business partners to market the soy powder. To increase the supplement's appeal and bring it into closer alignment with the Indian diet, these women would teach their neighbors new cooking habits and skills. They hosted home cookery days that attracted their friends and neighbors and offered home cooking consulting services, shared recipes, and cookbooks for using soy powder.

Bayer Crop-Science used a similar concept of relying on local community members for distribution and sale. It worked with farmers in Kenya to educate them about the responsible use of the pesticides and trained a network of rural agro-dealers who created consultancy centers and engaged with the farmers about proper handling. The agro-dealers sold the crop protection products to farmers in small packets they could afford and handle safely. The dealers were enmeshed in their communities and were chosen based on their reputation and their ability to be top sales performers. The parent company provided marketing support via radio connections.

Energy

Husk Power Systems, started in 2007 by graduate engineering students from India and business students from the United States, focused on a well-known problem that existed in the small villages in the Indian state of Bihar: lack of electricity. The students developed a gasifier that made electricity from inedible rice husks. Compared to kerosene and wood, the traditional fuels in the region, using the rice husks as fuel was cheaper and less polluting. Husk Power has become a public–private partnership supported by foundations and serves over 130 villages throughout Bihar. It sells electricity at low cost and employs local villagers to manage its electric power plants.

British Petroleum (BP) has been involved in another energy-related project in rural India. Women in villages often use ticks, shrub, grass, other biomass materials, and cow dung as cooking fuel. They spend two to three hours a day gathering this material, yet it yields harsh and unpleasant polluting smoke that is a health hazard. The way in which the material is gathered and used for cooking varies in rice- and wheat-growing areas. BP's solution was flexible to these different needs. It developed, manufactured, and sold a biomass pellet in collaboration with the Indian Institute of Science (IISC) and several NGOs. It also developed an easy-to-use, smokeless stove that met global safety standards and was affordable ($20) and aesthetically appealing. The NGOs identified village entrepreneurs to generate awareness and sell the pellets and the stoves. The goal was to reach 20 million consumers globally in less than a dozen years.

Critiques

Critics of the bottom of the pyramid point out that few large corporations have been able to build sizable businesses by serving the poor and that the profits they have made in doing so have not been significant. When surveying the options for new initiatives, many large corporations have come to the conclusion that they have better options elsewhere. The emerging middle classes in developing countries are a more attractive market than the poor. Serving this market requires fewer adjustments in the way large corporations do business. As the examples given show, it is complicated to serve the poor. The challenge is not just in creating appropriate technology, but also in bringing it to the communities in which the poor are located. Adapting to these markets often means working intensively with NGOs and government and foregoing easy and quick profits. Supply chains have to be created where none existed previously, delivery systems have to be put in place, and production modified to create affordable products with sufficient quality.

Low-margin, high-volume methods usually are out of the question because the markets for the poor are so diverse. Poor populations are often geographically dispersed and culturally heterogeneous, which increases distribution and marketing costs and makes it very difficult to take advantage of economies of scale. Weak infrastructure in all areas—transportation, communication, media, and legal—increases the cost of doing business. Transactions are usually small in size, and poor people are very price sensitive. Marketing costs are high. Although technology reduces these costs via the redesign of business processes, whole new ecosystems have to be created to reach different populations of the poor. These problems have led some to conclude that for large corporations the fortune at the bottom of the pyramid is not achievable. Smaller, local firms working together with governments and NGOs are better suited to serving this market.

The definition of poverty has generated controversy. Examples of serving the poor are not targeted at people at the lowest rungs. They are often targeted at general populations, women, or entire regions. Another critique is that the poor are often viewed as consumers rather than agents capable of creating economic value. Better assessments of what has been achieved and the lessons to be learned are needed. They must address both the economic and social impacts.

Conclusion

This chapter has provided insights into the problems of global inequality both as they manifest themselves in the gaps between countries and within countries. Particular attention has been paid to the widening wealth gap in the U.S. and its causes. As an example of the opportunities at the top of the pyramid, this chapter highlighted hedge funds using quantitative methods only available to the wealthy. The sophisticated models of these hedge funds act to preserve and enhance the wealth of the rich. As for the opportunities at the bottom of the pyramid, this chapter has highlighted efforts to lift the poor out of poverty by providing them with improved telecommunication services, drinkable water, and access to health services, nutrition, energy, and housing. The limits of these efforts have been discussed, too.

The emphasis in this chapter has been on this dual nature of technology, both as a cause of global inequality and as means for its mitigation. It has shown that the rich have access to technologies that have helped to perpetuate their wealth, whereas the poor provide fertile ground for technological innovations. However, business models that can bring these innovations to the poor profitably and on a widespread basis still need to be developed. The next chapter continues the discussion of the relationship between technology and the business environment with a focus on energy.

Endnotes

1. Kerry A. Dolan and Luisa Kroll, eds., "The World's Billionaires," *Forbes*. March 2, 2015. http://www.forbes.com/billionaires/.

2. "The Purse of the One Percent," *The Economist*. Oct. 14, 2014. http://www.economist.com/blogs/graphicdetail/2014/10/daily-chart-8.

3. Jill Treanor, "Richest 1% of People Own Nearly Half of Global Wealth, Says Report," *The Guardian*. Oct. 14, 2004. http://www.theguardian.com/business/2014/oct/14/richest-1percent-half-global-wealth-credit-suisse-report.

4. "Gini Index," *Investopedia*. http://www.investopedia.com/terms/g/gini-index.asp.

5. United Nations Development Programme, *Human Development Reports*, United Nations, 2014. http://hdr.undp.org/en/data>. Central Intelligence Agency, *The World Factbook* n.d. https://www.cia.gov/library/publications/the-world-factbook/.

6. Nan Wu, "Income Inequality in China and the Urban-Rural Divide," *Journalist's Resource*. Aug. 19, 2014. http://journalistsresource.org/studies/international/china/income-inequality-todays-china.

7. Prachi Salve, "India's Wealth Is Rising. So Is Inequality," *India Spend*. Jan. 9, 2015. http://www.indiaspend.com/cover-story/indias-wealth-is-rising-so-is-inequality-96987.

8. World Bank, "Countries and Economies," *World Bank Data*. World Bank, n.d. http://data.worldbank.org/country.

9. Ibid.

10. Ibid.

11. Ibid.

12. See *Human Development Reports* and *The World Factbook*.

13. Jennifer Erickson, ed. "The Middle-Class Squeeze," *Center for American Progress*. Washington: Center for American Progress, 2014. https://cdn.americanprogress.org/wp-content/uploads/2014/09/MiddeClassSqueeze.pdf.

14. Facundo Alvaredo, Tony Atkinson, Thomas Piketty, and Emmanuel Saez, *The World Top Incomes Database* n.d. http://topincomes.parisschoolofeconomics.eu/#Database:.

15. Thomas Piketty and Emmanuel Saez, "Inequality in the Long Run," *Science*. May 23, 2014: 838-842. http://eml.berkeley.edu/~saez/piketty-saezScience14.pdf.

16. Robert Putnam, *Our Kids: The American Dream in Crisis*. New York: Simon and Schuster, 2015. Charles Murray, *Coming Apart*. New York: Crown Publishing, 2012.

17. "About Hedge Funds: What Is a Hedge Fund?" Magnum Funds, 2011. http://www.magnum.com/hedgefunds/abouthedgefunds.asp.

18. Matt Simon, "Hedge Funds and Multi Asset Algorithmic Trading—Perfect Partners?" *Automated Trader*. July 2, 2006. http://www.automatedtrader.net/articles/marketplace/513/hedge-funds-and-multi-asset-algorithmic-trading-_-perfect-partners.

19. Lawrence Delevingne, "Are You Rich and Sophisticated Enough for Private Funds?" *CNBC*. Aug. 20, 2014. http://www.cnbc.com/2014/08/20/are-you-rich-and-sophisticated-enough-for-private-funds.html.

20. Gregory Zuckerman, "Yen Bets Don't Add Up for a Fund Giant," *The Wall Street Journal*. April 25, 2013. http://www.wsj.com/articles/SB10001424127887324474004578444933337979710.

21. C.K. Prahalad and Allen Hammond, "Serving the World's Poor, Profitably," *Harvard Business Review* (September 2002): 4–11.; C.K. Prahalad, *Fortune at the Bottom of the Pyramid: Eradicating Poverty Through Profits*, Upper Saddle River, NJ: Wharton School Publishing, 2004.; Allen Hammond, William Kramer, Robert Katz, Julia Tran, and Courtland Walker, *At the Base of the Pyramid: The Next Four Billion*. Washington: World Resources Institute, 2007.; Aneel Karnani, "The Mirage of Marketing to the Bottom of the Pyramid: How the Private Sector Can Help Alleviate Poverty," *California Management Review* 49.4 (Summer 2007): 90–111.; Hsain Ilahiane and John Sherry, "The Problematics of the 'Bottom of the Pyramid' Approach to International Development: The Case of Micro-Entrepreneurs' Use of Mobile Phones in Morocco." *Information Technologies & International Development* 8.1 (2012): 13–26.; Ashish Karamchandani, Mike Kubzansky, and Nishant Lalwani, "Is the Bottom of the Pyramid Really for You?" *Harvard Business Review* 89.3 (2011): 107–111.; Ans Kolk, Miguel Rivera-Santos, and Carlos Rufín, "Reviewing a Decade of Research on the 'Base/Bottom of the Pyramid' (BOP) Concept," *Business & Society* 53.3 (2014): 338–377.; Costas Markides, "Disruptive Reality," *Business Strategy Review* 3 (2013): 36–43.; Jerry Calton, Patricia Werhane, Laura Hartman, and David Bevanj, "Building Partnerships to Create Social and Economic Value at the Base of the Global Development Pyramid," *Journal of Business Ethics* 117.4 (2013): 721–733.

8

Abundance, Scarcity, and Global Sustainability

The world depends on fossil fuels like coal, oil, and natural gas for essential services like electricity, heat, and transportation. In 2013, more than 78 percent of the world's energy came from fossil fuels, 19 percent came from renewables like biomass, hydro, wind, solar, and geothermal, and the rest came from nuclear energy.[1] By their very nature, the supplies of fossil fuels are finite. Their consumption yields greenhouse gases, which bear the most responsibility for global climate change. Utilization of these fuels produces common air pollutants that cause smog and endanger human health. Petroleum is found in dangerous and unstable regions of the world controlled by repressive regimes. The world can reduce its dependence on fossil fuels through energy efficiency and by becoming more reliant on renewable energy and nuclear power.

Renewable energy is derived from plant material, the sun, wind, and waterfalls, which are theoretically inexhaustible. With regard to renewable energy, progress has been made. The International Energy Agency's (IEA) continually revises its forecasts for renewable sources such as wind and solar upward[2] Since 1977, the price of photovoltaic (PV) solar energy has declined exponentially.

Irrespective of the fossil fuel and renewable fuel mix, the world will need an ample supply of energy to enable future economic growth. Nuclear power is not a main source of air pollution or a contributor to climate change, but expensive construction costs, spent fuel storage problems, and accidents have slowed its growth. Nor is the supply of uranium on which nuclear power plants depend infinite; and although the ability to recycle uranium is possible, it is dangerous. Global public support for renewable energy, on the other hand, has been high.

However, for additional progress to take place, obstacles to the commercialization of renewable technologies must be overcome. The costs of energy efficiency and renewable energy must continue to decline. In 2015, because of a continued decline in solar prices, the investment bank UBS issued an optimistic report about solar power. It predicted that

PVs have the potential to account for 10 percent of the world's global electricity supply, overtaking other technologies as the default source for electricity generation by 2025.[3] This result, however, is not inevitable. With respect to future world energy supplies, both fossil fuels and renewable energy may be abundant. On the other hand, both may be scarce. Mixed cases that favor either fossil fuels or renewables also are possible. The balance will tip in the direction of one of these scenarios (see Exhibit 8.1) depending on technology. If fossil fuels are to flourish, there must be advances in the low-cost and pollution-free exploitation of unconventional, hard to access, and extract sources of supply. Similarly, if renewable energies are to flourish, there must be advances in low-cost, energy-efficient, and renewable technologies. This chapter evaluates these possibilities.

Exhibit 8.1 Four Energy Future Scenarios

Fossil Fuels	Abundant	Limited
Renewable & Energy Efficiency		
Abundant	Romance	A World of Renewables
Limited	A World of Fossil Fuels	Scarcity

Fossil Fuels

Higher-priced fossil fuels mean less overall global economic activity, all else being equal. With the exception of the early 1990s (and even then there was a threat of higher petroleum prices because of the Kuwait War), higher energy prices have been associated with reduced economic growth. Governments have rightfully been reluctant to try to control the booms and busts that exist in fossil fuel energy markets, yet taxation and subsidies alter them, providing signals that change the fuel mix. In the short run, higher prices are needed to stimulate the search for fossil fuel alternatives, but in the long run, fossil fuel prices must go down. The dilemma is that fossil fuel prices should not be so elevated as to stifle economic growth and fossil fuel demand, nor so low as to remove the incentives for exploration and production of new sources of energy.

Oil Price Declines

Since 2014, there has been a rapid decline in oil prices. Supply and demand dynamics in oil price markets are worth examining in more detail. In 1956, the geoscientist M. King Hubbert suggested that U.S. oil reserves would eventually fall. They would peak and descend starting in about 1970. He was right that in that year, U.S. reserves did peak, but he did not take into account the build-up in reserves that subsequently took place by means of exploiting unconventional sources through improved technology.

On the one hand, many geologists and petroleum engineers maintain that once about half the oil in the ground has been exhausted, extraction becomes so difficult and expensive that prices are bound to remain high, regardless of the technological advances that are made. Many economists, on the other hand, hold that resource limits do not exist, that it all depends on price, and that the oil in the ground will never be exhausted because whenever prices rise, technology will emerge to reduce extraction costs.

There is no doubt that a crisis occurred in the United States around 1970, and after that, the United States became increasingly reliant on the import of foreign oil (see Exhibit 8.2). Other countries increased their foreign reliance about the same time. Given these trends, the likelihood of fossil fuels continuing to dominate the world's fuel mix depends on technologies for enhanced oil recovery.

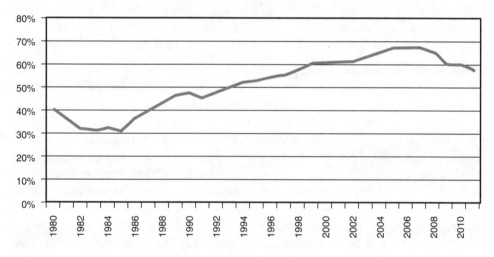

US Oil Imports as % of Oil Consumed – Btu Basis

Exhibit 8.2 Growth and Decline of U.S. Oil Imports

Data Source: Based on data derived from the U.S. Energy Information Agency

The output of an existing oil field typically declines 5 percent per year.[4] In the past, large oil companies typically gave up on a field after 30–40 years; prior to World War II, they extracted just 10 percent of the oil from a typical field. Since then, by means of technological breakthrough, they have learned to extract another 30 percent or more by injecting a combination of water, pressure, and chemicals into old oil fields. Normally, when a field reaches a 50-percent exhaustion level, it is necessary to transition from relatively inexpensive primary recovery to more expensive secondary and tertiary recovery. After obtaining about half the output, oil companies today still do more. They remove another 30 percent or so of oil out of a field by means of horizontal drilling and using gas, carbon dioxide, engineered microbes, and chemicals to drive as much of the remaining oil from fields as possible, although not all fields respond well to these methods, and extraction costs in the old fields can be twice or more the costs of extraction in new ones.

Hydraulic Fracking

Horizontal drilling in conventional oil fields led to hydraulic fracturing of shale rock in basins found in many parts of the United States and elsewhere in the world where previously it had not been economically feasible to extract oil and natural gas from the rock. The rock is now accessed via horizontal drilling, in a process called fracking. The oil and natural gas embedded in the rock are torn apart by hydraulically pressurized liquids made up of water, sand, and chemicals. The high-pressure mixture that is injected into the ground creates cracks in the rock so that petroleum and natural gas are released and flow freely to the surface. Instead of having to mine the rock and break it into tiny pieces, which are then heated to obtain fuel, the whole process takes place underground. When the hydraulic pressure is removed, small grains of sand or aluminum oxide keep the fractures open, creating the channel for fuels to come to the surface and be captured.

Fracking started as an experiment in 1947 and was used sporadically in commercial applications as early as 1950, but it took off only in 2005–2010, when the U.S. industry grew by 45 percent a year.[5] As a proportion of the country's overall gas production, shale gas grew from 4 percent in 2005 to 24 percent in 2012. In the second decade of the 21st century, fracking was quite common. Although hydraulic fracturing is an effective way to release oil and natural gas that otherwise would go unused and has greatly expanded the world's supplies of fossil fuel, it is also a controversial method because of the environmental risks involved, which include contaminating ground and surface water, depleting water that could be used for other needs (because it is intensive in its use of water), degrading air quality, causing earthquakes (mostly small but with the possibility of high magnitude quakes), and creating other public health and environmental hazards. Environmental groups have protested and alerted the world to these risks, but U.S. government studies have generally found the risks to be acceptable relative to the benefits.[6]

Fracking has restored U.S. fossil fuel production to levels not found since 1970. The real growth in future U.S. energy reserves, according to the U.S. Department of Energy (DOE), will come about because of fracking (see Exhibit 8.3). Conventional oil exploration and development have been flat or declining. However, it is unclear if the pace of fracking can be maintained with the Organization of the Petroleum Exporting Countries (OPEC) countries flooding oil markets worldwide.

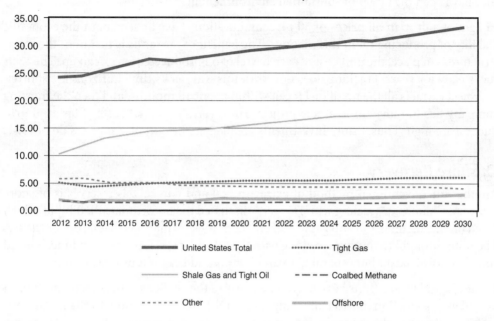

US Department of Energy Projections of Oil and Gas Supply
(trillion cubit feet)

Legend:
- United States Total
- Shale Gas and Tight Oil
- Other
- Tight Gas
- Coalbed Methane
- Offshore

Exhibit 8.3 The Dominance of Unconventional Oil and Gas Supply Sources

At the end of 2014, after several months of plummeting crude oil prices, OPEC was under pressure from its poorer members who needed the money. They wanted OPEC to lower its oil production quotas to shore up prices.[7] Against the wishes of its poorer members, the cartel announced a continuation of its past policies of high production quotas and low prices. OPEC's decision accelerated the fall in the price of crude oil and led to further drops in the number of new fracking projects. A number of other unconventional means of fossil fuel production exist, too. In each instance, in addition to the removal of residual fossil fuels previously left in the ground via fracking, the exploitation of unconventional oil sources, like tar sands found extensively in the central provinces of Canada, and advances in discovery and exploitation of oil in remote offshore locations, have become the most important sources of increased global fossil fuel supplies.

Tar Sands

Tar sands have enabled Canada to become the world's fifth-largest oil producer, but making oil in this way is technologically challenging. Like hydraulic fracking, it can be produced by injecting steam into deep underground wells to heat up the oil or by strip-mining and extracting petroleum from the mined earth. Up to 20 percent more energy and water are consumed this way than in producing oil by conventional means. These methods yield much greater amounts of harmful carbon emissions. For these reasons, they have been the target of substantial environmentalist criticism.[8]

In light of a drop in oil prices of 50 percent, questions have arisen about the economic viability of producing oil in this manner. The benefit of tar sands is that once the infrastructure is in place, the unit cost of each barrel of oil produced does not go up. The costs stay steady for years. Fracking does not work this way, as its time horizons are shorter. A project extracts all the fossil fuel it can within about 18 months, and then the fracking company has to move on to a new project. However, the capital costs of tar sand production are high. Thus, future investments are likely to be curtailed if prices do not rise.

Offshore Recovery

Another unconventional method of extracting oil and natural gas reserves is offshore recovery. Chapter 4, "Dealing with Danger," discussed the unfortunate BP oil spill, which relied on this method. Oil and gas are taken out of rock formations that lie under the sea. The water brought to the surface along with the oil and gas is impure—it is brackish and contains dissolved and unseparated hydrocarbons and is a pollution problem.

Technological innovations have overcome many of the challenges that make this type of oil and gas production more challenging than land-based production. In shallow waters, mobile units are anchored to the sea bottom. In deep water, the units float with mooring systems to keep them steady. The floating systems reduce operating costs, but the sea's dynamism makes it hard to extract oil in this way. The platforms cannot be fixed to the seabed and must float. Huge ballast tanks must be placed under water to prevent excessive rolling in unstable seas. Thrusters compensate for the platform's movement. The platforms must keep their positions steady even in severe weather.

Offshore oil production also presents logistics and human resources challenges. Crews go to the platforms by helicopter and stay for long periods. The platforms are full-blown communities with cafeterias, sleeping quarters, and areas for exercise. The crews have to receive high levels of compensation to work under these stressful conditions. All the supplies are brought by ship, and their waste is sent back to land in the same way. The crews work around the clock under great pressure to ensure that the platform is steady and that accidents are avoided. Bad weather is a regular occurrence. In emergencies, such as fires or explosions, lifeboats offer the only method of escape.

Offshore production of oil started in the 1940s, and by 2010, about one-third of world oil output was not land based.[9] Offshore production was the main source of growth in the world's oil supply in this period. All offshore production until the 1990s was in shallow water, but shallow water output had become flat, and deep water production was growing. Ultra-deep water production was on the horizon. It started in the U.S. Gulf of Mexico in 2005. By the second decade of the 21st century, it is expected to comprise about 4 percent of offshore sources.[10]

Intensive deep-water exploration efforts have stimulated technological breakthroughs in drilling and seismic technologies. Brazil, Angola, and Nigeria as well as the United States are deeply involved. This type of production is risky. Environmental and economic goals tend to conflict; to meet return on investment, goals sometimes involve compromising environmental goals. More breakthroughs are needed to produce environmentally friendly, safe, and cheap oil that is deeply embedded under the world's oceans.

Cleaner Energy

If oil prices follow conventional logic, then low oil prices should mean more consumption, but in 2014, despite a drop in prices, energy consumption grew by just 0.9 percent, the slowest rate in almost 20 years.[11] Although lower gasoline prices motivate Americans to buy bigger vehicles, bigger vehicles have become more efficient. If more people choose alternatives like the electric car or hybrids, petroleum consumption could fall even more. From a small base, global sales of electric vehicles and hybrids have increased, but they represent just a tiny percentage of the vehicles actually sold.[12]

Scientists and engineers continue to work on ways to reduce fossil fuel use for transportation. The auto company Audi reports having developed a "blue crude" fuel, which it makes into carbon neutral e-diesel through a simple process.[13] The German government supports the technology because it could be a game changer in the effort to reduce dependence on fossil fuels. Whether such technologies make it to the mainstream depends on affordability. Their costs must go down. In this section, the promise and limits of different types of energy efficiency and renewable energy technologies that have the potential to reduce reliance on fossil fuels are reviewed.

The promise of these technologies is that they can reduce noxious emissions, lower the chances of climate change, and decrease dependence on a commodity imported from unstable regions of the globe. They may also enable the creation of new industries and jobs. In response to high gasoline prices, George W. Bush, in his term in office, backed policies that were meant to stimulate energy efficiency and renewable-energy technologies. Obama's election suggested that the issue resonated well with the public. As part of the effort to recover from the financial crisis, Congress included energy efficiency and cleaner energy technologies in the stimulus package. The Obama administration declared that they were an important priority, setting aside more than $90 billion for this purpose. Other governments throughout the world committed close to $190 billion to this goal, and it was estimated that China would spend two to four times this amount.

However, the favorable conditions that spurred governments to support cleaner energy technologies started to wear thin. Chinese solar power firms receiving cheap loans from their government flooded the U.S. market with inexpensive solar cells, which led to the bankruptcy of solar-panel maker Solyndra, the recipient of more than half a billion dollars of U.S. government aid, and unleashed a barrage of criticism. Because of the financial crisis, many energy efficiency and renewable energy projects were canceled. Start-ups focusing on energy efficiency and cleaner energy with innovative technologies had trouble scaling up their operations and competing. The attempt by Congress to pass cap-and-trade legislation to control greenhouse emissions failed in 2009, and fracking seemed to offer the United States the potential for abundant and cheap fossil that could lead to U.S. energy independence, a long sought-after goal.

Progress was made, and some technologies started to compete with fossil fuels on a dollar-for-dollar basis, but the advances were not enough to make a significant dent in fossil fuels' dominance. Under the U.S. DOE's 2010 projections, by the year 2035, the U.S. economy and society will still be largely dependent on fossil fuels. In the base case, energy use grows slowly in response to greater energy efficiency—reliance on petroleum falls from 37 to 32 percent, the use of natural gas expands from 25 to 26 percent, and coal declines from 21 to 20 percent, but renewable energy only increases from 8 percent of U.S. primary energy consumption to 15 percent.[14] The promise of change lies in the domains of efficiency, solar power, wind, energy storage, and, to a lesser extent, biofuels.[15]

Building Energy

Buildings consume a high percentage of U.S. energy at 39 percent. They consume 71 percent of the electricity, and 54 percent of the natural gas, and they are responsible for 40 percent of carbon emissions. Yet building energy efficiency consists of a host of numerous small fixes that are hard to implement. These fixes must be designed and introduced into new buildings or retrofitted into old ones. However, the turnover in buildings is low. The incentives for the introduction of energy efficiency technologies have to be right for the owners to make changes needed. They include new seals, sensors, building controls, lighting fixtures and sources, windows, insulation, appliances, water, and heating and cooling systems.

Utilities play an important role. By altering their pricing structures, increasing demand monitoring, and restructuring billing, utilities can foster change. A major problem is that a good business model is needed to entice residents and building owners to incorporate energy efficiency. New technologies have to be cost and time effective; however, the payoffs often require long lead times. Getting renters to make changes is particularly challenging. Who is responsible for making the changes: the owner or the tenant? The person bearing the risk is not necessarily the same as the person enjoying the reward. Documenting actual savings is even more complicated. After an owner pays for an improvement, maintenance might be spotty, and the anticipated gains are not realized.

When there are maintenance gaps and building systems do not function as expected, investments do not pay off.

Only in some jurisdictions are strong codes in place to encourage needed changes. Even rarer are rigorous inspections to ensure compliance. Also, only some jurisdictions provide sufficient assistance via low-interest or subsidized loans. Government agencies like the EPA have developed programs such as Energy Star for testing appliance energy efficiency, but participation in these programs is voluntary. Consumers' reasons for not choosing energy-efficient appliances include price, convenience, and features. Independent and private sectors certifying agencies like the U.S. Green Energy Business Council's LEED (Leadership in Energy & Environmental Design) program play a role in promoting green buildings, but obtaining certification is costly, and the number of buildings certified, although growing, is small.

Some energy-efficiency technology for buildings is simple and involves nothing more than painting roofs and asphalts white. Other technologies are more sophisticated and complicated, such as, for example, software for monitoring and controlling buildings' energy use. The flagship product of Nest is a networked learning thermostat for home use. Nest began to sell these thermostats in 2011. The users set the thermostat by spinning and clicking a control wheel, which unveils menus for heating, cooling, setup, energy history, and scheduling. With time, the thermostat learns self-adjustment techniques and patterns, such as when the house is occupied, that conserve energy.

Spring Networks is another company involved in building technologies to promote energy efficiency. It provides smart grid software and other products that enable utility companies to manage data from customers' meters. The data shows how much money customers spent on electricity and how much money they can save if improvements are made. Echelon, another company, has a multiapplication energy-control-networking platform for smart grid applications that are designed to help customers save energy. Its network platform is able to reduce the duration of outages or even prevent them from occurring. The company provides a visible platform with data to analyze past decisions and collaborative tools to act promptly.

The company Opower offers a simple tool to improve building energy. It is a social comparison report sent to electricity users. The report shows an occupant of a building how she is doing in comparison to her neighbors. If the occupant is doing as well as her most efficient neighbors, the report shows a double smiley face, if not as well as the most efficient neighbors, but better than the average, it has a single smiley face, and if worse, the report is marked with a frowning face. These reports, based on the research of psychologist Robert Cialdini, have the potential to reduce energy usage by 2.5 percent, a reduction that translates into a 0.5 percent saving in greenhouse gas emissions. The reports motivate customers to improve by giving them advice about how to save money as well as information that shows their performance relative to others.

Among the most promising technology for building energy efficiency is LED lights. Originally used as indicator lamps for electronic devices, their potential for saving energy lies in their use as replacements for electric lighting. Their use is rapidly catching on. LEDs last 50 times longer than the typical incandescent bulb and have low carbon emissions and slow failure rates but a high initial price.

The use of dynamic glass in buildings can also reduce energy consumption by as much as 20 percent. Dynamic glass blocks solar radiation during peak summer heating periods and adds insulation during peak winter cooling seasons. The gains are significant because windows account for as much as 40 percent of a building's energy consumption. Dynamic glass consists of standard glass that is coated with an efficient, light-absorbing surface. The product changes from clear to tinted glass as needed. With these windows in place, buildings provide for healthier indoor spaces that have the potential to improve the occupants' spirits and productivity, too.

Industrial and Commercial

There are many promising avenues to explore in the domains of industrial and commercial energy efficiency. With regard to industrial efficiency, the company Transphorm has a semiconductor platform for making power converters that change AC to DC current and vice versa, using gallium nitride (GaN), the same material used in white-light LEDs. The converters currently used are made of silicon, and they operate at efficiencies of about 90 percent with power losses in the form of waste heat. Transphorm promises to reduce these losses by 5 percent or more. The company's initial product was aimed at the data server market, which has been heavily criticized for its high electricity consumption.

eASIC has also developed a product that can save energy in industry: a gate-array design for manufacturing application-specific integrated circuits for transistors and other devices. This design reduces development costs, turnaround times, power consumption, and unit costs.

To reduce energy use in commercial building, Bloom Energy stacks small, solid oxide fuel cells using natural gas and oxygen close together to generate electricity. The stacked cells achieve energy conversion efficiencies of 50 percent, which is close to the 60 percent efficiencies of combined cycle natural gas, but transmission and distribution losses are lower because the power is produced closer to a facility. However, the cost of the units, each of which has to be custom built, is high.

Solar

Two different types of solar power have to be considered: solar thermal (ST) and photovoltaics (PVs). The former involves a collector amassing heat and directly absorbing sunlight for the purposes of electrical power or heating. It was first used for power generation in the 1980s. The largest ST installation in the world was in the Mojave Desert in California. Under ideal conditions, when cloud cover does not obscure the sun, the Mojave Desert installation's capacity to produce electricity is 354 megawatts (MW), but the sun does not always shine during the day. Furthermore, because it utilizes sunlight, ST installations do not operate at night, unlike coal or nuclear powered plants, which have the potential to produce three times or more the amount electricity any time of day or season of the year.

To capture the sunlight, different ST systems exist. The most common has a parabolic collector, but there are alternatives, such as power towers, dishes, and other designs. Tracking systems that follow the motion of the sun increase the cost and complexity of ST systems. There are designs that integrate thermal energy storage into modular flat reflectors that focus the sun's heat onto elevated receivers, which allow for a longer solar power generation cycle.

Arguments for ST depend on the willingness of utility companies to pay the premium of installing ST systems. The companies may agree to do so because, whereas cloud cover tends to instantaneously drop PV output, ST systems produce power in a more consistent way because the turbines they enable have inertia. Even more important is that ST can be augmented with molten salt-based storage systems, which produce power at night. ST systems can also be used in other applications than to generate electricity; the hot steam they make can be used in industrial processes like petroleum refining. They also can be used to help convert saltwater into freshwater.

Heliostats form the foundation of ST systems. Second-generation heliostat designs have larger mirrors and smaller and more easily implanted bases. They have streamlined software electronics, cabling, and robotic cleaning to lower costs. There are patented systems based on complex algorithms to track the exact position of the sun and coordinate the control of the heliostats.

PVs, unlike ST systems, directly convert sunshine into electricity. When the sunlight strikes the surface of semiconductor material from which the cell is made, it energizes electrons to break loose. The freed electrons are channeled through a grid on the cell's surface to junctions where they combine to form an electric current that can be captured by an inverter as useable direct currency (DC) electricity.

A cell's efficiency is the maximum amount of power that can be obtained from the current. The highest level of efficiency ever obtained in a laboratory is about 45 percent, but the actual efficiency of PC cells in use is far less than that amount. Typically the cells are sold as panels consisting of multiple cells in a group that are oriented in the same direction. The most common cells found in solar panels are thick-film crystalline silicon (c-Si) cells. They can achieve efficiencies in converting sunlight to useful energy of about 13 to 19 percent in use, but they are subject to price volatility of silicon and are heavy and hard to transport. Thin-film cells are lighter in weight than c-Si cells and easier to mount on rooftops. However, they are less efficient and require more panels, sunlight, and space to generate the same amount of electricity as cells made of c-Si. If made of cadmium tullride (Cdte), they are 6 to 13 percent efficient in converting sunlight to useful energy. Other thin-film cells can be made of amorphous silicon, copper indium selenide (CIS), or copper indium gallium selenide (CIGS).

Failed solar manufacturer Solyndra placed its bets on CIGS. The high cost of silicon was a main reason for using thin-film cells, but then silicon costs dropped. Makers of thin-film gallium selenide (CIGS) PV modules tried to lower costs with manufacturing efficiencies. Those with experience in the hard disk and semiconductor industries tried to deposit CIGS on a flexible stainless steel substrate through a continuous sputtering process. By re-engineering the manufacturing process to improve efficiency, it became possible to lower costs, but manufacturing these cells in high volume proved to be a significant challenge. Other companies tried to focus sunlight onto multijunction thin-film cells. Multijunction cells stack together many cells for better patterning and sunlight absorption. Transitioning from testing in the lab to full-scale production, however, was, again, a significant obstacle to commercialization.

Low-cost silicon cells from China trumped the potentially superior designs and manu-facturing methods. The Chinese government provided tax forgiveness, free land, fast track permitting, research and development (R&D), and export financing to solar pro-ducers, not to mention that wages in China already were low. The Chinese-made solar panels were originally meant for the domestic market, but Chinese companies sold them globally in response to European subsidies. Chinese manufacturers boosted their global market share from 10 percent in 2005 to more than 50 percent in 2010. Euro-pean governments had far-reaching renewable energy goals and large subsidies, which were phased out by design and because of the post-2007-08 stagnation in the European economies. More than half of the U.S. states had renewable energy goals, but they were not as far reaching as those in European countries, and the subsidies they offered were not as generous.

Wind

Wind turbine technology has improved dramatically. Whereas a wind turbine of the early 1990s typically had a 20-to-25-percent capacity factor, a turbine in 2014 might have a 40-percent capacity factor in reasonably good wind and up to 50-percent capacity in the best wind conditions. Although conventional wind turbines have greatly increased in size and height, their design has not changed much. They are based on the physical prin-ciples of the 18th century windmill, in which the turbines open to the elements. Another design includes a cover that allows the turbines to takes advantage of aerospace industry innovations in engine design and alters the airflow patterns around the turbine. This type of design increases energy output while delivering useable energy in a quieter way.

Still another possibility is a two-bladed, rather than a three-bladed, turbine. Smaller units of this nature can be used in community wind-generating sites. The first prototypes were built in Sweden. These systems are lightweight and affordable, more easily assembled and erected than three-blade systems, and suffer from less fatigue. Therefore, they do not require as much maintenance. They are less obtrusive and quieter than three-bladed turbines, and they can be located closer to population centers.

Still another innovation is poised to take place in the way turbines are manufactured, transported, and delivered for onsite assembly. Modular designs make possible automated parts that are mass manufactured and delivered over ordinary roads in regular trucks. The turbines can be assembled onsite, which reduces project development and construction timelines and lowers costs. GE has been working on a truss-structured, fabric-covered turbine blade that can be shipped in containers and assembled economically onsite even as the blades get bigger. The company's three-dimensional tower has struts that lock together and are, therefore, able to bear heavy burdens with limited material and support. The GE tower uses 20–30 percent less steel than older towers, and its broad base needs less support. GE houses advanced power electronics and battery storage inside the tower's base to protect it from weather and vandalism. Concrete can be substituted for steel in a project if the project is located near a concrete source, thus lowering costs even more.

Another possibility is to improve the management of the power generated from variable sources like wind. Better control can be achieved by using sensors with the turbine's computer systems. Remote operators can wirelessly manage variables like erratic wind and grid changes that automated systems are unable to control. Full application of remote operated automated wind can cut the cost of integrating it into the grid by as much as 30 percent if better ways are found to assimilate and use weather data and improve turbine performance at low-wind speeds.

A growing scarcity of land with high potential for wind is forcing developers to take more expensive offshore wind installations seriously. The offshore movement began in Europe, where the number of locations with good wind speeds and turbines close to transmission lines was nearly exhausted. Throughout Europe, in countries like France, Germany, the UK, and Denmark, where renewable energy remained a priority, there were targets to boost offshore development. Despite higher initial and operating costs, offshore wind farms may make economic sense because offshore wind tends to be stronger and steadier than it is onshore. The economic viability of offshore wind, though, still has to be proven. The cost gap relative to onshore wind is substantial. It is not certain that offshore wind will ever achieve grid parity. The turbines have to be larger and stronger, and the transmission and interconnection are more complicated.

Rather than offshore, another way to find stronger and steadier is to place the wind turbines on taller towers. A taller tower can be built at little extra cost yet can substantially reduce costs. Alternatively, a high-altitude airborne platform, like a kite or another device, can be used. If under autonomous control, the wind pulls the kite and changes its angle so the energy obtained is steady and produced at a low cost.

Energy Storage

For solar and wind to make further improvements in their ability to supply electrical energy, storage must improve. Batteries must be lighter and store more energy for a given weight or volume. Many new storage technologies are commercially available, in development, or being researched to accomplish this purpose. The promise they hold is both in electrical generation and for transportation. Because multiple potential pathways to improvements exist and because the pathways cut across many disciplines, it is challenging to identify which technologies have the most promise.

Lead-acid batteries have been manufactured on a mass scale for the purpose of transportation for more than a century. Outside of lead acid, the main battery types of interest are lithium-ion and nickel-based aqueous. Because they are durable and lightweight and offer highly specific energy and relatively fast charge and discharge times, lithium-ion batteries are commonly used in consumer electronics. Tesla uses these batteries. The main nickel-based aqueous alternatives to the lithium ion battery are nickel-cadmium and nickel-metal hydride. Nickel-cadmium batteries are limited by the cost and toxicity of cadmium. The European Union has banned them. Nickel-metal hydride batteries, on the other hand, have found a home in some hybrid electric vehicles; however, because of lower energy density compared to lithium-ion batteries, they are not as likely to be deployed.

In grid applications, lead-acid batteries found in conventional vehicles could serve as uninterruptible power supplies in substations. Sodium-beta and liquid electrolyte flow batteries are alternatives to the lead-acid battery. Sodium-beta batteries include sodium-sulfur units first developed in the 1960s and commercially available in Japan. On the other hand, sodium-nickel-chloride batteries are in the early stages of development. If they move in the direction of a stacked planar cell design, sodium-beta batteries can cut cell costs in half. This departure from prior designs has the ability to increase both specific energy and power.

In flow batteries, a liquid electrolyte drifts through a chemical cell to produce electricity, and the chemical components are separated in a liquid state or conductor. Vanadium flow batteries use vanadium ions in the different oxidation states of the battery. Vanadium electrolytes do not disappear or lose capacity after many cycles, resulting in capacity that remains constant even after 25 years of operation, but they do not have the efficiency of lithium-ion batteries. Although vanadium is abundant, it is expensive to obtain.

Zinc-bromide, another flow battery that has gained attention, is still is in the demonstration stage. Aquion Energy has developed a technology that uses water as the main electrolyte along with sodium and magnesium oxide. The combination of cheap input materials and high efficiency makes this option attractive.

Game-changing battery companies like Graphene Energy exist. They are involved in next-generation nano-tech-based ultra-capacitors for energy storage. Ultra-capacitors can store and deliver energy in short time, making them suitable for high-power density applications. Graphene's technology relies on a material structure of bonded carbon atoms that are densely packed in a honeycomb crystal lattice. When of high quality, this material weighs little, is strong, light, and almost transparent, and is an excellent heat and electricity conductor. It is extremely flexible. It can be applied in regenerative braking systems in electric and hybrid vehicles as well as in the balancing of the energy power grid and solar and wind storage.

Although solid and flow batteries rely on a chemical reaction for storage, older technologies do not. Flywheel technologies use kinetic energy for storage. As the flywheel spins, it converts kinetic to electrical energy. Another older type of storage is pumped hydro. It stores water pumped from a lower to a higher reservoir. During times of peak energy demand, the water is released. Thirty-eight pumped hydro facilities already exist across the United States.

Biofuels

First-generation biofuels that use corn, sugarcane, and soy to make ethanol and biodiesel have fallen out of favor because of controversy about food versus fuel and the question of whether biofuels provide net environmental improvement. In any case, it has been estimated that if the entire U.S. corn crop is converted to energy production, it can provide just 12 percent of the gasoline the United States needs. There is not enough good arable land to grow corn for fuel transportation.

Second-generation biofuels consist of prairie and switch grass, wood, and animal waste. This material has to be dried and fermented. More than 70 percent of these substances is made up of lignum. It has to be removed and starch and sugar extracted from it. For it to be processed for fuel, it must be transported long distances. Because these materials for making fuel are so dispersed, economies of scale are hard to achieve.

The company Kior, which went bankrupt, offers an example of how hard it is to create biofuels from second-generation material. Kior used wood chips delivered by dump trucks to make fuel. The wood chips were conditioned and prepared for a conversion process and then fed into a device where they interacted with a proprietary catalyst system, similar to the fluid catalytic cracking used in petroleum refining. The byproducts of the process were oil, light water, gases, and coke gas, which were sent to a separator that removed the catalyst and recycled it.

Kior touted the process as mimicking the natural cycle of making petroleum, which takes millions of years. The fuel that was made, however, had to be upgraded and refined before it could be fed into trucks and delivered to refineries to be used as an additive to conventional gasoline. The process by which this additive was made was complex and expensive and unable to consistently compete with the price of conventional petroleum. Only at high gasoline prices was Kior competitive. After a long and hard struggle to become a viable business, Kior ultimately failed.

Other start-up companies that tried to make bioproducts in various ways have not fared much better:

- Amyris created and used synthetic biological processes to design microbes, mainly yeast. It used the yeast to convert plant-sourced sugars into renewable hydrocarbons that had many uses, from cosmetics and personal care products to additives, lubricants, flavors, and fragrances, specialty chemicals jet fuels, diesel, and other transportation fuels. Amyris went through an initial public offering in January 2011. Its stock peaked at about $35 a share, but by January 2012 its share price had plunged to less than $5 a share.

- Gevo also went public in 2011. It had acquired a 22-million-gallon-per-year ethanol production facility in Luverne, Minnesota. Gevo intended to retrofit this facility to produce isobutanol, a chemical with broad applications as a replacement for petroleum-based raw materials. Isobutanol could be integrated and added to existing refining processes without modification. Gevo cleared isobutanol with the U.S. EPA for use as a fuel additive in gasoline. Nonetheless, like Amyris, Gevo's stock quickly plunged after the company went public. Within two years, the stock price had declined about 70 percent. The company temporarily halted production in 2012 after contamination issues, and it only resumed output on a small scale. In 2014 Gevo revealed that its working capital was not adequate to meet its cash requirements.

- Mascoma's bioprocessing technology made ethanol out of hardwood pulp with proprietary yeasts that did away with the need for expensive enzymes. Hardwood pulp had the major advantage of being cheap and abundant. Mascoma demonstrated its conversion process at a facility in Rome, New York. However, its plan to expand production to 20 million gallons per year in Michigan was put on hold when its major financial backer and the facility's main owner, Valero Corporation, refused to provide its part of the needed funding. Citing unfavorable market conditions, Mascoma withdrew its attempt to go public in 2013.

- Coskata made cellulosic ethanol from agricultural and municipal wastes in a Pennsylvania plant using proprietary microorganisms in a licensed fermentation process that it made available for sale to other biofuel producers. This company also canceled its plan to go public in 2013 due to unfavorable market conditions.

With so much failure among second-generation biofuel companies, who would take the next step and make investments in third-generation biofuel companies that, for example, relied on processes for making petroleum from algae?

Conclusion

Abundant energy resources are needed to sustain global economic growth and development. This chapter has shown that they can come from two major sources: fossil fuels, which are finite, and the efficient use of theoretically infinite renewables. The latter have many advantages over the former, including less contribution to climate change, less pollution, and less dependence on unstable regions of the globe.

The fossil fuels upon which the world increasingly relies are hard to access. Unconventional oil from fracking, tar sands, and deep-water recovery are expensive, environmentally questionable, and potentially unsafe. Cleaner energy alternatives have progressed, but not as fast as they are needed. Many serious obstacles still stand in the way of their widespread adoption. Fully commercializing these technologies remains a stubborn challenge. The best outcome for the world would be technological advances in both fossil fuel technologies and renewables, but whether these advances will take place is still highly uncertain.

This chapter concludes the assessment of societal challenges and their relation to technology. Part IV, "Coping with Technological Disruptions," consists of a series of paired case studies that relate to the way specific companies have coped with technological disruptions.

Endnotes

1. International Energy Agency, *Statistics.* http://www.iea.org/statistics/.

2. Stephen Lacey, "Renewables Continue to Outpace Conservative Global Projections," *Greentech Media.* July 1, 2013. http://www.greentechmedia.com/articles/read/Renewables-Continue-to-Outpace-Conservative-Global-Projections.

3. Giles Parkinson, "UBS Lays Out 'Dream Solar Scenario: 50% of Global Generation by 2015," *Clean Technica.* June 15, 2015. http://cleantechnica.com/2015/06/15/ubs-lays-out-dream-solar-scenario-50-of-global-generation-by-2050/.

4. Dennis Coyne, "Peak Oil Barrel." *Peak Oil Barrel.* June 25, 2014. http://peakoilbarrel.com/oil-field-models-decline-rates-convolution/; also see "Oilfield Decline Rates," *The View from the Mountain,* n.d. https://grandemotte.wordpress.com/oil-and-gas-5-production-decline-rates/.

5. "Shale of the Century," *The Economist*. June 2, 2012. http://www.economist.com/node/21556242.

6. See, for example, the summary "EPA's Study of Hydraulic Fracturing for Oil and Gas and Its Potential Impact on Drinking Water," *United States Environmental Protection Agency*. June 5, 2015. http://www2.epa.gov/hfstudy.

7. Benjamin Leeney, "OPEC Monthly Report Shows Likely Continuation of Low Oil Prices," *WBP Online*. Dec. 10, 2014. http://wbponline.com/articles/view/39978/opec-monthly-report-shows-likely-continuation-of-low-oil-prices.

8. Greenpeace Canada, "Tar Sands," *Greenpeace*, n.d. http://www.greenpeace.org/canada/en/campaigns/energy/tarsands/.

9. International Energy Agency, *Statistics*.

10. Ibid.

11. Ibid.

12. Alfred Marcus, *Innovations in Sustainability: Fuel and Food*. Cambridge, UK: Cambridge University Press, 2015.

13. Sophie Vorrath, "Blue Crude: Audi Pilot Produces Diesel Fuel from CO2 and Water, *Renew Economy*. April 29, 2015. http://reneweconomy.com.au/2015/blue-crude-audi-pilot-produces-diesel-fuel-from-co2-and-water-66638.

14. U.S. Department of Energy, *Annual Energy Outlook 2013 with Projections*, Washington: USA, 2013. http://www.eia.gov/forecasts/aeo/pdf/0383(2013).pdf.

15. The remaining sections in the chapter rely on material contained in Marcus, *Innovations in Sustainability: Fuel and Food*.

PART IV

COPING WITH TECHNOLOGICAL DISRUPTIONS

9

Missing the Boat on Mobile Technology: Intel and AMD

I n 2014, Intel enjoyed the world's largest market share in all segments of the global microprocessor market—servers, laptops, and desktops.[1] It controlled close to 98 percent of the server market, more than 90 percent of the laptop market, and over 80 percent of the desktop market. In the desktop market, where AMD, its rival, was most competitive, Intel's gross margins were over 60 percent, whereas AMD had gross margins of 30 percent. Since 1976, Intel and AMD had cross-licensing agreements, which stipulated that the two companies could use each other's patents. For years the two companies had been battling it out for dominance in the microprocessor market. (See the section at the end of this chapter, "Glossary of Computer Terminology.") In the mid-2000s, AMD achieved a technical lead in server technology. In 2003, it was the first to produce a 32-64-bit processor, and in its history it had other firsts, including at one time producing the top GHz clock speed and the earliest dual core central processing unit (CPU). Indeed, in 2006, AMD's gross margins actually exceeded those of Intel, but Intel fought back with its own 64-bit design and advances in manufacturing, whereas AMD chose to divest its manufacturing unit.

While the two companies battled for leadership in the server, laptop, and desktop segments, both missed the mobile revolution that took place largely without them and both suffered as a result. Intel and AMD needed a plan for the future. From where would their future revenue and profits come? To what extent should they continue to compete for the same customers, each gaining at the other's expense? To what extent would they be able carve out separate niches in different markets?

The Mobile Revolution

Intel and AMD did not anticipate and were not prepared for the mobile revolution. Because of the ascendance of smartphones and tablets over PCs, Apple, and not Intel or Microsoft, became the world's leading computer company (see Exhibit 9.1). Apple's iOS software, released in 2007, along with Google's Android, which was launched in 2008, became the most-used software in tablets and phones. Apple was in command of more than 40 percent of the U.S. smartphone and tablet device markets, and Android had about 50 percent, but whereas iOS is exclusive to Apple, Android can be found in devices produced by a variety of companies, the most prominent being Samsung.

Intel made several false starts to enter the smartphone and tablet markets, but it was largely shut out. Taiwan Semiconductor and Samsung made most of the devices, including many of Apple's, using ARM architecture. The British company ARM Holdings developed this architecture based on a reduced instruction set computing (RISC) design that depends on far fewer transistors than the complex processors Intel and AMD have created for servers, PCs, and laptops. ARM develops this architecture, but it does not manufacture products. In 2015, its architecture supported more than 95 percent of the smartphones and tablets used in the United States. Its simple design kept energy usage to a minimum, whereas Intel's comparable architecture was complex because of its need to be compatible with the company's servers and desktop CPUs. Relying on Windows Phone software and Microsoft's Surface tablet in the United States and relying on devices from companies such as ASUS, Lenovo, and Motorola in the developing world, the products Intel marketed to mobile markets were not profitable. Intel sold them at a loss so that it could gain a foothold.

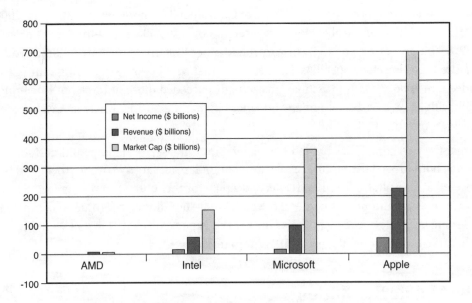

Exhibit 9.1 Income, Revenue, and Market Cap in the Computer Industry, 3rd Quarter 2015

Compared to mobile markets, the server, laptop, and desktop markets responsible for most of Intel's and AMD's revenue were in decline. In addition, Intel was vertically integrated and had high fixed costs because it both designed and manufactured its products. To support its world-leading microprocessor fabrication facilities, it had to spend a high proportion of revenue (about 20 percent) on research and development (R&D), and it had to sell products at high margins and volumes.

Because the products that Intel could offer for mobile markets had low margins, the company had been reluctant to sell them. ARM, Apple, Google, and, beginning in 2009, AMD, when it divested its microprocessor fabrication facilities, had different structures than Intel. None of these companies were manufacturers; they just designed products. They had contractual relations with other firms to make the products they sold.

As suppliers of CPUs for laptops, PCs, and servers, how could Intel and AMD survive in a mobile world, where the business model was so different from the one to which they were accustomed? AMD was in particularly bad shape and barely profitable. Intel had taken away almost every advantage AMD had once had in microprocessors for PCs, servers, and laptops. AMD had negative revenue growth (see Exhibit 9.2) and a net annual loss of more than $0.5 billion in the second quarter of 2015 (see Exhibit 9.3). In that quarter, Intel had no revenue growth.

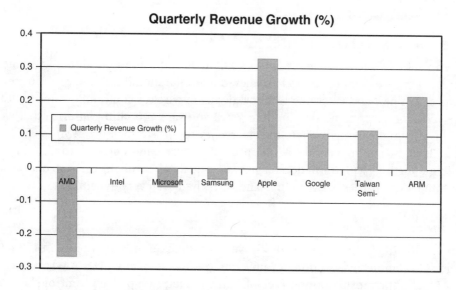

Exhibit 9.2 Revenue Growth in the Computer Industry, 3rd Quarter 2015

Exhibit 9.3 Computer Company Finances, 3rd Quarter 2015

	AMD	Intel	Microsoft	Samsung	Apple	Google	Taiwan Semi	ARM
Net Income ($ billions)	−0.563	11.77	12.19	4.52	50.74	14.39	9.70	0.47
Gross Margin (%)	0.33	0.64	0.65	0.39	0.40	0.62	0.50	0.95
Operating Margin (%)	−0.01	0.28	0.30	0.13	0.30	0.26	0.39	0.42
Quarterly Revenue Growth (%)	−0.26	0.00	−0.05	−0.03	0.33	0.11	0.12	0.22
Revenue ($ billions)	5.14	55.89	93.58	47.12	224.34	69.61	27.31	1.36
Market Cap ($ billions)	2.02	151.71	364.58	167.62	704.40	430.31	113.26	21.85
Employees	9,700	106,700	118,000	480,000	92,600	57,148	43,591	3,524

The Battles Between Intel and AMD

When Paul Otellini took over as Intel's CEO in 2005, he announced that he wanted to increase the pace of innovation.[2] He believed that Intel should play a key role in creating half a dozen new and emerging technologies from wireless communications to health-care. The company could develop integrated software and chip platforms that would be of use from the living room to the emergency room. Hector Ruiz, AMD's CEO from 2002–2008, was unimpressed. He quipped, "People are smart enough to pick quality.... Calling something a platform doesn't guarantee quality."[3] Evolving through many stages, the competitive battles between Intel and AMD had been very dynamic.[4]

Memory

Facing what Intel's first CEO Andy Grove refers to as an inflection point in 1985, Intel decided to completely abandon dynamic random access memory (DRAM) production.[5] DRAMs are the most common type of semiconductor chip. They control short-term computer operations, such as software applications used, the number of applications open at the same time, and the speed at which a computer processes an application.

DRAMs had been Intel's main source of profits and revenues, but Japanese manufacturers, such as NEC, Mitsubishi, Fujitsu, Hitachi, and Oki, had captured 80 percent of the world market, and firms from Korea, like Samsung and Hyundai, were not far behind. Intel's executives reasoned that U.S. companies could not compete with large, vertically integrated Japanese and Korean firms that were the beneficiaries of substantial government assistance. Grove, in his book *Only the Paranoid Survive,* wrote that getting through this inflection involved considerable "confusion, uncertainty, and disorder, both on a personal level...and on a strategic level..."[6]

Microprocessors

Gordon Moore founded Intel in 1968 along with Robert Noyce, who was a co-discoverer of the integrated circuit. In 1972, Moore made the famous prediction that became known as "Moore's Law" on the doubling of microprocessor speed every 18 months Microprocessors are complex electronic circuits with transistors that allow simple instructions from hard disks, floppy disks, CD-ROMs, remote Internet servers, plug-in cartridges, and other storage devices to be carried out on a PC. In 1981, IBM selected Intel's microprocessor for its PCs. The one caveat IBM made was that Intel could not be the sole supplier. Intel had to license its design to other chipmakers. The first companies to receive a license from Intel were National Semiconductor, Zilog, NEC, Fujitsu, and AMD. Because they could not compete with Intel, all of them ended up dropping out of the business except AMD.

In 1993, Intel introduced the first Pentium processor. The initial launch was shaky because of a flaw in this processor. Over many calculations, the microprocessor made simple mistakes. Intel recalled all affected systems and fixed the problem, and the reissued Pentium became the processor of choice for most users. The Pentium's success enabled Intel to establish the strong brand identity of "Intel Inside" as a symbol of quality.

The Sub-Zero Segment

Jerry Sanders, AMD's charismatic founder and first CEO, came out of the same company that bred many of Intel's leaders: Fairchild Industries. From 1987–1995, while Intel grew more than eight times, from $1.9 billion in revenues to $16.2 billion in revenues, AMD's sales more than doubled, from $1 billion to $2.5 billion. Sanders sued Intel for monopolistic practices in 1987. In the 1995 arbitration that ended the suit, Intel agreed not to take away AMD's license to make microprocessors so long as AMD did not make microprocessors that plugged into Intel's motherboard and worked with Intel's chipsets. This outcome meant that AMD had to have partners to help develop its own motherboard and chipset. Because AMD, unlike Intel, had to rely on partners, Sanders referred to the company as a "virtual gorilla," whereas Intel was the real gorilla.[7]

By partnering with Via Technologies, AMD succeeded in creating a Pentium clone. It sold at a much lower price than the Pentium. Grove, Intel CEO's at the time, called the less than $1,000 computer made possible by this microprocessor the "sub-zero segment."

He saw it as a real threat to Intel. Therefore, Intel introduced a budget processor of its own in 1998, which it called the Celeron. By 1998, it had a full-fledged segmentation strategy: the Xeon for the high-end server/workstation market, the Pentium for the market's middle, and the Celeron for the low end of the market. Prior to the burst of the dot-com bubble in 2000, Intel flourished like few other companies (see Exhibit 9.4), as it rapidly grew its revenue, margins, and operating income every year.

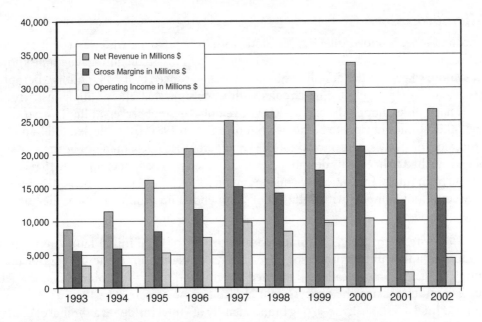

Exhibit 9.4 Intel's 1993–2002 Performance

Speed and Continued Price Wars

Having failed to dislodge Intel from the market's low end, AMD took aim at the high end. It achieved a speed of one GHz in its microprocessor in year 2000, shortly before Intel. For the first time in 19 years, a company other than Intel had the world's fastest processor. However, after the year 2000, the business landscape for Intel and AMD changed. Speed was no longer the key factor in a consumer's choice of a microprocessor. The speed of most microprocessors exceeded the typical consumer's needs. The strategy of producing ever-more-powerful processors no longer made sense. With the exception of very high-end servers, most consumers could make do with slower and less costly computers.

AMD's response to this situation was to try to increase its market share by lowering prices by as much as 50 percent. Intel responded by discounting its products by 40 to 85 percent and, to ensure that PC makers remained loyal, by granting advertising subsidies, volume discounts, and exclusive deals to them. Intel also managed to take the performance, not just the price lead, away from AMD.

Branching Out

The changing business landscape led Intel to decide that it had to branch out into other areas. It could not rely just on microprocessors to sustain it. With its core business not as strong as it once was, the company had to find new business opportunities. Craig Barrett, who became CEO in 1997, launched a strategy of moving Intel beyond PCs and servers and into such markets as communications, information appliances, and Internet services.[8] The company invested more than $10 billion in these efforts. However, by 2001 it was apparent that these investments had yielded little in return (see Exhibit 9.5). They erased more than $4 billion in profits from Intel's bottom line in 2001. Without them, Intel would have been a much more profitable company.

Exhibit 9.5   Intel's Business Units' Performance 1999–2001

(millions $)	1999	2000	2001
Architecture (microprocessors)			
Revenues	25,459	27,301	21,446
Operating profit	11,131	12,511	6,252
Communications			
Revenues	2,380	3,483	2,580
Operating profit	437	319	−735
Wireless			
Revenues	1,264	2,669	2,232
Operating profit	−96	608	−256
Other			
Revenues	286	273	281
Operating loss	−1,705	−3,043	−3,005
Totals			
Revenues	29,389	33,726	26,539
Operating profit	9,767	10,395	2,256

Intel, therefore, was under great pressure to cut the investments back. When the tech economy was booming, it made sense for Intel to "throw spaghetti against the wall to see what stuck," but with dot-com bust in effect, this strategy no longer made sense. Analysts criticized the company for moving into too many new markets too quickly and losing focus. Its 2001 drop in performance forced the company to cut 5,000 jobs.

Nonetheless, Intel continued to spend heavily on R&D. Its corporate venture capital invested in what it believed to be leading-edge small companies. Intel did not stop spending on improving its microprocessor production facilities, introducing the latest technologies and pushing the limits of state-of-the-art manufacturing. Although not profitable, the wireless division helped to develop a chip for laptop computers called the Centrino, which allowed laptops to receive wireless signals, and Intel worked on new 64-bit microprocessors for servers. It had started development of a new server chip in 1994 to compete with Sun's 64-bit chip. However, development costs turned out to be much higher than expected. When launched two years late, in 2001, Intel's new 64-bit processor had to run on software written for 32-bit processors at speeds slower than the new processor's capacity.

The Hammer

This failure provided AMD with the opening that it needed. AMD bet its future on Hammer technology, the only technology able to flawlessly run 32-bit as well as 64-bit software.[9] In 2003, to obtain the cash AMD needed to challenge Intel, it spun off its large and successful flash memory business in a joint venture with Fujitsu. It divested entirely from the flash memory business two years later. The company focused exclusively on microprocessors, augmenting its capabilities with a purchase from National Semiconductor of embedded-processor products used in systems like casino slot machines and customer kiosks. The plan of AMD's CEO and former Motorola executive Ruiz was to flawlessly introduce the Hammer (commercially called the Opteron) to boost AMD's share of the microprocessor business, especially in the lucrative server segment to as much as 30 percent. With a market share of 30 percent, AMD would finally become Intel's formidable foe.

Intel, meanwhile, was not standing still. It benefitted somewhat when Apple CEO Steve Jobs announced in 2005 that Apple would transition from its PowerPC architecture to Intel's architecture for its PCs and servers.

AMD, however, kept advancing. Its performance lead over Intel in the 32-to-64-bit server market lasted for nearly two years. In that time, AMD signed up major customers like IBM, HP, Dell, and Sun, and its server market share grew from nearly 0 to about 22 percent at the end of 2006. As a result of the inroads AMD made, Intel's revenues fell from $38.8 billion in 2005 to $35.4 billion in 2006, and it had to lay off workers again, this time a tenth of its workforce of 100,000.

Intel did not have a product for the 32-to-64-bit server market that directly competed with the Hammer until the end of 2006, but at the start of 2007, with this product in hand, it started to recapture microprocessor business it had lost to AMD. It exploited its manufacturing lead over AMD by bringing down chip sizes before AMD did, and making a smaller chip allowed it to match AMD's multiple core technology and apply it to high-end applications like digital media creation and gaming.

Global Antitrust

AMD did not like the aggressive way in which Intel went about recapturing its market share. Already in 2004, it launched antitrust litigation against Intel in many countries.[10] The findings arrived at by at least six government bodies in 30 nations was that from 2001–2007, Intel had paid computer makers, including Dell, HP, Lenovo, and Acer, to not use or to limit their use of AMD products, even when some of these products, including AMD's Opteron server system, were superior to Intel's comparable offerings. None of the companies involved in the suits, including Intel, admitted to any wrongdoing, but they did sign consent decrees and made payments to AMD that helped to compensate AMD for some of the losses it alleged it had experienced.

Graphics and Other Products

AMD's response to the situation it then faced was to acquire the Canadian graphics processor company ATI Technologies.[11] This acquisition was big for AMD; the company paid $4.3 billion in cash and 58 million shares of its stock to buy ATI Technologies. AMD immediately retired the ATI brand name and started an initiative called Fusion. Its purpose was to merge CPU and graphics capabilities in one chip. In 2007, the company released an integrated graphics chipset for applications requiring high-performance 3D and video.

AMD also released dual-core, triple-core, and quad-core processors for desktops and nine quad-core processors for servers. Although these processors cost less than Intel's comparable offerings, they were not competitive in performance with Intel's high-end processors.

To differentiate itself from Intel, AMD put its focus on platform specialization. It refreshed its products every year with new processors, chipsets, and graphics. As a virtual and not vertical gorilla, it opened itself up to the components that other vendors made. Despite these moves, the company lost market share to Intel. By 2007, it had just 13.4 percent of the microprocessor market for PCs and corporate servers, a far cry from Ruiz's goal of 30 percent. In contrast, Intel accounted for 86.6 percent of the market—clearly ahead again. AMD also was in a dreadful financial situation.

Divesting Manufacturing

To compete with Intel, AMD had added to its manufacturing capacity between 2003 and 2005. In a reversal of strategy, AMD, because of its poor financial performance, had to divest all its manufacturing operations in 2008.[12] The company needed an infusion of cash, and it divested its manufacturing in the form of a multibillion-dollar joint venture with the Advanced Technology Investment Company, which was run by the government of Abu Dhabi. This joint venture was called GlobalFoundries, and it became a competitor of Taiwan Semiconductor. Its main manufacturing facilities were located in Dresden, Germany, and it licensed third-party manufacturers to make integrated microprocessors in Taiwan.

The deal with Advanced Technology Investment Company gave AMD the money it needed to survive. It also allowed the company to focus exclusively on what it considered that it did best: chip design. Nonetheless, this move did not yield a turnaround. In 2008, AMD announced its seventh consecutive quarterly loss. CEO Ruiz had to step down, and his replacement, Dirk Meyer, cut 1,100 jobs the following year because of the company's ongoing financial crisis.

Searching for New Markets

With PC sales flat and weak growth in the server market, Intel and AMD were searching for new markets. Intel made the biggest acquisition in its history to that point in 2010. It purchased the computer security company McAfee for $7.68 billion.

In 2013, Intel CEO Otellini claimed that the company's revenue and earnings growth were poised to double.[13] He saw Intel doing well in notebooks and smartphones as well as in wearables, cars, and any device in which microprocessors were needed and security was required. He admitted to the prolonged weaknesses that existed in the desktop market. He projected high annual growth rates in notebooks and laptops, yet he referred to these markets as a small niche. He held that the company's real opportunity lay in putting its chips and related software into an assortment of devices, in which computing typically had not been found before, such as televisions, power-meters, and washing machines, and to make them into "smart devices." As Intel's growth rates remained low, Otellini declared that Intel should move into software and services. He proclaimed that it had to grow more in emerging markets like China, India, and Brazil.

Although engaged in the search for new markets, Intel did not neglect its manufacturing capabilities. In 2011, it announced plans to build a new microprocessor manufacturing facility in Chandler, Arizona, at a cost of $5 billion. The company reaffirmed its commitment to manufacturing in the United States. It made three-quarters of its products in the U.S., although three-quarters of its revenue came from abroad. The new facility in Arizona was a large one and would accommodate up to 4,000 employees.

ARM Architecture

In 2011, former Lenovo executive Rory Read replaced Dirk Meyer as AMD's CEO. To reduce costs in the face of declining sales, he engaged in a series of successive layoffs. Read first let go of more than 10 percent of AMD's employees and then let go of an additional 15 percent. On many benchmarks, AMD's server and desktop processors were no longer competitive with Intel's. In some instances, they were even slower than the older AMD models they were supposed to replace.

AMD then came up with the idea that it should introduce the simpler ARM architecture server chip. To do so, it acquired the low-power server manufacturer SeaMicro in 2012, but it was slow in following up on this initiative. In 2012, the company had a rough year; revenues dropped 17 percent, and AMD experienced a net loss of nearly $1.2 billion.

The decline in earnings was largely due to Intel's having a lock on the waning PC microprocessor market. In the first quarter of 2013, worldwide shipments of PCs fell by 14 percent, the fourth consecutive quarter of decline and the worst PC sales drop in history.

Mobile

In 2011, Intel reorganized its business units to form a new mobile and communications group. It partnered with Google to place its Atom microprocessors in Android phones and began a pilot project to produce smartphones with the Atom microprocessors for the Chinese market. Intel recognized that the simultaneous advent of mobile computing and the decline of the PC were serious problems with which it had to contend. The company considered them to be the main reasons for its decline in net income of 25 percent the first quarter of 2013.

Intel had to confront ARM, whose processors powered more than 95 percent of the world's smartphones, as ARM announced that it had plans to make inroads into Intel's PC and server markets. Intel struck back with its own plans to introduce competitive energy-efficient processors for smartphones and tablets, but it was not at all clear whether Intel could successfully compete with ARM. ARM had been powering portable devices for decades, whereas Intel was a relative newcomer. ARM was dominant on the iPad, iPhone, and Samsung platforms. Its architecture was designed to be simple and to keep energy wastage to a minimum, whereas Intel's chips had a complex design meant to make them compatible with Intel's PC and server microprocessors.

Gaming

Intel's overwhelming domination of the microprocessor market had but one important exception. AMD's chips were in all three of the major next-generation game consoles. Both the Sony PlayStation 4 and Microsoft Xbox console had eight-core AMD processors that combined the CPU with graphics capabilities. Nintendo used AMD's graphics chipset, but not its CPU, which it obtained from IBM.

AMD's dominance of the gaming market was a boon for developers, who were able to work on products for multiple consoles. The company's turnaround depended on the $67 billion global video game market thriving. However, the proliferation of mobile smartphones and tablets had changed consumers' gaming habits, and console sales were not projected to be as strong as they had once been.

Mounting Mobile Losses

Intel's move into mobile devices did not succeed.[14] The mobile division lost $4.2 billion dollars in 2014. The company sold 46 million mobile processing units that year, exceeding its goal of selling 40 million. However, even then, its share in a market in which 229 million units were sold that year was low in comparison to other companies, such as, for example, Apple's 63 million units. Apple, moreover, used ARM architecture, and Intel was at cost disadvantage relative to ARM.

There was a major difference in the way the two architectures handled the numeric code instructions that told processors what to do. Intel architecture employed a second layer of instructions called a microcode, which took up more space on chips and contributed to their cost. ARM architecture did not have the second layer, and it did not require the extra space for decoding. The ARM architecture, therefore, was less power hungry and more efficient than the Intel architecture.

Intel mitigated the power disadvantage of its architecture by means of power-saving techniques that it introduced. However, these power-saving techniques brought with them greater complexity. The price Intel paid to achieve power performance parity with ARM exceeded what the mobile device market was willing to pay Intel for its products. To penetrate this market, Intel subsidized its customers; hence, it experienced losses on sales despite the fact that its sales were growing.

Paul Otellini stepped down as CEO of Intel in 2012 at the age of 62, three years before his mandatory retirement, replaced by Executive Vice President and Chief Operating Officer Brian Krzanich. The company again had to lay off thousands of employees in response to weak market trends. The mobile unit kept racking up losses, and Krzanich chose to do away with it.

New Leadership at AMD

In 2015, Rory Read stepped down as AMD's CEO after another 7 percent of AMD's workforce was laid off and was succeeded by Lisa Su, who had been his chief operating officer. Su, the first female CEO at a company like AMD, reorganized the company groups into: (i) Computing and Graphics, which included desktop and notebook processors and chipsets; and (ii) Professional Graphics and Enterprise, which included server and embedded processors, engineering services, and royalties. Su's aim was for AMD to do fewer things better.[15] Her hope was for the company to achieve greater market share in a few select leading-edge technologies involving devices where both computing and visualization were essential.

Su admitted that it would take time before the company could return to profitability. PCs were its largest business, and its revenue had suffered because of weak growth and because Intel had taken market share from it. With AMD's market share in servers falling to less than 3 percent, AMD had to find new markets in which buyers were willing to spend more for advanced technology, such as virtual reality, where AMD was ahead of Intel. At the same time, AMD had to de-emphasize products for consumer markets like PCs and laptops, where prices were low and graphics not that important.

A reason that AMD's business had slowed was that customers had no incentive to purchase the latest graphics cards to play new video games. With the launch of PC virtual reality headsets, Su was convinced that this situation would change. However, NVidia would continue to be a major competitor in this market. AMD's history in this market, like in PCs, was that it was a customer's second option.

The company planned to release a 64-bit ARM chip in 2015 that could be used in servers. It would be a low-power alternative to current Intel microprocessors. AMD anticipated increased spending by data center operators because its chips could perform power-hungry tasks there, like analyzing big data with Hadoop's distributed file system and using high-end graphics without sacrificing speed. Although small, AMD's data center business offered promise. The chip also had graphics capabilities that were found only in gaming consoles.

AMD continued to have a portfolio of dedicated graphics processors, including the Radeon for consumers, the FirePro brand for professionals, the Eyefinity for multimonitor applications, TrueAudio for audio applications, and Unified Video Decoder and Video Coding Engine for video applications. The company had a partnership with Samsung for a new line of all-in-one cloud monitors featuring integrated thin client technology that coupled high-performance computer and graphics in an integrated, low-power design. It also had partnerships with many other companies, such as Sun (owned by Oracle), HP, Compaq, ASUS, Acer, and Dell. Su was certain it would make a comeback. A problem, to which she admitted, however, was that Intel was ultimately able to able to copy most of what it did.

The issue for AMD was whether it would be able to survive before it returned to profitability. AMD denied the rumor that it was considering spinning off part of the company or breaking it up into separate graphics and server businesses. Su stood by the strategy of combining high-quality graphics with microprocessors for servers and other applications.

Field Programmable Gate Array (FPGA)

With PC sales declining and its failure in mobile, Intel had excess capacity in its manufacturing plants. It therefore reached agreement to produce chips for Altera and four other companies: Achronix, Tabula, Netronome, and Microsemi, which made field-programmable gate array (FPGA) chips. Intel made general-purpose microprocessor chips programmed for many computing tasks. However, some functions are better carried out using custom-tailored chips specific to a single task. The problem is that the cost of making these chips is high. Along with other companies, Altera, therefore, pioneered a middle course with FPGAs. FPGAs were sold ready for users to configure to handle specific tasks.

In 2015, Intel acquired Altera for $16.7 billion, in its largest acquisition ever.[16] It was 56 percent more than the price at which Altera traded prior to the acquisition. Because of the premium that Intel paid, on the day the deal was announced, Intel's shares declined 1.6 percent, whereas Altera's rose 6 percent. This transaction was meant to bolster Intel's position in corporate data centers' server markets. Altera's programmable chip technology offered a way for Intel to protect its position in selling chips for servers, a market that generated a high percentage of the company's revenues and operating profits. Companies were already using FPGAs alongside Intel's chips to help speed up their servers. Intel needed access to this technology to avoid falling behind in the server market.

Altera was set to become an operating division of Intel, with cost savings expected as duplicate general and administrative functions were eliminated and headcount reductions took place. The two companies knew each other well because Altera's headquarters were located just a few miles away from Intel's in Silicon Valley. Altera chips were sold widely in networking and wireless applications, which were good markets for Intel.

Some analysts, however, questioned whether Intel really could rely on Altera to bolster its revenue growth in the midst of the slowdown in demand for PCs.[17] The upside potential for Altera's programmable chips was not that large. The company was quite profitable. Its gross margin, at 64 percent of sales in the first quarter of 2015, was higher than Intel's at 60.5 percent in this period. However, growth in Altera's revenues was a question. Its sales declined 6 percent in the first quarter of 2014, and its total 2014 revenues were just $1.9 billion. Intel had to find a more sizeable boost in revenues than it could obtain from Altera.

The Internet of Things (IOT)

Intel was pinning its hopes on the Internet of Things (IOT).[18] Its claim was that the acquisition of Altera could help jump-start this market. IOT promises to place processors in everyday items from refrigerators to luggage to clothing. Intel's idea was to combine its low-end Atom chips with Altera circuitry for a host of new applications.

Projections for the growth of the IOT market were even greater than those for growth of mobile. Intel chips could be combined with specialized instructions programmed into Altera's circuitry so that the chips could improve automotive driver-assistance systems or provide vision capabilities for robots and drones to move around their environment by way of specialized vision algorithms incorporated into FPGA. The robots could carry out new functions. The drones could fly autonomously for purposes such as delivering packages. The devices could double their speeds and operate at lower costs.

Intel had already initiated a number of projects in this realm. In 2014, it teamed with the Council of Fashion Designers of America, Barneys New York, and Opening Ceremony to develop tech wearables. It had a design for wearable smart earbuds, which supplied biometric and fitness information. The earbuds had stereo audio and monitored the wearer's heart rate, while phone applications kept track of distance and calories burned. Intel had also invested in Basis Science, a maker of an innovative health tracker designed to improve fitness and sleep, and in Lemoptix, a start-up with a focus on low-power wearable displays, 3D-sensing automotive head-up displays, and embedded projectors in smartphones.

Smart Glasses and Augmented Reality

Within the ARM device market, Intel was poised to be a strong player in smart glasses and augmented reality. In 2013, it acquired Recon Instruments, a maker of smart glass display products for sports based on ARM technology. Along with Altera, Recon furnished Intel with the capabilities to compete in the ARM device market.

Intel had already invested heavily in smart glasses and augmented reality companies. Some of the companies that it had acquired or supported included these:

- Eyefluence, a company with eye tracking and control technology that can speed up wearable display adoption.

- Vuzix, a manufacturer of next-generation fashion-based smart glasses and wearable displays.

- Composyt, a company with smart glasses that feature direct retina projection and holographs.

- Orcam, a smart glasses start-up, focused on helping the visually impaired, and blinOmek Interactive, a gesture recognition technology company whose technology can be used in mobile and wearable devices, gaming, automobile, and casino markets.

Intel was trying to emerge as a leader in smart glasses and augmented reality. Its acquisitions gave it a head start over other companies like Apple, Samsung, and Microsoft. If the companies in which it invested took off, it would not be shut out of this market as it had been in the mobile market.

Risks Ahead

With the Altera purchase, Intel could make progress in two key areas: data centers, whose revenues grew by 19 percent in 2014 and 2015, and IOT, whose revenues grew by 10 percent in that time period. The problem with this strategy was that Intel's PC business remains much larger than business in either of these domains, and regardless of how fast they grew, they would not bolster Intel's revenues by a significant amount in the short run.

Intel, moreover, could not afford to lose focus on its global manufacturing lest it be overtaken by a company like Taiwan Semiconductor (TSMC). TSMC surpassed Intel in operating margins and revenue growth in the second quarter of 2015. In 2014, TSMC's revenues grew by 21 percent to $24.1 billion, whereas Intel's revenues grew by just 6 percent to $55.87 billion; TSMC had healthy profits of $8 billion, whereas Intel's profits were $11.7 billion. TSMC was good at manufacturing IOT devices, but IOT devices were not the kind of high-volume, high-margin business upon which Intel could rely to support the capital costs of its advanced production capabilities.

Conclusion

The question that Intel and AMD faced was this: with a shrinking PC and laptop business, a slow-growing server segment, and their failure to exploit mobile markets, what should they do next? Both companies had many options from which to choose and choices to make. The competition between them had been intense. To what extent could they afford to continue to collide in seeking the same group of customers? To what extent should their paths continue to diverge in ways yet to be determined? Intel and AMD had to decide what to do next.

The following options were of importance to both:[19]

- **Speed**—Neither AMD nor Intel had entirely given up on speed. Intel was working on a chip the size of a fingernail that was capable of processing one trillion calculations in a second. This chip, which would be the fastest ever, could be commercially available for applications in such areas as financial trading, complex physics, and Nintendo-like games.[20]

- **Power consumption**—Most organizations with data centers were concerned about power supply and cooling. Even small savings could add up in large data centers of universities and Internet companies like Google and Yahoo. Both AMD and Intel were focusing on power consumption of their chips.

- **The next billion**—The next billion represented a vast potential market in the developing world. Both Intel and AMD had shown interest in designing PCs suited to the needs of customers in emerging markets. These computers, though, had to achieve new levels of affordability, access, connectivity, and power usage and had to be available at low prices.

Glossary of Computer Terminology

8-through-64-bit architectures—The number of binary digits, or information bits, a microprocessor can retrieve.

chipset—All components communicate with the CPU through the chipset, which is the hub of data transfer. The chipset is usually second in size to the CPU.

CPU clock speed—Also called clock rate, it is measured in gigahertz (GHz) and refers to how many clock cycles a CPU can perform per second.

direct random access memory (DRAM)—Temporarily stores information from the system, applications, and data that are currently in use and determines how many programs can be run simultaneously and how quickly they perform.

flash memory—Small memory device that holds a lot of data that is mainly found in PDAs, wireless phones, and laptops.

microprocessor or central processing unit (CPU)—The mechanism that interprets information from various devices and executes it, such as telling a printer to print. The faster the processor is, the faster the computer works.

Endnotes

1. Roger Kay, "Intel and AMD: The Juggernaut Vs. The Squid," *Forbes.* Dec. 25, 2014. http://www.forbes.com/sites/rogerkay/2014/11/25/intel-and-amd-the-juggernaut-vs-the-squid/.

2. David Kirkpatrick, "Intel v. AMD: The Joy of Blood Feuds," *Fortune.* March 19, 2007. http://archive.fortune.com/magazines/fortune/fortune_archive/2007/03/19/8402328/index.htm.

3. Cliff Edwards, "Inside Intel," *Business Week.* Jan. 8, 2006. http://www.bloomberg.com/bw/stories/2006-01-08/inside-intel.

4. Alfred Marcus, *Winning Move.* Lombard, IL: Marsh Press, 2009.

5. Andy Grove, "Intel's Andrew Grove on Competitiveness," *Academy of Management Executive* 13.1 (1999): 15.

6. Andy Grove, *Only the Paranoid Survive*. New York: Doubleday, 1999.

7. Mike Magee, "AMD Now a Virtual Gorilla—Sanders," *The Register*. May 4, 2000. http://www.theregister.co.uk/2000/05/04/amd_now_a_virtual_gorilla/.

8. Andy Reinhardt, "The New Intel: Craig Barrett Is Leading the Chip Giant into Riskier Terrain," *Business Week*. March 13, 2000. http://www.businessweek.com/2000/00_11/b3672001.htm.

9. Paul Keegan, "Man with a Hammer," *CNN Money*. Nov. 1, 2002. http://money.cnn.com/magazines/business2/business2_archive/2002/11/01/331620/.

10. Arik Hesseldahl, "AMD Files Antitrust Suit Against Intel," *Forbes*. June 28, 2005. http://www.forbes.com/2005/06/28/amd-intel-lawsuit-cx_ah_0628amd.html.

11. Cyrus Farivar and Andrew Cunningham, "The Rise and Fall of AMD: A Company on the Ropes," *Ars Technica*. April 23, 2013. http://arstechnica.com/business/2013/04/amd-on-ropes-from-the-top-of-the-mountain-to-the-deepest-valleys/2/2013.

12. Dave Smith, "Why GlobalFoundries Bought Out AMD and Went Rogue," *International Business Times*. March 5, 2012. http://www.ibtimes.com/why-globalfoundries-bought-out-amd-went-rogue-420796.

13. Alexis C. Madrigal, "Paul Otellini's Intel: Can the Company That Built the Future Survive It?" *The Atlantic*. May 16, 2013. http://www.theatlantic.com/technology/archive/2013/05/paul-otellinis-intel-can-the-company-that-built-the-future-survive-it/275825/.

14. Ibid.

15. Michal Lev-Ram, "Exclusive: Fortune 500's Newest Woman CEO Talks About Her First 90 Days on the Job," *Fortune*. Jan. 8, 2015. http://fortune.com/2015/01/08/lisa-su-advance-micro-devices-ceo/.

16. Don Clark, Dana Cimilluca, and Dana Mattioli, "Intel Agrees to Buy Altera for $16.7 Billion," *The Wall Street Journal*. June 1, 2015. http://www.wsj.com/articles/intel-agrees-to-buy-altera-for-16-7-billion-1433162006.

17. Ibid.

18. Ibid.

19. Marcus, *Winning Moves*.

20. Don Clark, Dana Cimilluca, and Dana Mattioli, "Intel, Micron Claim Chip Breakthrough," *The Wall Street Journal*. July 28, 2015. http://www.wsj.com/articles/intel-micron-claim-memory-chip-breakthrough-1438099234.

10

From Mass Customizing to
Mass Commodity: Dell and Acer

As Dell and Acer planned for their future, they had to decide how they were going to deal with the commoditization of their business. It had moved from mass customization—where novel products that combined flexibility and personalization with low cost had been profitably sold to customers at a rapid pace—to commoditized products that had razor-thin margins and sold mostly based on price.

The main products of Dell and Acers were desktop and laptop PCs. Although smartphones and tablets cannot accomplish what these products do, especially in business settings, in a more mobile world, their role became less important. Dell and Acer faced an important question: with so many smartphones and tablets sold each year, how strong would the market for the desktop and laptop PCs be? The essential point for Dell and Acer was that unit sales and prices of PCs had been decreasing, and the decline of the PC industry, spurred by the rapid rise of mobile computing, was mounting. In 2015, mobile phones and tablets—not desktops, laptops, or notebooks—made up nearly 88 percent of global PC, mobile phone, and tablet shipments.

In 2014, the global PC market contracted by *only* 2.9 percent after declining 9.5 percent the previous year.[1] Business that upgraded from Windows XP to the next operating system and the business replacement cycle for PCs slightly moderated the downward trend. Tablets also witnessed a small drop in shipments. Dominated by the iPad, the premium end of the market weakened, but the market for lower-priced tablets with less functionality had picked up. In emerging markets, people tended to prefer "phablets," hybrid devices between the size of large phones and small tablets with the functionality of both.

Michael Dell once again held the top leadership position in the company he started in 1986.[2] On the one hand, he was convinced that the demand for conventional PCs would rise as they were improved—there was still room for improvement in screen size, touch, speed, weight, and battery power. On the other hand, Michael Dell had prepared the company for reduced reliance on PCs, making dozens of acquisitions, starting with information technology services provider Perot Systems in 2009 and culminating in Dell's purchase of EMC in 2015. Dell had made additional acquisitions in storage and networking systems, with the aim of expanding Dell's offerings from computers to complex solutions for enterprise customers.

After severe losses and a management shake-up, Jason Chen, a former Taiwan Semiconductor Manufacturing executive, became Acer's CEO in 2014.[3] He challenged the predictions that the PC industry was in demise and placed his company's bets on next-generation PCs, as well as inexpensive laptops that used Google Chrome software and combined tablet and laptop features. However, Chen also hedged his bets and stayed committed to the initiatives Acer had taken in mobile phones and cloud computing.

To what extent were the responses that Dell and Acer had made to the growing commoditization of their businesses adequate? The two companies had to decide what to do next.

Financial Woes

Neither Dell nor Acer had exhibited stellar financial performance in recent years. Prior to becoming a private company in 2014, Dell had not seen much improvement in its financial performance over the five-year period starting in 2009 (see Exhibit 10.1). Acer's revenue had been in a free fall since 2009 (see Exhibit 10.2). It had to streamline its product line because of weak 2011 performance, and it went through a massive restructuring because of even weaker 2013 performance.

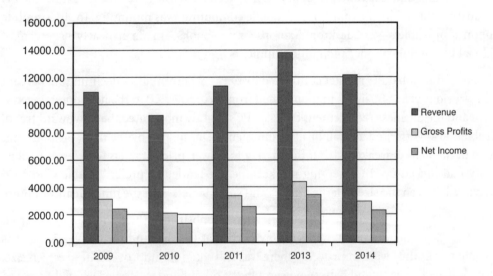

Exhibit 10.1 Dell's Revenue, Profit, and Income 2009–2013, Millions of Dollars

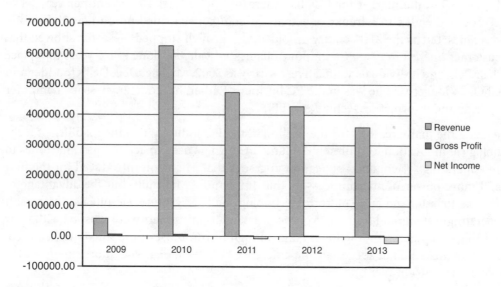

Exhibit 10.2 Acer's Revenue, Profit, and Income 2009–2013, Millions of Dollars

Annual accounting reports

Worldwide PC shipments declined by 5.2 percent in the first quarter of 2015, and among major PC makers, Dell and Acer experienced the biggest declines (see Exhibit 10.4).[4] Dell's sales were 5.1 percent less than they had been in the first quarter of 2014 and Acer's 6.8 percent less. Lenovo, in contrast, grew its shipments by 5.7 percent, and HP grew its shipments by 2.5 percent. Business desk-based PCs were affected the most, and shipments fell rapidly. Notebooks and notebook-tablet hybrids grew in comparison to the prior year.

Exhibit 10.3 Change in Worldwide PC Vendor Unit Shipment, First Quarter 2015

Company	First Quarter 2015 Market Share (%)	First Quarter 2014 Market Share (%)	Quarter One 2014–2015 Growth
Lenovo	18.9	17.0	5.7
HP	17.3	16.0	2.5
Dell	12.6	12.6	−5.1
ASUS	7.4	7.2	−2.9
Acer	7.2	7.3	−6.8
Others	36.5	39.8	−13.2

Based on Gartner data

An Industry in Decline

In the 1990s, the market for PCs had increased by at least 15 percent per year.[5] The decade had ended in a frenzy of activity as companies loaded up on new Y2K-ready machines; but as the 21st century unfolded, this growth stopped. Research showed that customer interest in new PCs was low. Businesses waited as long as 3.5 years to replace their PCs, and individuals waited five. As early as 2002, Michael Dell, Dell's founder and CEO, no longer said he was in the PC business. Rather, his company was in "computer systems and information technology (IT)."[6]

Among the many reasons for the decline in the PC industry was the inability of technological innovation to spur new demand. PC owners used to acquire new machines to run operating system and application upgrades that Microsoft introduced for the new and more powerful microprocessors that Intel and AMD built, but the advantage of moving to faster and more powerful technology had lost ground. Despite new Microsoft operating systems and faster microprocessors, many customers were satisfied with their existing computers, finding them good enough to run most of the software they used. Many of them did not appreciate the difference between a high-end, more expensive PC and a low-end, cheaper one.

With the advent of ever cheaper computers, competition was increasingly about price. A growing number of consumers believed that a cheap PC from Walmart operating Windows software was acceptable. Customers could walk into a Walmart store and take home a no-frills product right off the shelf. They did not have to wait for Dell to ship the PC to their home. User interest in PCs had been waning for quite some time, but industry competition continued to be intense. With capacity high and demand low, no large PC maker made much money.

The Fat Years: Dell's Ascent

Dell traced its roots to 1984, when Michael Dell, a student at the University of Texas at Austin, created the company, selling IBM-like PCs built from components he bought on the market from his dorm room. He left school to develop the business after obtaining a $1,000 investment from his family. In 1985, the company produced a computer of its own design, which it assembled and sold directly to customers for $795. The company advertised in national computer magazines and had revenue of more than $73 million in its first year of operation.

After the company's 1988 IPO, Michael Dell hired Morton Meyerson, a former Electronic Data Systems CEO, to help him manage the company's growth. Dell's products stood out in the 1990s for their reliability, quality, and customer support. The company expanded beyond desktops and laptops and started to sell servers, beginning at the low end of the market. Unlike other providers of servers at the time—IBM, Sun, HP, and Compaq—which had proprietary systems that made their servers more expensive, Dell's PowerEdge servers did not require major investments in proprietary technologies because they ran Microsoft Windows software and Intel chips. By 1998, 13 percent of Dell's revenues came from servers.[7] By 2001, Dell had a market share of 31 percent in servers, surpassing Compaq as the top provider of Intel-based servers.[8]

Originally, Dell ignored the consumer market due to the high costs and low margins of selling to individual consumers. However, when the company's online retail site took off in 1996, it was able to sell directly to this segment at low cost. Because a high percentage of Dell's sales was to second- and third-time computer buyers who wanted to upgrade, Dell's average selling prices rose, whereas those of the industry fell.

From 1997–2004, Dell's growth was strong and steady as it gained market share from competitors even during times of overall industry decline. Compaq, Gateway, IBM, Packard Bell, and AST Research struggled as Dell advanced. Eventually each exited the market or was acquired. Dell became the dominant PC manufacturer in the United States, taking that position away from Compaq in 1999. HP and Compaq merged in 2002.

Compared to rivals such as HP, Dell had low operating costs relative to its revenue. It added televisions, digital audio players, and printers to its product line and benefited from the slowdown in the U.S. economy in 2002–2003 because it had the lowest cost structure in the industry. When component prices dropped, it passed the savings on to customers. It made more money in this period by slashing prices than by selling fewer products at higher prices.

A Competency in Mass Customization

Dell's competency was in mass customization,[9] a competency its competitors could not match. Dell made its computers to order and delivered them directly to customers, giving them exactly what they wanted.[10] The customers paid Dell weeks before Dell paid its suppliers. Dell perfected a system that gave it a substantial cost advantage, not just because it did away with the reseller and retail markup, but because it eliminated the risk of unsold inventory piling up and having to be sold at a discount.

Born of necessity, mass customization played a central role in Dell's business model. The company concentrated on pleasing suppliers as well as customers, functioning as an intermediary between them. Its purpose was to maximize value to both parties. The information these relationships generated allowed Dell to engage in planning and just-in-time manufacturing (see Exhibit 10.4). The system eliminated channels that stood in the way of a direct relationship with customers.

These relationships enabled fast movement of inventory and the ability to forecast demand. They allowed Dell to excel on the other metrics on which it relied to measure its performance—in particular, return on investment. Dell's role as trusted technology adviser to its customers gave it intimate knowledge of their needs (see Exhibit 10.5).

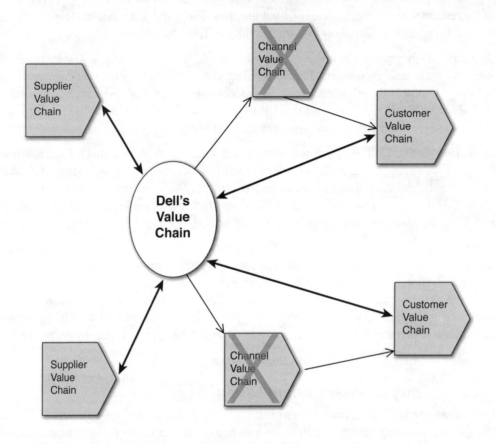

Exhibit 10.4 Dell's Direct Model

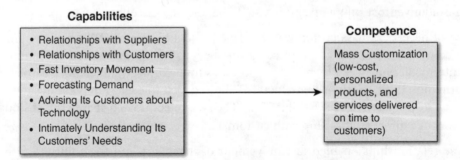

Exhibit 10.5 Dell's Capabilities and Its Core Competence

At the inception of the PC industry, competitors like IBM had to create all the components for a PC themselves. They made the disk drives, memory chips, and software. As the industry matured, specialized firms made each of the components, which allowed Dell to leverage the investments other companies made and focus on delivering solutions to customers. It evaluated what the component manufacturers produced and picked the best of what they made for its customers. Dell's integration was virtual; it was not vertical like IBM. Virtual rather than vertical integration allowed a small company like Dell to defeat a much larger rival like IBM (close to 500,000 employees at the time) in the nascent PC industry.

Inventory velocity was the key performance measure upon which Dell relied. The company made its products in response to a customer's order, thus avoiding the typical industry stop-and-start cycle when companies stuffed channels to get rid of excess inventory and meet their short-term revenue goals. Dell did not invent the technology it sold; instead, it assembled and passed on this technology to its customers, making it easy for them to use and keeping their costs down. If competitors adopted Dell's approach, they had a long road to travel. As sellers of devices through resellers, they confronted channel conflict if they attempted to sell directly to customers.

Gateway Abandons the Direct Model

A large divergence existed in the PC industry between companies that sold through resellers, like HP, Compaq, and Acer, and those that only relied on direct customer sales, like Dell. Initially, Gateway also used the Dell model, although it differed from Dell in the following way: it mainly sold to individual consumers, whereas Dell mainly sold to institutions.[11] As Dell gained ground on Gateway in the 1990s (see Exhibit 10.6), Gateway phased out of the direct model in favor of selling through retail outlets.

Exhibit 10.6 Sales and Operating Margins for Dell and Gateway, 1994–1999

	1994	1995	1996	1997	1998	1999
Dell sales ($ in billions)	2.8	3.5	5.3	7.8	12.3	18.2
Gateway sales ($ in billions)	2.7	3.7	5.0	6.3	7.7	9.0
Dell operating margin (percentage)	−1	7	7	9	11	11
Gateway operating margin (percentage)	5	7	7	5	6	7
Dell inventory turnover ratio	11	9	10	24	41	52
Gateway inventory turnover ratio	19	14	15	21	37	37

Data source: Dell and Gateway Annual Reports

Gateway sold more than computers. It combined computing with content and communication. It sought to establish a rich relationship with a customer that was based on more than a simple transaction. In 1997, it opened what it called *Country Stores* to give its customers the chance to "kick the tires" before buying by offering them many distinct and related products—systems, peripherals, software, warranties, and financing. It also provided training and Internet. These products had better profit margins than computer hardware.

Gateway referred to itself as the "PC maker for the Internet generation." The PC, in its view, was just a conduit to market Web and other higher-margin services. It introduced the first "Net Appliance," a small notebook-like computer with little utility other than getting on the Internet. At the same time, it went in the other direction, beyond PCs, by starting in 2002 to market 42-inch, flat-panel, and plasma televisions.

Gateway developed a different set of capabilities and a different competence than Dell (see Exhibit 10.7). Despite its efforts, it continued to fall far behind Dell. Its revenues increased to more than $9 billion in 2000, and employment grew to 19,000, but its sales and profits collapsed in 2001, and it had to implement massive layoffs.[12]

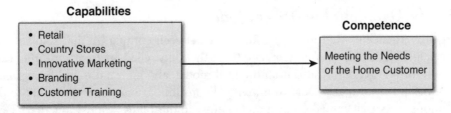

Exhibit 10.7 Gateway's Capabilities and Its Core Competence

The Lean Years: Michael Dell's Resignation

Dell's success also did not continue forever. In 2004, Michael Dell stepped aside as CEO, but he retained the position of board chair. Kevin Rollins, who had been the president and chief operating officer of the company since 2001, replaced him.[13] Growth in earnings and sales slowed in 2005, and the company's share price fell by a quarter. Rollins did not know how to cope with the commoditization of the PC industry. PCs made up 66 percent of Dell's sales, and desktop PCs sold to commercial customers accounted for 32 percent of its revenue. Their prices were quickly dropping. Dell no longer could make up in increased sales what it lost in reduced margins. Analysts advised Dell to move into non-PC business segments such as storage, services, and servers, but it was taking time for Dell to make this transition.

The advantage Dell had in mass customization was no longer especially relevant. The company needed to make strategic moves in new markets and products and not emphasize more refinements in its highly efficient mass customization system. Rollins was an operations person. He had been one of the main architects of this system, but it became less important as additional savings were harder to realize and competitors developed their own versions.

In an era of declining PC prices, the priority Dell gave to this system made less and less sense. The laptop segment was the fastest growing in the PC market, but the way Dell produced laptops was not unique. Like other companies, it did not assemble laptops on its own; rather, it had them produced in China by contract manufacturers according to its specs. This method of production did not give it a cost advantage. Moreover, its dependence on Internet sales meant that it missed out on growing laptop sales in retail channels.

Unlike the other PC companies, Dell also was heavily dependent on the U.S. market. Sixty-four percent of its revenue came from North and South America in 2006. Despite plans to expand outside the United States and into other product segments, it was not gaining much ground in foreign markets where the direct sales model was hard to implement.

Corporate IT departments had decided to take a break from upgrading. They saw no need to make any changes until Microsoft introduced a new version of Windows. However, the 2007 version of Windows did not result in as big a boost in corporate buying. To boost sales, all the PC companies had the same dilemma. They had no alternative other than to slash prices.

Dell's rivals—HP, Gateway, and Acer—did have a strong retail presence, and they could take part in the booming laptop market. Most consumers did not buy their laptops on the Internet. The lack of a retail presence also prohibited Dell from fully benefitting from the latest trends in electronics, such as flat-panel TVs. Dell experimented with mall kiosks, but these did not produce the results it wanted.

In product design, Apple was leading the way. Product design expertise was not a capability Dell had acquired. Its PCs were efficient and functional but not exciting; they lacked flair. They did not generate intense loyalty. They were not fashionable among the set of customers to whom Apple was appealing. Apple could obtain large premiums for the products it sold. Dell, on the other hand, had to compete with other PC makers based on price. Dell's low R&D spending, which had helped it to survive in a commoditized market, started to work against it.

Unlike HP, IBM, and sundry IT consulting firms such as Accenture, Dell did not have the capabilities to deliver complete IT solutions. By moving its call centers overseas, it let its customer service slip, which exacerbated the problems it was having. There was also criticism because of faulty components in some of the PCs and servers it sold to businesses and governments between 2003 and 2005. Finally, a battery recall in 2006 as a result of a laptop catching fire in an airplane only added to the company's woes.

By 2006, Dell's growth rate for the first time in its history did not exceed that of its peers. It fell behind HP's global market share, which led to Rollins' resignation and the return of Michael Dell as CEO in 2007.[14]

Acer's Acquisition of Gateway

Although Dell's worldwide shipments declined, the overall global PC market grew, mainly fueled by companies operating out of Asia, like Acer. In 2007, Taiwan-based Acer acquired Gateway in a deal designed to give Acer the size it needed to become a major force in the global PC industry.[15] "Joining with Acer will enable us to bring even more value to the consumer segments we serve and capitalize on Acer's highly regarded supply chain operations and global reach," said Gateway Chief Executive Ed Coleman in a joint statement signed by the two companies at the time of the acquisition.[16]

From 2004–2006, Gateway's gross margins slipped from 14.4 percent to 5.2 percent, which led to a reshuffling wherein Coleman was appointed CEO. The prior CEO, Wayne Inouye, brought in after Gateway's acquisition of eMachines in 2004, dealt with gross margin compression brought on by commoditization by means of expense reduction, but the strategy did not work because commoditization had advanced so completely.

Gateway marketed PCs under two brand names: Gateway and eMachines. It positioned these brands to represent the best value for the money in two different segments: mainstream and budget computers. In 2006 Gateway was the third-largest U.S. PC company and among the ten largest worldwide. It sold products in more than 7,000 retail outlets in the United States and Canada, such as Best Buy, Circuit City, CompUSA, Costco, Office Depot, Micro Center, and Walmart. It sold its eMachines in Japan and the UK as well as the United States. Inouye created a common supply chain management system for the two brands to keep costs low but failed in his efforts to revitalize Gateway.

Acer estimated that by acquiring the company, it could create savings from operating synergies of more than $150 million a year.[17] The multibrand company, which also sold computers under the Packard Bell label in Europe, could reach $15 billion in revenue and have shipments in excess of 20 million units per year. With its acquisition of Gateway, its per-unit procurement and component costs would go down, and its opportunities for cross-selling its products would go up. Because of its increased size, it would be able to get supplier discounts like those received by the other PC makers. Its reach extended deeply into retail outlets in three different continents, a feature no other computer company could match.

Acer had been founded by Stan Shih, his wife Carolyn Yeh, and a group of five others in 1976. In 2000, it spun off its manufacturing operation to focus solely on marketing PCs to third parties. Although its labor force contracted from 39,000 people in 2002 to 7,800 people in 2003, its sales grew.[18] Rejecting the Internet sales model Dell pioneered, Acer relied on retailers and resellers to reach consumers with PCs that were less expensive in their segments than those of its competitors. It had a major lead over competitors in notebooks. Acer sold more notebook PCs as a proportion of its total sales than any of its competitors. As notebook sales took off in 2007, it did very well.

Previously, Acer's small U.S. presence had been a weakness.[19] It had just 2.2 percent of the market in 2006 prior to the Gateway acquisition. Its first attempt to crack the U.S. market in the 1990s had failed. It flooded distributors with more PCs than they could sell before it retreated. The debacle cost Acer nearly $3 billion. Acer's main U.S. partner had been Ingram Micro, with whom it signed an agreement in 2004 to put Acer notebooks in Circuit City, Walmart, and CompUSA, among other U.S. retail outlets. With the Gateway acquisition, Acer was fully ready to take on the U.S. market.

Acer's 2008 global market share at 9.5 percent was third in the world behind HP at 18.3 percent and Dell at 14.9 percent.[20] Trailing badly was Lenovo at 6.7 percent and Toshiba at 4.3 percent. Acer's unit growth at 25.2 percent in 2007 topped the industry.

Acer tried to build on capabilities it had for new product development.[21] It had a highly motivated workforce and a talent for exporting that none of its competitors matched. Its Product Value Lab was dedicated to creating "Empowering Technology" that would provide customers with integrated solutions to their problems. The lab's aim was to develop easy-to-use and reliable products with good user interface, ultra-mobility, and such advanced features as video conferencing. Although Acer had a young and highly educated product design team, its product design capabilities were no match for Apple's.

Dell's Plans for a Recovery

In 2007, Dell continued to have difficulties. An admission of accounting irregularities led to a restatement in earnings. Andrew Cuomo, New York's attorney general, sued the company, alleging that it had deceived customers by failing to honor warranties and other service agreements. Dell's backlog of new products was insufficient to satisfy consumers' desire for novelty. While Dell stood still, the balance of power in the computer industry had shifted to innovative design. Apple benefitted. It grew the number of units it sold by 31.8 percent. The momentum in its favor kept growing (see Exhibit 10.8).

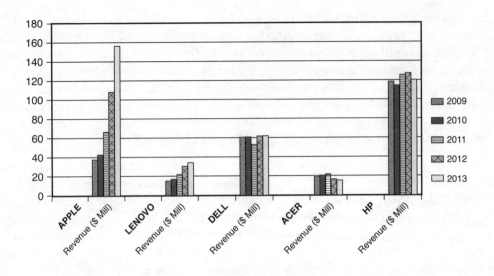

	2009	2010	2011	2012	2013
Apple					
Revenues ($ mil)	37.5	42.9	66.2	108.3	156.5
Total Employees (000)	32	36.8	46.6	60.4	72.8
Lenovo					
Revenues ($ mil)	14.9	16.6	21.6	29.6	33.9
Total Employees (000)	22.5	22.2	27	27	35
Dell					
Revenues ($ mil)	61.1	61.1	52.9	61.5	62.1
Total Employees (000)	76.5	76.5	94.3	100.3	109.4
Acer					
Revenues ($ mil)	18.6	19.6	21.5	16.2	14.7
Total Employees (000)	6.7	7	7.8	7.9	8
HP					
Revenues ($ mil)	118.3	114.5	126	127.2	120.3
Total Employees (000)	321	304	324.6	349.6	331.8

Data source: Annual accounting reports

Exhibit 10.8 Revenue and Employees of Major Computer Vendors, 2009-2013

A prior initiative Dell had made to sell computers in retail outlets quickly had been aborted when the company realized that the margins in retail selling were so low. In a mea culpa, however, Michael Dell admitted that the company would have to take retail more seriously. In a talk to analysts, he said that many people did not want to buy directly. Therefore, Dell was going to give customers a chance to buy its products in retail outlets. Dell announced that it would start indirect channel sales by placing $700 desktops in U.S. Walmart stores.[22]

This step was only the beginning in the changes that Michael Dell was making. He reduced the number of the company's employees by 10 percent and started to further diversify the products Dell sold. He closed some North American call centers and shut down most of Dell's domestic and its Irish manufacturing. These moves accelerated the transition Dell had to make from mass customization to selling computers in highly commoditized markets. With many of its manufacturing sites no longer functioning, most of Dell's computers were made like the computers of other companies, in the same high-volume, low-cost Asian, and in some cases Mexican, contract factories. Dell only continued to make very profitable servers in its Austin, Texas, facility.

Apple's release of the iPad negatively affected Dell because many consumers chose tablets over laptops. Dell created a division that focused on mobile devices, but this division was slow to create competitive products. The products never became popular. The failure to effectively enter this market may be attributed to Dell's view that smartphones and tablets were just short-term fads that would never have much influence on the market for computers. This fundamental miscalculation was a stumbling block to Dell making a rapid turnaround. In the third quarter of 2012, Dell had serious operating losses in the consumer segment.[23] In December of that year, Dell experienced its first decline in holiday sales in five years.

In a shrinking and commoditized PC industry, Dell also continued to lose global market share to Lenovo and HP. Lenovo, the former PC division of IBM, which was now an independently owned Chinese company, dominated the Asian market and did surprisingly well even in the United States where its ThinkPad series of laptops often were preferred by business customers to Dell's products.

Acer, a Taiwanese company, was disadvantaged in China because of the historic antagonism between the two states. With a strong foothold in slow-growing Europe (Packard Bell), Acer lost sales and global market share. All the major Asian vendors—Lenovo, Asus, and Ace—had lower production costs than Dell and HP and accepted lower profit margins than these companies (see Exhibit 10.9). As publicly traded U.S. companies, neither Dell nor HP could sacrifice profit for market share to the same degree as the Asian companies. The Asian companies, therefore, were in a better positon than U.S. PC companies to thrive in a market that had become commoditized.

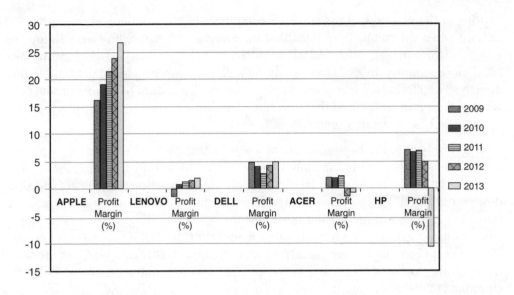

	2009	2010	2011	2012	2013
Apple					
Profit margin (%)	16.3	19.2	21.5	23.9	26.7
Revenue growth (%)	52.5	14.4	52	66	44.6
Lenovo					
Profit margin (%)	(1.5)	.8	1.3	1.6	1.9
Revenue growth (%)	(8.9)	11.4	30	37	14.5
Dell					
Profit margin (%)	4.8	4.1	2.7	4.3	5.0
Revenue growth (%)	6.5	(.1)	(13.4)	16.2	.9
ACER					
Profit margin (%)	2.1	2.0	2.4	(1.4)	(.7)
Revenue growth (%)	16.5	5.1	9.6	(24.4)	(9.6)
HP					
Profit margin (%)	7	6.7	7	5	(10.5)
Revenue growth (%)	13.5	(3.2)	10	1	5.4

Data source: Annual accounting reports

Exhibit 10.9 Profit Margins and Revenue Growth Changes Major Computer Vendors, 2009–2013

The Enterprise Market

Dell was in a difficult position. Competing on price in a commoditized PC market was a stretch, but so was entering and seriously competing with the likes of IBM and HP in the already crowded enterprise service market. In 2010, IBM's service and software business brought in more than $85 billion in sales, HP's brought in more than $40 billion in business, whereas Dell's brought in a paltry $18 billion. IBM's R&D over sales was 5.6 percent, HP's was 2.3 percent, and Dell's was a meager 1.1 percent.[24]

Nonetheless, Dell tried to offset its declining PC business, which still accounted for most of its revenue, by expanding into the enterprise market not only with servers, where it already had a strong business, but in networking, software, and services. In these businesses, the margins were far superior to the declining margins in PC hardware.

HP, too, was trying to expand in this segment, but it made mistakes with poor acquisitions that ended up in write-downs and management turnovers. Dell by and large avoided these problems. It aimed to take advantage of the close contacts it had established with IT professionals within organizations when it had pursued its mass customization strategy. The first really serious enterprise service acquisition Dell made was in 2009, when it acquired Perot Systems, which was mainly active as a technology services and outsourcing company in the health sector. It acquired Perot Systems, in 2009, in a $3.9 billion deal and amalgamated the company with Dell Services. Perot gave Dell capabilities it needed to compete in services, applications development, systems integration, and strategic consulting. The acquisition of Perot was followed by many other acquisitions and collaborations in this segment.[25] For example, in 2010, Dell acquired KACE Networks, a leader in Systems Management Appliances, and software-as-a-service integration leader Boomi. In 2011, Dell acquired Compellent to extend its storage solution portfolio, SecureWorks, for its information-security services, and Force10, for its intellectual property in networking portfolio.

In 2012, Dell made even more acquisitions. It bought the following:

- Backup and disaster recovery software solution provider AppAssure Software
- SonicWall, a company with 130 patents that develops security products
- Clerity Solutions, which provides services for application rehosting
- Gale Technologies, which supplies infrastructure automation products
- Credant Technologies, a provider of storage protection solutions

Credant was the 19th acquisition in four years; Dell spent $13 billion on acquisitions after 2008 and $4 billion dollars in 2012. Dell collaborated with Telefonica on communication products, Integrity on government security, Cisco and Juniper on IT and networking solutions, and SAP on cloud and in-memory computing.

Despite spending so much money on acquisitions to diversify its portfolio beyond hardware, Dell did not convince shareholders that it had made a fruitful transformation from mass customization to enterprise service provider. The company's share price remained weak. Its market share in the corporate segment, which had been its strong point, no longer seemed impregnable from the inroads of competitors, and Dell faced a turning point.

Becoming a Private Company

In 2013 Dell delisted its shares from the stock market and went private by means of a $24.4 billion leveraged buyout deal.[26] No longer would it have to endure the pressures of stock market investors and analysts.

Michael Dell and Silver Lake Partners, supplemented by a $2 billion loan from Microsoft, made an offer for all the publicly traded shares of the company for $13.65 a piece in what would have been the largest technology buyout ever and the largest leveraged buyout since the 2007 financial crisis. The proposed buyout price, however, was not much of premium over the stock price, and it was considerably lower than the $65-per-share stock price peak achieved in 2000 and $40-per-share price in 2005 before the company's decline. Michael Dell's stake at $750 million was relatively small.

In a typical leveraged buyout (LBO), the buyer attempts a turnaround by breaking up the company into pieces, reducing the workforce, introducing cost-cutting measures, and bringing in outside management to replace the existing top management team. Then the buyer sells the pieces and tries to return the firm to public ownership at a higher valuation than its original acquiring price. The Dell LBO was different because the buyer was not an outside company with these intentions in mind, but the company's largest shareholder and CEO. Michael Dell forged the deal, and he would retain his position as CEO and would be entrusted with the task of trying to turn the company around. By going private, he could continue the transformation of the company from mass customization to enterprise solution provider that he had started, without the pressure of Wall Street to achieve quarterly performance results and without the pressure of analysts questioning his moves.

Soon after the announcement of the proposed LBO, the Blackstone Group and Carl Icahn considered making a higher offer for the company, but then they expressed reservations and withdrew because of their assessment that the company's business prospects were weak. Without a competing offer, Dell's board raised the buyout price to $13.75 a share plus a special dividend of 13 cents per share and accepted the offer Michael Dell and Silverlake made, terminating Dell's 25-year run as a publicly traded company. The buyout led to a voluntary separation program, which was meant to reduce the workforce by about 7 percent.

In 2014, Dell announced another new acquisition designed to make it a more capable enterprise solution. It acquired StatSoft, a global provider of analytics software, to strengthen its big data solutions capabilities. In 2015, in the biggest tech takeover of the year, Dell bought EMC for $67 billion. Adding data storages to its network and other offerings was the riskiest and most ambitious move Dell took to transform itself.

Acer's Efforts at Revitalization

Unlike Michael Dell's plans to revitalize Dell, Jason Chen's plans to revitalize Acer did not involve much departure from Acer's prior business model.[27] Acer would stick to its core of designing and selling PCs and PC-related devices through global retail outlets. Rather than shifting to entirely new businesses, the company intended to make steady progress in PCs and PC-related products. By exploiting its core instead of exploring new opportunities, the hope was that the company could regain profitability and start to grow again.

Notebooks

Acer's biggest opportunity was probably in small, lightweight, and inexpensive notebooks, which ran on Chrome software and easily hooked up to the Internet. These devices had great appeal in Asia and could be sold globally in the niche between a tablet and a laptop. For most users, a notebook accomplished everything that a laptop accomplished, yet it lacked the limitations of a tablet. There was some evidence that the product's appeal was growing among people who were not satisfied with their iPads. With 35 percent of the global market share, Acer dominated this segment. According to many market analysts, the segment was poised to grow fairly rapidly. In 2015, Acer introduced its 15.6-inch Chromebook, an industry first, in the hope that it would attract new customers. Acer also saw promise in convertible notebooks with detachable keyboards that could be transformed into tablets. Another arena in which Acer could excel was high-end PCs. If it had solid offerings, it could attract customers interested in games for whom price was less of an issue than performance.

Smartphones

Acer was also venturing into smartphones. From a small base, it had tripled its sales in a few years. The company wanted to be a force in mobile devices in developing countries other than China and in developed countries other than the United States, where its brand name was a disadvantage. In the fourth quarter of 2013, Acer's sales percentage was higher in the rest of the Asia than it was in China (25 percent in the rest of Asia as opposed to 13 percent in China), and in Europe it was higher than it was in the Americas

(46 percent in Europe as opposed to 18 percent in the United States). Its market share in India (about 8 percent) surpassed its market share in China (about 4 percent). In China, it continued to suffer in comparison to Lenovo because it was a Taiwanese company (see Exhibit 10.10).

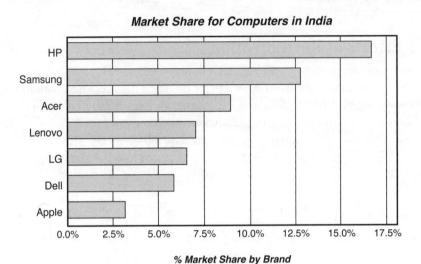

Market Share for Computers in India

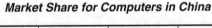

% Market Share by Brand

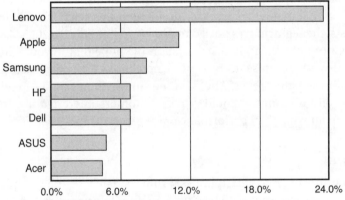

Market Share for Computers in China

Exhibit 10.10 Acer's 2014 Market Share for Computers in India and China

Source: Euromonitor

Free Cloud

An important initiative Acer made was the relaunch of a free cloud computing service that it called Build Your Own Cloud. This service hosted users' data on its platforms, allowing them to expand the capabilities of devices they purchased from Acer. For this initiative to work, Acer had to avoid the pitfalls of hacking and privacy breaches. It was taking precautions that it claimed made it more immune to problems than comparable services. To compete with Google and Amazon services, Acer opened its cloud platform to programmers, who could develop unique apps for Acer users.

IOT

IOT (the Internet of Things), which includes Web-enabled home appliances and centrally linked industrial equipment and which is expected to grow rapidly, offered the potential to provide Acer with the opportunity it needed. Acer sold wearable devices like its Liquid Leap wristband, which tracked a person's activities and had a touch-screen that linked it to Acer's Build Your Own Cloud. Companies such as Cisco, AT&T, ARM, GE, and Intel had invested heavily in bringing connectivity to software, hardware, and components and wireless gadgets ranging from smoke detectors to industrial equipment and wristwatches. Through these, Acer might capture growing demand for data storage and applications powered by the rise of Web-connected devices in homes, cities, and workplaces.

Acer was convinced that its low-key, gradual approach would allow it to survive and ultimately thrive in the hyper-competitive commoditized PC and PC-related market. The plans were also to keep costs down while exploring these markets and discovering a successful formula. Analysts, however, were not convinced that these moves would restore profitability and increase growth. They might stabilize the company, prevent further losses, and provide a short-term boost, but they were not the kind of breakthroughs that would have a big impact. Some analysts wanted Acer to move further outside the field of PCs. Cofounder and chairman of the company Stan Shih proclaimed that the goal should be that more than 50 percent of company profit should come from areas outside of PCs and PC related devices, but how the company could achieve this goal remained uncertain. Acer did not have the capabilities to make the kind of transformation Dell was making. Moreover, as a publicly traded company, it had to meet shareholders' expectation for steady growth and improvement in profitability.

Conclusion

For Dell, storage, the cloud, and service were the main options it had decided to pursue to make a comeback. These service businesses were growing globally, but historically they had not been Dell's forte. Nonetheless, Dell was trying to remake itself as a service company able to compete with companies like IBM and HP. What was required of it to effectively make this transition?

For Acer, on the other hand, retail was essential for its survival. Starting with notebooks, where it had a dominant global market share, it was basing its turnaround on offering a broad array of standard PC and PC-related products, the most unique of which was Build Your Own Cloud.

In which directions would Dell and Acer have to take their initiatives to ensure their survival? Could they again become vital forces in the computer industry?

Endnotes

1. "Gartner Says Worldwide Traditional PC, Tablet, Ultramobile and Mobile Phone Shipments to Grow 4.2 Percent in 2014," *Gartner.* July 7, 2014. http://www.gartner.com/newsroom/id/2791017.

2. Joshua Brustein, "Michael Dell Gets His Chance to Save Dell." *Bloomberg Business Week.* Sept. 12, 2013. http://www.bloomberg.com/bw/articles/2013-09-12/michael-dell-gets-his-chance-to-save-dell.

3. Eva Dou, "Acer CEO to Take Chairman Role in Three Years," *The Wall Street Journal.* Oct. 16, 2004. http://www.wsj.com/articles/acer-ceo-to-take-chairman-role-in-three-years-1413455293.

4. "Gartner Says Worldwide PC Shipments Declined 5.2 Percent in First Quarter of 2015," *Gartner.* April 9, 2015. http://www.gartner.com/newsroom/id/3026217.

5. Alfred Marcus, *Winning Moves.* Lombard, IL: Marsh Press, 2009.

6. Kathryn Jones, "The Dell Way" *Business 2.0.* Feb. 1, 2003. http://money.cnn.com/magazines/business2/business2_archive/2003/02/01/335960/; Andrew Park, "What You Don't Know About Dell" *Business Week.* Nov. 3, 2003 http://www.bloomberg.com/bw/stories/2003-11-02/what-you-dont-know-about-dell.

7. Marcus, *Winning Moves.*

8. Andy Serwer, and Julia Boorstin, "Dell Does Domination." *Fortune.* Jan. 21, 2002: 70.

9. C. K. Prahalad and Gary Hamel, "The Core Competence of the Corporation." *Harvard Business Review* May-June 1990. (Also online at https://hbr.org/1990/05/the-core-competence-of-the-corporation.)

10. Joan Magretta, "The Power of Virtual Integration: An Interview." *Harvard Business Review* March-April 1998. (Also online at https://hbr.org/1998/03/the-power-of-virtual-integration-an-interview-with-dell-computers-michael-dell).

11. Frances Frei, Youngme Moon, and Hanna Rodriguez-Farrar, "Gateway: Moving Beyond the Box." Case Study. *Harvard Business School.* Boston: Harvard Business Publishing, 2002. Steven Brull, "Gateway's Big Gamble." *Business Week.* June 5, 2000. http://www.bloomberg.com/bw/stories/2000-06-04/gateways-big-gamble.

12. Frances Frei, Youngme Moon, and Hanna Rodriguez-Farrar, "Gateway: Moving Beyond the Box."

13. Christopher Lawton and Joann S. Lublin, "Dell's Founder Returns as CEO As Rollins Quits," *The Wall Street Journal.* Feb. 1, 2007. http://www.wsj.com/articles/SB117027913335994112.

14. Christopher Lawton, "How H-P Reclaimed Its PC Lead Over Dell." *The Wall Street Journal.* June 4, 2007. http://www.wsj.com/articles/SB118092117687623314.

15. Gary Gentile, "Acer Buying Long-Struggling Gateway." *Associated Press.* Aug. 27, 2007. http://www.washingtonpost.com/wp-dyn/content/article/2007/08/27/AR2007082701074.html.

16. Jason Dean and Christopher Lawton, "Acer Buys Gateway, Bulks Up for Global Fight," *The Wall Street Journal.* Aug. 28, 2007. http://www.wsj.com/articles/SB118820817365109596.

17. Ibid.

18. Marcus, *Winning Moves.*

19. Ibid.

20. "Gartner Says in the Fourth Quarter of 2008 the PC Industry Suffered Its Worst Shipment Growth Rate Since 2002," *Gartner.* Jan. 15, 2009. http://www.gartner.com/newsroom/id/856712.

21. Jason Dean, and Jane Spencer, "Taiwan's Acer Rebounds." *The Wall Street Journal Asia.* April 5, 2007:1.

22. Matt Richtel, "Dell Will Sell 2 Computer Models at Wal-Mart," *New York Times.* May 25, 2007. http://www.nytimes.com/2007/05/25/technology/25iht-dell.1.5862729.html?_r=0.

23. "Dell Reports Third Quarter Financial Results." *Dell.* Nov. 15, 2012. http://www.dell.com/learn/us/en/uscorp1/secure/2012-11rtewq155-133pr.

24. MarketLine Industry Profile, "PCs in the United States." *MarketLine* November 2014.

25. Ibid.

26. Michael J. De La Merced and Quentin Hardy, "Dell in $24 Billion Deal to Go Private," *New York Times*. Feb. 5, 2013. http://dealbook.nytimes.com/2013/02/05/dell-sets-23-8-billion-deal-to-go-private/.

27. Tim Culpan, "A Future for PCs? Acer's Chen Is Betting Company On It," *Bloomberg Business*. Jan. 5, 2015. http://www.bloomberg.com/news/articles/2015-01-06/a-future-for-pcs-acer-s-chen-is-betting-company-on-it.

11

Finding Growth and Profitability in Bookselling: Barnes & Noble and Amazon

B arnes & Noble and Amazon were the bookselling industry's leading companies. Yet Barnes & Noble's revenues were declining by 10 percent per year, and in the second quarter of 2015, Amazon had lost more than $0.4 billion dollars (see Exhibit 11.1). The bookselling industry was experiencing vast technological change with the introduction of e-books and tablets, and Barnes & Noble and Amazon had to figure out what to do next.

Exhibit 11.1 Financial Performance of Major Booksellers, 2nd Quarter 2015

	Barnes & Noble	Amazon
Market Cap (billion $)	1.66	203.83
Employees	33,645	154,100
Quarterly Revenue Growth (%)	−0.10	0.15
Revenue (billion $)	6.07	91.96
Gross Margin (%)	0.31	0.30
Operating Margin (%)	0.02	0.00
Net Income (billion $)	.0128	−0.406.00

Data source: Quarterly financial reports

Barnes & Noble and the Superstore

Leonard Riggio, Barnes & Noble's founder, believed shopping was a recreational activity. Relying on the philosophy that people bought books based on emotion, he transformed bookselling into a giant industry.[1] Too poor to attend college full time, Riggio had worked during the day as a clerk in the New York University bookstore. In 1965, he created a campus bookstore of his own. During the next six years, he established four other bookstores on campuses in New York City.

In 1971, Riggio bought Barnes & Noble, then an unprofitable New York textbook seller, and in 1974 he opened a Barnes & Noble annex in Manhattan where he aggressively marketed low-priced books that had been returned to publishers. By 1986 he owned 142 college bookstores and 37 Barnes & Noble's stores. When he bought B. Dalton from Dayton-Hudson, Barnes & Noble became the largest U.S. bookseller.

Barnes & Noble's main competitor had been Borders, an Ann Arbor, Michigan, chain.[2] At the time, Walden Books was a part of Borders. Kmart had bought Walden in 1984. In the late 1980s, B. Dalton and Walden owned more than 600 mall-based stores. Borders pioneered the concept of the bookstore as a superstore. Barnes & Noble was an aggressive follower. The son of a professional boxer, Riggio learned from his father to be quicker on his feet and more nimble than his opponents. Barnes & Noble acted more quickly than Borders and expanded more rapidly than Borders.

The superstores had a special atmosphere. They were meant to serve as gathering places for people. They tried to get people to linger with comfortable seating, coffee to drink, and late-night hours. Some stores were decked out like small or full-scale libraries. Most had comfortable chairs and writing tables. They hosted readings by famous authors and other events. They played pleasant jazz and classical music in the background. The stores made an effort to build a sense of community. Advertisements featured pictures of literary greats like Hemingway and Virginia Woolf. Barnes & Noble, in particular, tried to create a literary climate. It paid a great deal of attention to décor, layout, furniture, display, signage, and selection of books. The special atmosphere meant that customers spent time browsing, and of course, the more time they spent browsing, the more they bought. Customers bought twice as much merchandise at a superstore as at a mall-based store.

Barnes & Noble chose about 50,000 titles to display at each superstore. Local managers adapted the rest of their selections to local tastes. The result was that the typical store offered about 175,000 titles packed into 30,000 square feet.

The competition between Barnes & Noble and Borders was fierce. They were in a race to see which would expand most rapidly. Both feared that Walmart and mass-market retailers would take away their business. Kmart spun off Walden in 1995 because it could not keep up. In that year, Barnes & Noble and Borders captured about one-quarter of the U.S. market for books, with Barnes & Noble having a market share of about 15 percent and Borders having a market share of about 10 percent.[3] The focus of both companies was on aggressive expansion. The number of superstores in the United States kept growing. It jumped to nearly 800 in the mid-1990s. Many independent bookstores could not keep up and folded.

Barnes & Noble and Borders were focused on the competition between them and their commitment to continued expansion. When Amazon.com began operations in 1995, neither company paid much attention.[4] Barnes & Noble's goal was to expand at a pace of about 100 new stores per year. Yet by 1997, the estimate was that there were several hundred online booksellers operating on the Web and that, by 1998, they already had captured 2 percent of the adult book market.[5]

Amazon and Internet Commerce

Jeff Bezos, the founder of Amazon, was a summa cum laude graduate of Princeton in 1986 with a degree in computer science.[6] He had worked for a telecom start-up and a hedge fund. Seeking to begin a business of his own, he examined 20 possibilities for Internet commerce before settling on bookselling. He understood the opportunities in books to be high because the industry was very fragmented and because Internet selling offered many advantages over conventional book stores, including enabling larger selection, greater inventory turnover, higher sales per square foot, and higher sales per operating employee.

Bezos moved from New York City and started his business in Seattle, Washington, to take advantage of the software talent and proximity to Ingram's large bookstore and electronics wholesale warehouse in Oregon. Before building its own warehouse complex, Amazon relied on Ingram. There also happened to be no state taxes on retail purchases in the state of Washington, which made Internet sales more competitive with retail. To begin operations, Amazon had to innovate. It had to pioneer in the development of software for Internet shopping. It created the look and feel of an Internet shopping site that now has become common. It provided information about the books it sold, posted author interviews, offered free book reviews, and gave links to other sites and features. Amazon spent vast sums of money on research and development (R&D), in 1999 obtaining a patent for its one-click technology, which allowed customers to order from its site with a simple click of the mouse instead of going through several steps. In contrast to a physical store, which had fixed times when it opened and closed, Internet shopping could take place at any time of the day.

The venture capital firm Kleiner Perkins Caufield & Byer invested $8 million dollars in Amazon to help it get started, and the business grew rapidly. In less than a year, Amazon had nearly $1 million in sales. Repeat customers provided more than 50 percent of its business, and the average transaction was greater than $50. Technical and business books made up a high percentage of the early orders.

The company went public in 1997, and its market capitalization rose to $560 million on the first day. Bezos suddenly was a multimillionaire because he owned 42 percent of the stock. Investors continued to have confidence in Amazon's business model year after year, although Amazon did not report that it was profitable, and it was not clear when it would be. The company stayed afloat by means of the positive cash flow it generated. Customers paid Amazon with credit cards; Amazon collected the sale price within a few days from the credit card company, but it was weeks before it paid its suppliers.

Barnes & Noble launched its own book-selling website in the spring of 1997.[7] The website featured personalized book recommendations and deep discounts every bit as good as Amazon's on most items. Barnes & Noble used its brand name to capture leadership in the general interest and fiction categories. Because of its warehouses and greater experience in shipping books, it tried to beat Amazon's delivery times. It built new warehouses, in Atlanta and Reno, which it added to its existing warehouse in New Jersey to ensure prompt distribution. It also built its own version of the one-click technology, which it called "express lane" ordering. However, the company was not able to seamlessly integrate brick-and-mortar operations with the Internet, which permitted Amazon to make the claim that it, not Barnes & Noble, was "earth's biggest bookstore."[8] Since 1970, Barnes & Noble's slogan had been that it was the "world's biggest bookstore." Barnes & Noble sued, arguing that Amazon was not a bookstore at all, but a book broker. Amazon, in turn, counter-sued, and it sought an injunction against Barnes & Noble for stealing its one-click technology.

In 1999, Barnes & Noble had an IPO, which spun off BarnesAndNoble.com, its online business, as a separate company. Bertelsmann, a German mass media corporation, owned 36 percent of the new company, Barnes & Noble owned 36 percent, and 36 percent of the shares were sold to the public. One month before the spin-off, Amazon took a number of aggressive steps to counter any success that BarnesAndNoble.com might have by adding 1.5 million more titles to those it already listed, introducing a personalized book recommendation service, and starting to sell bestsellers at a 50-percent discount. The 50-percent discount was especially galling to BarnesAndNoble.com, which was forced to match the discount and thus sell books at cost.

Amazon's aggressive moves had their desired effect. The stock of BarnesAndNoble.com climbed just 27 percent on the first day of the IPO, a huge disappointment in an era when stocks routinely doubled or tripled the initial asking price. Amazon was beating BarnesAndNoble.com on the most important Internet criterion: "eyeballs."[9] It had 8.4 million registered Internet customers compared to BarnesAndNoble.com's 1.7 million, and its Internet market share was 75 percent whereas BarnesAndNoble.com's was 15 percent. Barnes & Noble made an offer to buy Amazon's Oregon supplier, Ingram's Book Group in 1998, only to be rebuffed because of antitrust scrutiny.

Amazon's Reinvention

Worn down by the battle with Barnes & Noble, in 1997 Amazon came up with a new plan to reinvent itself as a general merchandiser and Internet service provider.[10] It began to sell music online and quickly became the biggest online music seller; this was followed by video and DVD sales later in the same year. In both these cases, it engaged in the full range of e-commerce activities, including buying, warehousing, merchandising, shipping, and customer service. By the end of 1999, it had moved beyond books into other retail categories such as electronics, home improvement goods, and toys, while BarnesAndNoble.com only sold media-related products and limited its increased consumer offerings to a few items like music, posters, and prints. In 2000, Amazon added lawn and patio and kitchen products, cell phones, and wireless services to the array of products it sold.

Amazon also decided that in some of its initiatives it would not own the goods sold or take responsibility for order fulfillment. Like eBay or Yahoo, it would be an e-commerce partner for individuals and for small and large businesses, earning fees for bringing people together and providing a technology for the marketing, distributing, and warehousing of their goods. In 1999, it launched an auction initiative oriented mostly toward higher-end arts and antiques in partnership with Sotheby's. In a few short years it morphed from an online bookstore to a purveyor of everything from CDs and Palm handheld devices to power tools and waffle irons.

In 1999, Amazon created an area on its website where it facilitated transactions between customers and sellers. It signed agreements with dot-coms like Drugstore.com, Living.com, Audible, and the online car-sales company Greenlight.com. Each would pay Amazon fees for the opportunity to be showcased on Amazon's website. Unlike the launch of a new Amazon product category, which required spending on products and physical infrastructure, these deals cost the company virtually nothing, but even with the fees, it was not profitable. Amazon had become more like an Internet portal such as Yahoo. However, unlike Yahoo and other portals, its customers were not just surfers and chatters; they were experienced online shoppers.

In 2001, Amazon signed deals with brick-and-mortar retailers like Target, Circuit City, Virgin Records, and Borders. The company agreed to run all or part of their e-commerce operations. It sold the retailers' products on Amazon.com, and in some cases it would store products in its warehouse, distribute orders, and run the partner's website. Gross margins in these services outstripped the profitability of Amazon's bookselling business.

The start of the 21st century saw Amazon make an aggressive push into third-party selling (see Exhibit 11.2). Third-party sellers offered a variety of merchandise on Amazon's website. To support these services, Amazon built many U.S. warehouses in which it invested in technology to integrate the website with customer service, payment processing, and warehouse operations. It hired thousands of people to work in these warehouses and paid them minimal wages. By taking these steps, Amazon reinvented itself as a general merchandiser of goods and services on the Internet and an Internet service provider.[11]

Exhibit 11.2   Third-Party Sales as a Percentage of Amazon's Total Sales

Year	2000	2001	2002	2003	2004	2005	2006
% Total Item Sales	6%	13%	17%	22%	26%	28%	28%
Year over year growth	N/A	116%	31%	29%	18%	7%	0%

Source: Marcus, *Winning Moves*

Barnes & Noble's Focus on Books

Whereas Amazon branched out, Barnes & Noble remained focused on books. In 2007, it was still the largest U.S. bookseller, with 793 bookstores. Barnes & Noble ran many university bookstores, often not under its own name. Most Barnes & Noble stores had Starbucks-owned-and-operated cafés, the first of which opened in 1993. In 2004, the company began to offer Wi-Fi in the cafés. The BarnesAndNoble.com website, which Barnes & Noble repurchased from Bertelsmann in 2004, was among the top 30 e-commerce sites in terms of traffic, but it was far behind Amazon in terms of sales.

Barnes & Noble remained dedicated to the community store concept, trying to make each store an integral part of the community in which it was located by offering titles with local content, a café, children's and music section, and a magazine department. The company hired community business development managers to engage in outreach. They organized in-store events, such as author appearances, children's story times, and book groups; worked with local schools and groups to promote literacy and the arts; hosted book fairs; and collected book donations for local charities.

Some of the books that Barnes & Noble sold it published itself.[12] The company inexpensively reprinted noncopyrighted titles and acquired the rights to books from other publishers, while it commissioned reprint anthologies and omnibus editions using its own editors. Starting in the 1990s, it released a series of literary classics for adults and children under the Barnes & Noble Classics imprint. One of titles it published, *The Gentle Art of Verbal Self-Defense* by Suzette Haden Elgin, sold more 250,000 copies. It also released a new edition of *The Columbia History of the World* by John Garrity, which sold more than one million copies. The expansion of Barnes & Noble publishing was aided by the acquisitions of SparkNotes, an educational publishing house, and Sterling Publishing, a press that specializes in how-to-do-it books. Barnes & Noble established a paperback series called the Barnes & Noble Library of Essential Reading as well as, in 2007, the Barnes & Noble Review, an online literary site.

Bestsellers, like *Harry Potter*, accounted for 3–5 percent of Barnes & Noble's sales, most of which continued to come from outside publishing houses, although the firm also tried to promote books from university presses and independent publishers.[13] However,

Barnes & Noble typically had to discount bestsellers by as much as 30 percent to attract customers because of the intense competition from mass merchandiser stores like Walmart and Costco.

Sinking Profits

Barnes & Noble's major problem was sinking profits.[14] Gross margins had declined by more than a percentage point in the first quarter of 2007, and the company lost money. Profits were falling because of the severe pricing pressure from discounters, the existence of warehouse clubs, and online retailers. Barnes & Noble, therefore, raised the discounts it gave to customers who signed up for its $25-a-year membership club. Members had the right to a 40-percent discount on bestsellers, a 20-percent discount on all other hardcovers, and a 10-percent discount on everything else sold either online or in a store, including paperbacks and coffee.

Then-CEO Steve Riggio, the founder's brother, emphasized the importance of giving customers discounts. The company could afford discounting because it still had a strong financial position and was not in debt. Riggio wanted to lock in Barnes & Noble's best customers with the discounts. Independent bookstores had witnessed a resurgence because of their intimate knowledge of their customers.[15] The personal service they offered was hard for Barnes & Noble to match. Many of the independent bookstores gave steep discounts on special interest books. Riggio wanted to keep customers from defecting to the independent booksellers, a new source of competition, as well as Borders and Amazon.

The impact of Barnes & Noble's aggressive discounting was felt the most by Borders.[16] Borders started a membership club similar to Barnes & Noble's but quickly retreated and reduced its scope when its profits shrank. It was not earning enough money from the scheme to justify the expense. Neither was Barnes & Noble's, but that did not keep the company from persisting.

Instead of going the discount route, Borders was betting on a new store concept. The remake of its stores, however, was an expensive initiative. It would cost Borders about $2.4 million per store: $1.2 million in capital expenditures, $1 million for new inventory, and $0.2 million for preopening costs. Ultimately, this initiative was unsustainable. Along with other factors, like being too late to online retail, the amount of debt Borders accumulated in trying to remake its stores led to its bankruptcy in 2011. Barnes & Noble was the last-standing major bookstore chain.

Amazon's Fluid Identity

By 2014, most of Amazon's revenue did not come from books.[17] The company was secretive and protective of information about how it obtained its revenues; nonetheless, the estimates were that 7.5 percent of the company's annual revenue in 2014, or less than $7 billion, derived from books. Apparently, Amazon had not entered the bookselling industry because of a special attraction to books. As items sold over the Internet, books did have some advantages. There were too many of them to sell in a physical store, but it was possible to offer a large selection online. Books also shipped easily; they did not break. However, books mostly offered Amazon a way to attract an educated and affluent customer base and a gateway to selling to this customer base merchandise other than books on the Internet. Amazon collected vast amounts of data about these customers, which it used to sell them an ever-widening array of goods and services—music, electronics, lawnmowers, art, toys, diapers, shoes, bikes, appliances, games, jewelry, clothing, shoes, office products, software, pet supplies, tools, and many other items. Books were just an entry point for these customers to the Amazon website. Amazon did not have to make much profit on the books it sold so long as it could use books to acquire customers. Two decades after Amazon entered the bookselling business, it offered a bewildering array of products and services.

Amazon continued to expand the scope of what it did. In 2007, it created its own hardware—the Kindle tablet—and, in 2011, the Kindle Fire phone. The Kindle was billed as a "single-purpose reading device" meant to compete not only with books, but with newspapers and magazines. A handheld book reader that cost less than a tablet, a Kindle could hold more than 200 books in a paperback-sized package and display them on pages that appeared more like paper than an LCD screen. The device connected to the Internet wirelessly, permitting users to download books and other material any time they wanted. Initially, Amazon offered 90,000 titles for $9.99 each. The $9.99 price was meant to resonate with the $0.99 price of downloading a song from the Apple's iTunes store.

In many ways, Amazon was more like Apple than Barnes & Noble. It designed devices and produced and distributed its own entertainment, similar to Netflix, creating content such as Garry Trudeau's comedy "Alpha House" about a group of Republican senators living together on Capitol Hill. It also helped authors self-publish their own works.

But that was not all. Like FreshDirect, Amazon also offered a grocery delivery service. Too dependent on UPS and the U.S. post office for shipping, Amazon was hoping to find innovative ways to deliver packages on its own, including the possibility of an Uber-like service staffed by part-time drivers or of sending packages directly to businesses and to people's homes using drones.

Separate from the company, Bezos bought the *Washington Post*. There was much speculation about how acquiring this landmark newspaper would fit into his plans. The company's identity was hard to pin down; its tentacles stretched broadly into many areas. Even if it rarely earned a profit, shareholders seemed to be satisfied. Despite some rough patches at the beginning, Amazon's share price over time had soared (see Exhibit 11.3).

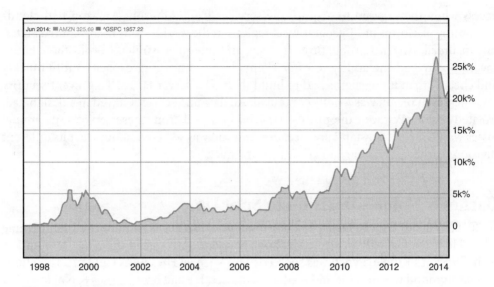

Exhibit 11.3 Growth in Amazon's Share Price

Profiting from the Cloud

Although pay-as-you go cloud data storage services were estimated to account for less than 6 percent of Amazon's 2014 revenue, or $5.4 billion, they were the source of a high percentage of any profits it earned.[18] At the end of 2014, more than one million customers relied on Amazon's web services. Its customers included large web companies like Netflix and big government users such as the U.S. Department of Defense with whom Amazon had a major contract.[19] The revenues of this segment were projected to reach $106 billion by 2016. In contrast, the total revenues of bookselling were not likely to exceed $29 billion in that year. Amazon had achieved a distinct lead over its major competitors—Microsoft, IBM, Google, Salesforce.com, and Rackspace—in the cloud segment.

Amazon developed its cloud-based services almost by accident.[20] The challenge it faced was to make better use of the excess cloud capacity it had. Amazon employed as little as 10 percent of this capacity at any time, saving the rest for spikes in demand during the holiday season. Higher-capacity use would mean steeper discounts to shoppers, which would translate into higher Internet sales, lower shipping prices per unit of sale, and more efficient warehouse utilization.

The solution to too much cloud capacity was to rent and sell the excess capacity to individuals and organizations. Amazon identified this opportunity early and developed a unique edge that other players in this segment had not matched. It mitigated the many concerns that clients—especially government clients—had about security, speed, and access when they agreed to acquire the services from Amazon. Amazon had cloud-computing platforms in 11 geographical regions in the world—four in the United States, one in Brazil, two in Europe, three in Asia, and one in Australia.[21] From these bases, the company had the ability to offer clients large computing-capacity more quickly and cheaply than if the clients had to build their own server farms. To prevent security breaches, each region was wholly contained. All data and services stayed in a designated, isolated region. Without the profits Amazon obtained from these services, its annual losses would mount substantially. Because Amazon was secretive about what its different divisions earned, it was hard to know by how much.

Barnes & Noble's Decision to Split Up

In 2010, William Lynch, formerly the president of Barnes & Noble's website, became CEO. He helped launch an electronic bookstore and introduced the Nook to compete with Amazon's Kindle. Lynch was succeeded by Michael Huseby as CEO in 2014. Huseby's background was in cable and media businesses. He had been Barnes & Noble's CFO in 2012 and had been its president since 2013. After three years of weak profits, Huseby decided to split up Barnes & Noble into three separate businesses in 2015: the bookstore, the Nook, and the college division.[22] While Amazon grew and became more diffuse, Barnes & Noble got smaller and became even more focused.

Spinning Off the Nook

When first unveiled, the Kindle's main competitor was Sony's Reader, but Barnes & Noble soon introduced an e-reader of its own: the Nook. Huseby decided to spin off the Nook as a separately traded company because it lost so much money. The outside investors in this new venture were Microsoft, owner of 17.6 percent, and Pearson, owner of 5 percent, whereas Barnes & Noble retained ownership of 84.4 percent.

In 2014, Barnes & Noble had scaled back the Nook business after it experienced large losses. Over the history of the Nook, Barnes & Noble sold about 10 million of these devices. When the Nook was launched in 2009, it did quite well, at one time capturing 27 percent of the e-reader market, but sales in 2014 were about half of what they had been the previous year, and the Nook kept losing ground to the Kindle.

The Nook did not have the latest e-ink technology like the Kindle did to give it the feel of reading on paper, and it was slightly slower in turning pages. It lacked features the Amazon device had, like the ability to export notes and highlights or access and copy and paste them from a Web interface. The Nook also had a smaller library of books from which to choose, and although book searching was somewhat easier and the prices better displayed, downloading a book was slightly harder on the Nook.

The task of the spinoff was not to abandon the Nook but to fix it so that it would be more competitive with the Kindle. Nook partnered with Samsung to launch a new generation of Nook devices.

Many people who read e-books owned an e-reader but did not own a Nook. Nearly 40 percent of U.S. adults who read e-books in 2013 owned a Kindle. The iPad came in second place. The Nook e-reader was behind these devices in market share. It fell even further behind when people were asked if they planned to buy one in the near future.

Tablet ownership in the United States had grown significantly since the 2010 introduction of the iPad. Although more consumers had a way to read e-books, they were using their tablets as their dedicated reading devices. They had many advantages as a book-reading device. Unlike e-readers, they could be used for many other purposes.

Spinning Off the College Division

Besides the spinoff of the Nook, Barnes & Noble also decided to separate its retail from its educational and college bookstore holdings. The move, which created two separate publicly traded companies, enabled the company to raise $775 million, which was critical to alleviating its financial distress. Michael Huseby, Barnes & Noble CEO, became the executive chair of the new college bookstore company. It had 714 stores on U.S. college campuses and was capable of reaching 23 percent of U.S. college students. The total sales of this division in 2014 were $1.75 billion. Same-store sales were down 2.7 percent from the previous year, but profits had improved, going up from $30.2 million to $35.1 million. Unlike the legacy retail stores, this division was profitable. Huseby intended to expand to new colleges and universities and grow the market for digital educational content and services.

The legacy bookstore chain hired former senior Toys R Us, Sears, and Kmart executive Ron Boire to be its chief executive. His prior experience in electronics products at Best Buy, Sony, and Brookstone was touted when he was appointed CEO of Barnes & Noble. Sales at the legacy chain had been weak for a number of years, although they were stabilizing. Comparable retail bookstore sales were experiencing declines in the low single digits.

Boire had 648 bookstores to manage. Barnes & Noble was aiming for an increase in comparable sales, excluding e-books, of 1 percent in 2015. The challenge at the legacy stores to generate new and profitable revenue was great, and it was not at all clear how it could be met. Barnes & Noble had to be a destination for customers who wanted the opportunity to browse and discover the content offered in its stores. Beyond books, the company was selling toys and games. These categories outperformed books growing at a 16-percent pace in 2015 compared to the previous year.

The company was also trying to find new ways to engage customers. It had launched a "Get Pop-Cultured with Barnes & Noble" campaign, which celebrated pop culture icons. It had a campaign called "Throwback Thursday" to celebrate the decades from the 50s to the 90s and "Vinyl Day" to celebrate the resurgence of vinyl disk recordings. Because it made so much of its money on bestsellers, Barnes & Noble looked forward to the publication of Harper Lee's *Go Set a Watchman,* Dr. Seuss's first original manuscript since 1990, and an E. L. James follow-up to *Fifty Shades of Grey.* The company was also launching an improved version of its website with better search capabilities. It hoped that the improved user experience would increase sales and lower its costs. Better integrating the stores with the website continued to be an issue for Barnes & Noble.

How Attractive Was Bookselling?

Was the bookselling industry, in which Amazon and Barnes & Noble competed, a good industry in which to compete? A number of factors had to be carefully examined: sales trends, people's reading habits, leisure time choices, and how people accessed books and other reading material.

Sales Trends

Book sales were roughly divided among trade books, college and K-12 textbooks, professional books, mass-market paperbacks, and religious books, with different trends within each of these segments. The industry's overall revenues were fairly stagnant, although some of these categories were doing better than others.[23] In 2014, the industry had sales of 2.7 billion units and about $28 billion in revenues. Its sales included both conventional books and e-books, as well as audiobooks. These results represented a 4.6 percent increase over the prior year. The main areas of growth were in the children and young adult category, e-books, and audiobooks. Sales of trade books (fiction and nonfiction) barely grew. Sales of K-12 instructional materials, higher education course materials, university presses, and professional books declined.

The top sales channel for trade book buyers was online retail, with 832 million units in sales and $5.90 billion in revenue. However, in 2014, in the trade book category, after years of decline, physical retail stores saw a 3.2 percent increase in revenues ($3.80 billion from $3.68 billion) and a 4.1 percent growth in units (577 million from 554 million).

The largest-growth category in trade books was children and young adults, which had a 20.9 percent growth in revenue and a 13 percent growth in units sold over the previous year. The children and young adults' fiction category had more unit sales (843 million) than the adult's fiction category (746 million units). Within the children and young adults' fiction category, growth was across the board. It took place in paperback, hardback, and downloaded audio and e-books sales.

Overall, paperbacks remained the most popular format, with sales of $4.84 billion in 2014 and 942 million units sold, compared to $4.42 billion in 2013 and 882 million units sold in that year. Sales of downloaded audio books had record growth in both units and revenue compared to the prior year, whereas sales of physical audio books slightly declined on these measures compared to the prior year.

After slightly declining in 2013, e-book sales grew by 3.8 percent in 2014 to an estimated $3.37 billion. More than 510 million e-books were sold in 2014, almost the same number as the number of hardback sales of 568 million that year. Subscription services provided publishers with another important distribution outlet. Twenty publishers had launched such programs. Audiobooks sold via subscription were more popular than e-books via subscription, with 3.88 million audiobooks and more than 2.47 million e-books sold this way.

Reading Habits

According to a Pew Survey, the average number of books that U.S. adults reported they read or listened to in 2013 was 12, and the median was five.[24] Women reported that they read more than men, whites and blacks reported that they read more than Hispanics, those older than 30 reported that they read more than those younger than 30, and college graduates reported that they read more than non-college graduates.

Leisure Time Choices

People had many substitutes for reading. They could go to a movie, the theater, or a concert; participate in voluntary activities like serving on the board of a charitable organization; be involved in sports, such as run a marathon, golf, or work out; or go to a sporting event like a hockey or football game. They also could attend religious services, browse the Internet, play a video game or a board game, bowl, or simply watch television. There were other activities from restaurants and yard work to shopping in department and outlet stores that competed with bookselling.

When asked by the U.S. Department of Labor (DOL) in 2013, Americans reported that their main leisure time activity was watching television (see Exhibit 11.4). They claimed to spend just 19 minutes per day reading. In contrast, they watched television for about 2.8 hours a day. Older Americans, those above 75 years old, claimed to spend much more time reading per day, a full hour, than younger Americans, who admitted to spending just six minutes a day reading. In general, older Americans had more time for all types of leisure activities than younger Americans.

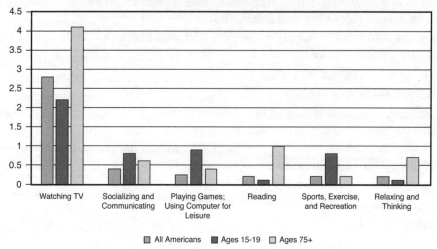

Hours Per Day Americans Spend in Leisure Activities

Legend: ☐ All Americans ■ Ages 15-19 ☐ Ages 75+

Exhibit 11.4 How Americans Report Spending Their Leisure Time, 2013

Adapted from U.S. Department of Labor Survey

Digital Devices

A 2013 Pew survey found that e-book reading devices were rapidly diffusing in the Unites States. About 42 percent of adults owned a tablet.[25] The number who owned an e-reader like a Kindle or Nook reader had increased as well, to 32 percent. Overall, half the Americans surveyed had a handheld device. Those with these devices were younger, had higher levels of education, and came from better-off households. Close to two-thirds (65 percent) of people living in households earning $75,000 or more annually owned one of these devices. Yet print books still played an important role; Pew found that most Americans continued to read at least one printed book per year in 2014, although e-reading was growing. For most people, it was not an either-or decision; they tended to access their reading material via both media.

The Publishers

Publishers released thousands of new titles each year, adding to the millions of titles already in print.[26] Barnes & Noble and Amazon purchased from thousands of publishers and many wholesalers as there were their own imprints, through which they assisted authors in self-publishing. Yet two wholesalers and just five publishers were the industry's main players.

Wholesale

Publishers sold books in two ways—through wholesalers and by direct sales. Ingram and Baker & Taylor were the largest wholesalers. They distributed more than just books. For example, Ingram also distributed personal computer hardware and software and home videos. When publishers sold directly to retailers, the discounts were 44–55 percent off the list price. When they sold to wholesalers, the discounts were 2–3 percent higher. Because the wholesaler had margins of no more than 1.5 percent, they had to be super-efficient.

To achieve high levels of efficiency and fast delivery times, the wholesalers invested heavily in warehousing, electronic ordering and inventorying, and robotics. They were experiencing vast changes moving from supplying books to distributing physical and digital texts and prints on demand. They were not seeing an end to the print medium, but rather complementary orders from customers of physical and digital texts. Therefore, they had to develop new capabilities in the rapid printing of books on demand.

Ingram and Baker & Taylor sold to most of the independent booksellers. They also worked with large companies like Amazon and Barnes & Noble, but publishers tried to supply these companies directly. Under a consent order the publishers signed, they agreed not to give large companies higher discounts than independent retailers, but suspicion existed that they favored the large companies. Popular movies like *You've Got Mail* cast suspicion on the treatment the publishers gave independent booksellers.

Wholesalers and retailers bought books on consignment so they could return what they did not sell for full credit. This practice originated during the Depression, when there was no other way for publishers to get their books on booksellers' shelves. More than 30 percent of new hardcover books were returned because they did not sell. For the publishers, this problem was addressed in a variety of ways. They might offer additional discounts if the retailer or wholesaler was willing to give up their return privilege. They might give rebates at the end of the year if the retailer or wholesaler returned a low percentage of books. Publishers also chose to print fewer initial copies. If demand went up, a publisher would either reprint the book or release a new edition.

The Big Five

Before overhead and advertising, the money earned by a book was split five ways: the retailer got about 35 percent, the publisher about 20 percent, the author about 10 percent, the wholesaler about 6 percent, and the rest was absorbed by printing, shipping, and miscellaneous costs. Celebrity authors like the Clintons obtained huge advances, but the typical author obtained just a small percentage of the price of each copy sold. Most books sold fewer than 5,000 copies. Unsold copies were shipped back to publishers to be remaindered and sold at a discounted rate or destroyed. With point-of-sale data available, publishers could track sales better today than they did previously. They also could make better forecasts about how well books would do, but even the experienced ones still made mistakes.

The number of publishers had been declining as large media companies and global conglomerates swallowed up smaller companies.[27] The five big publishers sold books under a variety of imprints, many of which bore the labels of once-thriving publishing houses. In order of their size, here were the Big Five:

1. Penguin Random House (about $4.1 billion in sales in 2011). This company was 47 percent Penguin and 53 percent Random House. It is the result of a merger between the UK Penguin Group, which owns Pearson, and the privately held German company Bertelsmann.

2. Hachette (about $1.6 billion in sales in 2011). This French-owned company absorbed Little, Brown & Company and Time Warner Book Group.

3. HarperCollins (about $1.2 billion in sales in 2011). This company is owned by Rupert Murdoch's conglomerate, News Corporation.

4. Macmillan (about $.9 billion in sales in 2011). This company was started in the UK but now has German owners, the Verlagsgruppe Georg von Holtzbrinck group, and it consists of such imprints as Palgrave Macmillan, Farrar, Straus and Giroux, and St Martin's.

5. Simon & Schuster (about $.8 billion in sales in 2011). CBS owns this prestigious New York publisher.

The Spat with Amazon

Book retailers, like Barnes & Noble, charged publishers promotional fees for prominently placing their books. Publishers also paid Amazon such fees to feature their books on its home page.[28] As Amazon gained power as a major book outlet, it raised the price of these fees. It took this route to increase its profitability as opposed to raising book prices and hurting sales.

Amazon's pressure on the publishers made it harder for them to do well financially, but they had little choice but to rely on Amazon. One of the motives for the ongoing consolidation of publishers was to gain bargaining power against Amazon. Another tactic they used was to reduce authors' earnings. When Amazon set the price of e-books at $9.99, it put the publishers in a bind. How would they pauy authors? They could do little initially since in 2010 Amazon held 90 percent of the market for e-book distribution.

The publishers worked out a deal with Apple to bypass Amazon for Apple and set prices on their own at the levels they wanted. The only holdout was Random House, which at that time was separate from Penguin, but in 2012 the U.S. Federal Trade Commission struck down this deal, and the Justice Department sued Apple and the five publishers for conspiring to raise prices and restraining trade. Macmillan had to pay $20 million in damages and Penguin $75 million. Apple, confronting up to $840 million in damages, appealed. Meanwhile, Amazon's share of the e-book market fell, plateauing at about 65 percent, with Barnes & Noble and Apple picking up most of the rest.

The government took the side of readers, wishing to guarantee them low prices, and not the publishers, who produced books and paid the authors. The tension between the publishers and Amazon remained ongoing and was subject to continuing tense negotiations. In the most noteworthy of these conflicts, Amazon withheld selling Hachette books for a time in 2015 before Hachette and Amazon came to an agreement.

Conclusion

Fortune's May 2003 cover story featured Jeff Bezos, founder, chair, and CEO of Amazon, jumping on a trampoline. It remarked that during the Internet bubble Bezos's "oversized personality made him seem fun and inspiring," but when Amazon's losses mounted, his behavior makes him look "clueless."[29] Amazon had evolved from a retailer to a commerce platform, department store mall, and service provider on the Web. What direction should Amazon take next? It had so many options.

Bezos bet that Amazon stood for high-quality customer service over the Web and that this service would attract customers regardless of what Amazon sold. If Amazon became the Walmart of the Internet, then Barnes & Noble's narrow focus—its commitment to books—could serve as a unique advantage. Barnes & Noble, however, was hedging its bets, too. It remained committed not only to books, but to a reading device, the Nook, despite its poor performance and lack of profitability. Barnes & Noble was also exploring what it should do next.

Was the book industry simply an unattractive one that both firms should leave? What changes should they introduce into the industry to make it more hospitable? Was a subscription service like Amazon Prime the answer?[30] Amazon was betting heavily on Prime. Did Barnes & Noble have an answer?

Endnotes

1. Alfred Marcus, *Winning Moves.* Lombard, IL: Marsh Press, 2009.

2. Todd Leopold, "The Death and Life of a Great American Bookstore," *CNN.* Sept. 12, 2011. http://edition.cnn.com/2011/US/09/12/first.borders.bookstore.closing/.

3. Marcus, *Winning Moves*; Also see Jeffrey F. Rayport and Dickson L. Louie "BarnesAndNoble.com (B) and (C)," Case Study. Boston: Harvard Business Publishing, February 2001.

4. Pankaj Ghemawat and Bret Baird, "Leadership Online: Barnes & Noble Vs. Amazon.Com (A)," Case Study. Boston: Harvard Business Publishing, April 2000. Stig Leschly, Michael Roberts, and William Sahlman, "Amazon.Com—2002," Case Study. Boston: Harvard Business Publishing, February 2003.

5. Rob Norton, "Why the Bookstore Wars Are Good," *Fortune.* Oct. 27, 1997. http://archive.fortune.com/magazines/fortune/fortune_archive/1997/10/27/233299/index.htm.

6. Marcus, *Winning Moves.*

7. Pankaj Ghemawat and Bret Baird, "Leadership Online: Barnes & Noble Vs. Amazon.Com (A)."

8. David Bahn and Patrick Fischer, "Clicks and Mortar," Metropolitan State University of Minnesota, Unpublished Manuscript, 2002.

9. Ibid.

10. Fred Vogelstein, "Mighty Amazon," *Fortune* 26 May 2003. http://archive.fortune.com/magazines/fortune/fortune_archive/2003/05/26/343082/index.htm; Robert Hof and Heather Green, "How Amazon Cleared That Hurdle," *Business Week.* Feb. 4, 2002. http://www.bloomberg.com/bw/stories/2002-02-03/how-amazon-cleared-the-profitability-hurdle.

11. Robert Hof, "Jeff Bezos' Risky Bet," *Business Week.* Nov. 13, 2006. http://www.bloomberg.com/bw/stories/2006-11-12/jeff-bezos-risky-bet.

12. Jeffrey Trachtenbergy, "Title Role: Barnes & Noble Pushes Books from Ambitious Publisher: Itself," *The Wall Street Journal.* June 18, 2003. http://www.wsj.com/articles/SB105588208069899900.

13. Marcus, *Winning Moves.*

14. James Covert, "Barnes & Noble Swings to a Loss; Books Retailer Blames Heavy Discounting, Warns of Weak Profit," *The Wall Street Journal.* May 25, 2007. http://www.wsj.com/articles/SB118001145703313367.

15. Verne Kopytoff, "The Indie Bookstore Resurgence," *Fortune.* Sept. 20, 2013. http://fortune.com/2013/09/20/the-indie-bookstore-resurgence/; Peter Osnos, "How 'Indie' Bookstores Survived (and Thrived)," *The Atlantic.* Dec. 2, 2013. http://www.theatlantic.com/business/archive/2013/12/how-indie-bookstores-survived-and-thrived/281974/.

16. Leopold, "The Death and Life of a Great American Bookstore."

17. George Packer, "Cheap Words: Amazon Is Good for Customers. But Is It Good for Books?" *New Yorker.* Feb. 17, 2014. http://www.newyorker.com/magazine/2014/02/17/cheap-words.

18. Ibid.

19. Frank Konkel, "Big Win for Amazon: First Provider Authorized to Handle Sensitive DOD Workloads in Cloud," *Nextgov*. Aug. 21, 2014. http://www.nextgov.com/cloud-computing/2014/08/big-win-amazon-first-provider-authorized-handle-sensitive-dod-workloads/92069/.

20. Marcus, *Winning Moves.*

21. See the website for Amazon Web Services (AWS): https://aws.amazon.com/?nc2=h_lg.

22. Ramkumar Iyer, "Barnes & Noble to Keep Nook Business, Spin Off College Books Unit," *Reuters*. Feb. 26, 2015. http://www.reuters.com/article/2015/02/26/us-barnes-noble-divestiture-idUSKBN0LU1NE20150226>; Matthew Townsend, Barnes & Noble to Spin Off College-Bookstore Business," Bloomberg Business Week. Feb. 26, 2015. http://www.bloomberg.com/news/articles/2015-02-26/barnes-noble-to-separate-college-unit-from-retail-chain-nook.

23. Jim Milliot, "Unit Sales Inched Up in First Half of 2015," *Publishers Weekly*. July 3, 2015. http://www.publishersweekly.com/pw/by-topic/industry-news/bookselling/article/67394-unit-sales-inched-up-in-first-half-of-2015.html; Jim Milliot, "Industry Sales Rose 4.6% in 2014," *Publishers Weekly*. June 10, 2015. http://www.publishersweekly.com/pw/by-topic/industry-news/financial-reporting/article/67074-industry-sales-rose-4-6-in-2014.html.

24. Kathryn Zickuhr and Lee Rainie, "A Snapshot of Reading in America in 2013," *Pew Research Center*. Jan. 16, 2014. http://www.pewinternet.org/2014/01/16/a-snapshot-of-reading-in-america-in-2013/.

25. Ibid.

26. Marcus, *Winning Moves.*

27. Valerie Peterson, "The Big Five Trade Book Publishers" *About.com* n.d. http://publishing.about.com/od/BookPublishingGeneralInfo/a/The-Big-Five-Trade-Book-Publishers.htm.

28. Packer, "Cheap Words: Amazon Is Good for Customers. But Is It Good for Books?"

29. Fred Vogelstein, "Mighty Amazon."

30. Marcus Wohlsen. "Amazon Prime Is One of the Most Bizarre Good Business Ideas Ever," *Wired*. Feb. 9, 2015. http://www.wired.com/2015/02/amazon-prime-one-bizarre-good-business-ideas-ever/

12

Escaping the Middle:
Best Buy and Charles Schwab

B est Buy and Charles Schwab were middle-of-the-road competitors that needed to nurture more distinctiveness. Best Buy could not match Amazon's online experience, nor could it equal the uniqueness of Apple's products and the excitement that Apple's stores generated, or offer the same low prices as Walmart.[1] Although its net income was higher than Amazon's (see Exhibit 12.1), it was falling behind these competitors on a number of key dimensions, including growth in revenues and gross margins in the second quarter of 2015.

Exhibit 12.1   Financial Performance of Best Buy and Its Main Competitors, 2nd Quarter 2015

	Best Buy	Amazon	Apple	Walmart
Net Income (billion $)	.814	−406	47.81	15.84
Qtrly Rev Growth (%)	−0.01	0.15	0.27	−0.00
Gross Margin (%)	0.22	0.30	0.40	0.25
Operating Margin (%)	0.04	0.00	0.30	0.05
Revenue (billion $)	40.26	91.96	212.16	485.52
Employees	125,000	154,100	92,600	2,200,000
Market Cap (billion $)	11.76	203.06	725.89	233.59

Data source: Quarterly financial reports

Charles Schwab was neither a premier full-service investment bank like Goldman Sachs and Morgan Stanley, nor a small discount broker like TD Ameritrade or E*Trade (see Exhibit 12.2).[2] Charles Schwab's second-quarter 2015 revenue growth did not come close to the revenue growth of Goldman Sachs or Morgan Stanley, although it exceeded that of TD Ameritrade and E*Trade. Its gross margins were the best among these firms, but its operating margins were behind those of TD Ameritrade and E*Trade.

Exhibit 12.2 Financial Performance of Charles Schwab and Its Main Competitors, 2nd Quarter 2015

	Charles Schwab	Goldman Sachs	Morgan Stanley	TD Ameritrade	E*Trade
Net Income (billion $)	1.23	8.85	4.04	.802	.236
Qtrly Rev Growth (%)	0.03	0.14	0.12	−0.02	−0.04
Gross Margin (%)	0.96	0.91	0.90	0.92	0.91
Operating Margin (%)	0.34	0.40	0.27	0.40	0.35
Revenue (billion $)	6.03	35.82	35.30	3.15	1.76
Market Cap	42.69B	89.88B	76.54B	20.10B	8.50B
Employees	14,900	34,400	56,087	5,895	3,221

Data source: Quarterly financial reports

As neither pure premium nor pure discount players, Best Buy and Charles Schwab were stuck in the middle. They needed to find ways to distinguish themselves. To what extent could they stand out?

The Evolution of Best Buy

Best Buy had gone through many evolutions since 1983 when it adopted the name Best Buy and became a discount retailer.[3] The ferociously competitive environment of retail electronics fueled each of its changes.[4] Best Buy had continually fine-tuned its approach of offering not just best prices, but the best value for the money. Some of its competitors were able to match its low prices. Other competitors were able to equal it on differentiation, but none could do both. Best Buy's goal was to combine these elements in an attractive value-for-the-money package.

Early on, Best Buy's top executives realized that price slashing by itself was not going to lead to success; in fact, continuous price wars were disastrous. Budget-minded consumers expected low prices, but that was not all they wanted. They were looking for knowledgeable service, fast checkout, interesting selection, and an exciting in-store atmosphere. They wanted a distinctive experience that would lead them to come back to the store again and again. As the percentage of retail sales based on discounts rose from 8 percent in 1971 to more than 80 percent after 2002, low prices simply were not that relevant.[5] Discounting was so common that customers took it for granted, and it no longer translated into brisk business expansion. Best Buy's evolution went through five stages.

Concept One: 1983–1989

Best Buy began as a high-quality audio electronics store called Sound of Music. Its name change, in 1983, signified the new format under which the company would operate, as a superstore with more floor space, greater product selection, and better prices. The company added new products, such as video equipment, microwave ovens, major appliances, and cameras. With higher-volume sales, it achieved economies of scale in such areas as advertising and distribution and gained greater clout over suppliers.

Concept Two: 1990–2001

The next stage in Best Buy's evolution was to move toward combining the best of the specialty retailer it had been (Sound of Music) with the best of the mass-merchant retailer it had become. It was fixated on creating the unique shopping experience that would differentiate it from its competitors. The company surveyed customers and found out that they wanted an enjoyable shopping experience in which they did not feel pressured to buy. Best Buy created a low-pressure selling environment by eliminating its commissioned sales force and using salaried workers instead. Rather than just low-priced products, it brought back value products in select categories, selling what it called "commodity" and "myth" items. Commodities, such as modestly priced PCs and household appliances, yielded sales volume and appealed to the customer's intellect. Myth items, such as plasma TVs and camcorders, resulted in higher profits and appealed to a customer's emotions. Together, commodities and myths increased interest in the stores and upped the traffic level.

By 1996, Best Buy had become the largest specialty retailer in the United States, but its profits were at a five-year low. The company had to place renewed emphasis on profitability. To do so, it pushed harder on both sides of the hybrid paradigm—commodity and myth—by upgrading the product mix with additional profitable categories and enhancing the in-store environment with more interactive opportunities and hands-on experiences. There were demonstrations of products in the stores, a new store layout, and a number of displays featuring upscale products.

At this point in time, Best Buy divided its customers into the following segments:

- Value-driven shoppers, the largest group (32 percent), were price conscious. They checked ads, waited for prices to come down, did comparison shopping, and bargained over warranties.

- Techno-savvy entertainment consumers, the next largest group (26 percent), wanted to buy what was newest and had the most features. Price was not the main consideration.

- Older customers (23 percent) required considerable handholding. They were intimidated by new technology and needed assistance in making their purchases. Service was more important to them than price.

- Pragmatic buyers (19 percent) looked for trusted brands and reliable service. They did not have the time or interest in a prolonged shopping experience.

Best Buy tried to appeal to each of these customer groups.

Under concept two, the company also took the following initiatives:

- It expanded the appliance department.

- It improved inventory management.

- It simplified the stores.

- It achieved tighter relationships with vendors.

- It reduced shrinkage (employee theft).

- It enhanced employee development and training.

- It introduced an extended service plan, sold at a 30-percent discount in comparison to price of its main competitor at the time, Circuit City.

Concept Three: 2002–2007

The following stage came after a string of successes. With the downturn in the U.S. economy in the early 2000s, the company hit a rough spot. It erred in buying Musicland Group (Sam Goody, Media Play, and On Cue stores), a mall-based entertainment software and music retailer. Consumer confidence plummeted with the economy's downturn, and Best Buy had large losses at Musicland. Brad Anderson took over from Best Buy's founder and chairman Richard Schulze as CEO of the company in the summer of 2002, and in 2003 he sold Musicland to a Florida-based private investment firm.[6]

Anderson concluded that because it was hard to get additional PC sales, there had to be renewed emphasis on exciting products. Digital technology was taking off. Anderson also wanted the company to offer additional services and to have a new loyalty program and a better website. He initiated an advertising campaign that called attention to the value-added information that Best Buy's sales associates provided. Another initiative was a joint venture with Black Box to install data, voice, video, and audio cables in new houses.

Best Buy updated its stores. With a new design, the stores had wide center aisles and bright overhead signs with slogans like *Fulfillment* and *Simplicity* and offered fast-growing, high-margin digital goods front and center. A single queue fed multiple lanes of customers. Customers were able to complete complex purchases at separate transaction spots. The store itself continued to be one of the ways in which Best Buy tried to differentiate itself.

The Geek Squad, too, was a differentiator. Geek Squad technicians provide 24-hour computer service from Best Buy stores, online, and in customer homes. Best Buy made good money from repairs by the Geek Squad of items such as home theater systems and wall-mounted televisions. Still another feature that differentiated Best Buy was in-store kiosks that sold mobile phones and mobile phone plans.

Finally, Best Buy introduced a strategy of meeting the individual needs of customers through a program called "customer centricity," aimed at five customer segments, with each store supposed to adapt to serve one or more of these segments:

- *Affluent professionals* who want the best in technology and entertainment and who demand excellent service

- *Active, young males* who seek the latest technology and equipment

- *Practical family men* who want technologies that improve their lives

- *Busy suburban moms* who desire to enrich their children's lives

- *Small business owners* who aim to use technology to enhance the productivity of their businesses.

A main reason for customer centricity was to differentiate Best Buy from Walmart.[7] In contrast to Best Buy, Walmart encouraged employees to relate to customers using a WALK method: **W**elcome a customer, **A**sk questions, **L**earn needs, and **K**now when to close. In other words, get customers to buy as quickly as possible and relate to them no further. This approach worked well with low-end consumer electronic products that did not require much explanation, installation, or setup. After closing the sale, Walmart kept customer contact to a minimum.

These moves, however, did not spare Best Buy from price erosion. Profitability was hard to maintain. Many of Best Buy's stores did not fully convert to customer centricity. Tests of the model showed sales gains of 7 percent in comparison to similar stores. However, the sales gains came at a price. Whereas gross profits increased by 50 percent, selling, general, and administrative expenses grew by 240 percent.

As of 2007, the company operated 917 Best Buy stores, 13 Magnolia Audio Video stores (specializing in high-end electronics), seven standalone Geek Squad stores, three Audio-Vision stores, and 17 Pacific Sales stores (in Southern California). It also operated 51 Best Buy and 128 Future Shop stores throughout Canada, one Best Buy store in Shanghai, and 151 Five Star Appliance stores in China. In 2007, the company faced the problem of falling margins at the same time that it had few additional opportunities for U.S. growth.

Expanding abroad did not alleviate the problem because the squeeze on margins abroad was just as acute. Best Buy ultimately got out of Canada and China, downsized some of its stores, and decided to place others in urban areas.

The Aftermath of the Financial Meltdown

In 2007, flat-panel televisions, MP3 players, digital cameras, GPS devices, and video games sold well, with U.S. consumers spending more than $150 billion on such merchandise.[8] However, the financial meltdown and the recession followed, and Best Buy's sales growth slowed considerably. Best Buy reduced its profit and revenue forecasts for 2008 because of the weak economy.[9] Its main competitor, Circuit City, was struggling.[10] In 2008, Circuit City announced that it would close 155 stores and lay off 17 percent of its workforce, and in 2009 it filed for bankruptcy and went out of existence. RadioShack, another consumer electronics retailer, was on shaky ground as well and was looking for a buyout partner, although such a partner did not appear.

With Circuit City's bankruptcy, Walmart became Best Buy's main competitor. The big-box discount chain expanded its merchandise to include items previously offered only by specialty retailers. It was an easy and familiar place for customers to shop. By providing the opportunity to buy nearly everything a person might need under one roof, it attracted a broad group of consumers. By 2007, Walmart had more than 15 percent of the U.S. retail market for consumer electronics and an estimated $31 billion in revenues in the segment, second only to Best Buy, which had 25 percent of the market.[11] Best Buy remained committed to a brick-and-mortar strategy of opening new stores, but these expansion plans became more and more risky. The company pinned its hopes on the federal government's stimulus package reviving the U.S. economy.

The Evolution of Charles Schwab

In positioning itself as a discount seller and at the same time a company that could help a client find premium services, Charles Schwab was like Best Buy in many ways.

Discounting

An upstart that fought the major Wall Street players, Charles Schwab pushed industry boundaries from its inception in the 1970s.[12] The company was among the first discount brokerages to take advantage of the end of fixed-rate commissions. Breaking with the full-service model of investment banks and eliminating advice, it gave clients the ability to make their own decisions.[13] Like Best Buy, Charles Schwab introduced a salaried sales force, one not made up of brokers who earned commissions from passing on tips to clients, but rather of brokers who took orders from clients. A salaried sales force was less expensive to maintain than a commissioned sales force and gave Charles Schwab the leeway to offer deep discounts on client transactions that could not be matched by the full-service brokerage firms.

High Net Worth Clients

However, Charles Schwab also tried to attract the profitable business of high-net-worth individuals usually assisted by full-service brokerage firms.[14] In this way as well, it overlapped with Best Buy in that it had an inexpensive commodity stock trading business, yet it also had myth-type products and services it offered to high-net-worth individuals. Charles Schwab did not hire a staff of full-time financial advisers like the full-service brokerages, but instead referred clients who wanted more handholding than it could provide to affiliated account managers for whom it provided the back-office technology. By providing them with this technology, Charles Schwab earned a slice of the affiliated account managers' business.

Charles Schwab had a great run during the bull market of the 1990s. In 1998, at the height of the Internet economy, it was the most highly capitalized firm in the industry. It even exceeded the valuation of Morgan Stanley.[15] The stock market rewarded it for its innovations. After the stock market bubble burst in the year 2000, the financial services industry as a whole faced a difficult environment of economic uncertainty and waning trust. Unaffected by the conflicts of interests afflicting the full-service brokerages that handled the investment banking needs of companies they recommended to clients, Charles Schwab bought a full-service investment firm, U.S. Trust, but the marriage with U.S. Trust did not work out, and by 2006 Charles Schwab divested the company.[16]

A Category of One

Charles Schwab referred to itself as "a category of one."[17] There were full-service brokers, like Goldman Sachs and Morgan Stanley, and discount brokers, like TD Ameritrade, E*Trade, and Scottrade. Charles Schwab fell somewhere in the middle.

The company decided to divide its customers into three main categories:

- *Self-directed* investors were generation-X people (21–35 year olds) with investments under $100,000.
- *Validators* were baby boomers (36–55 year olds) with investments between $100,000 and $1 million.
- *Delegators* were mature investors (>56 year olds) with investments above $1 million.

Charles Schwab reasoned that *self-directed* investors were looking for unbiased information and tools and wanted to manage their money by themselves, *validators* made their own decisions but were looking for some consultation, and *delegators* wanted a lot of help in managing their money.

The Affluent of the Future

Charles Schwab's aim was to capture the business of all three groups. In doing so it would appeal to the affluent of the future. The affluent of the future shared a number of characteristics: they were highly educated, held higher paying executive or professional jobs or business ownership, and had the possibility of accumulating large amounts of assets over a lifetime of work. Compared to other groups in the population, the affluent of the future were self-directed. They had upbeat outlooks and a tolerance for risk. Members of this group:

- Read a lot and worked hard.

- Valued marriage and were less likely to be divorced.

- Tried to take care of themselves; a very high percentage belonged to health clubs.

- Often lived in cities with more than two million in population on the East and West Coasts.

- Were sociable and optimistic and were involved with technology; they were also hungry for convenience and looking for innovation.

Seeking collaborative advice from a financial services provider, the affluent of the future were seeking the technological tools that would put them in control. They wanted to be independent and active participants in the management of their own money. They were looking for ways to aggregate all their financial transactions with one adviser. Charles Schwab's goal was to provide high-quality service at an affordable price that was designed to empower such investors with the information and technological tools they needed to make good, informed decisions. Its advertising and marketing emphasized putting its client in control of the client's investments, while the company was confined to being a trusted, neutral adviser.

Following Customers

Charles Schwab built its business on its understanding of how this core group of customers changed over time. When Charles Schwab saw its clients moving to mutual funds, it rushed into this breach. The problem was that clients had a dizzying array of choices. Charles Schwab, therefore, brought customers and mutual fund companies together by means of a business model it called a "switchboard." The switchboard meant that Charles Schwab operated independently of any single mutual fund company. It was neutral and objective and could bring its clients the best products and best advice. In every category of product—insurance, banking, retirement services, and so on—the company tried to apply this model of bringing the best advice to customers without being biased toward any asset class or company.

New Challenges

Best Buy and Charles Schwab were pioneers that had revolutionized the retail and brokerage industries in the past. However, the success formulas that previously worked for them were no guarantee of success in the future. They faced considerable challenges going forward as new concepts were needed in their industries for them to continue to thrive.

Competition in Consumer Electronics

With Circuit City out of the picture, Best Buy's three biggest competitors in consumer electronics were Walmart, Amazon, and Apple. It also confronted a number of other companies like Target, Dell, and RadioShack. Best Buy competed with Walmart on only some product lines. It competed with Amazon on virtually all its product lines. In overall retail sales, Best Buy was far behind Walmart. As a consumer electronics retailer, Best Buy was quite large, but in retailing in general it was not a particularly big company.

Online

Amazon was the undisputed e-commerce leader, but Walmart outpaced Best Buy in selling on the Internet as well. In 2014, Walmart's Internet sales grew faster than Amazon's.[18] Next to Amazon, Walmart obtained the highest number of monthly unique site visitors. Best Buy was not among the top 10 U.S. Internet retailers in the United States. More so than Walmart, Best Buy remained a traditional brick-and-mortar retailer and had not made the transition to an online world. Best Buy had to compete better online as online sales continued to grow. According to the U.S. Census Bureau, online sales accounted for 16.2 percent of total retail sales in the third quarter of 2014.[19]

Best Buy's online failures were surprising. The many initiatives it took did not yield success.[20]

- In 1999, Best Buy launched an online website.

- In 2006, it partnered with RealNetworks' Rhapsody and SanDisk to create a Digital Music Store. It acquired Speakeasy, one of the largest U.S. independent broadband voice data information technology service providers, in 2007.

- In 2007, the company also set up Best Buy Video Sharing, an online-based way for customers to store and share home movies and videos on the Web.

- In 2008, it completed the nationwide rollout of Best Buy Mobile.

- In the same year, it acquired Napster, the online provider of digital music. However, Rhapsody bought Napster from Best Buy in 2011.

- In 2013, Best Buy partnered with a number of major Hollywood studios to offer a disc-to-digital conversion service.

Although Best Buy made many moves in the online domain, it did not execute them well. It did not have a coherent online vision or strategy. Best Buy was losing in the clicks-versus-bricks battle. Integrating the two was a major challenge. Online selling gained in popularity because consumers preferred its convenience and low prices. Best Buy's more than 800 brick-and-mortar stores were a liability in comparison to less expensive online selling. They had high overhead and maintenance costs.

Showrooming

Showrooming, a phenomenon in which customers came into Best Buy stores to check out products and gain hands-on experience with gadgets but then made actual purchases online from a cheaper retailer, was negatively affecting Best Buy.[21] As online shopping exploded and smartphones became the norm, consumers routinely used their phones to comparison shop, even while in a physical store. A retailer could not demand that people browsing in its store deposit their phones for safekeeping before they went into the aisles. Consumers engaged in showrooming to have a closer look at a product's features before buying it. Home delivery, online discounts and rewards, convenience, and low prices were motivations that led them to make their final purchases online rather than in-store.

Showrooming negatively impacted the sales of many brick-and-mortar retailers. All brick-and-mortar retailers confronted this threat, but it affected Best Buy in particular because the practice was extremely common among its customers.[22] Among the categories of products affected the most by showrooming, consumer electronics were at the top of the list, and showrooming was more common in the consumer electronics trade than in any other product category including apparel, books, and appliances. Seventy-two percent of men and 56 percent of women surveyed showroomed for consumer electronics.

Competition Among Discount Brokers

Charles Schwab and the other discount brokers also had online challenges. In the recession that followed the financial meltdown of 2007, traders vigorously searched for ways to lower their costs. To spur the expansion of their businesses, discount brokers were willing to lower commissions.[23] However, there were limits to how far the price competition could go. The discount brokers were competing for an attractive customer group that cared not only about price, but also about the utility of the broker's online platform.

On average, their clients were younger, they traded more and traded larger sums of money, and their average household income was greater than that of other investors.

To gain a competitive edge not just based on price, the brokers invested more in their online trading platforms.[24] These investments took many forms. Some firms tried to increase the speed of transactions. Other discount brokers introduced mobile device applications. Nearly all the discount brokers also invested in sophisticated forecasting tools and relied heavily on software suppliers and IT consultants to assist them.

Innovation Dilemmas

The brand image of the brokers was wrapped up in these platforms, which allowed them to differentiate themselves beyond just price. Competition along these dimensions of price and the distinctiveness of their platforms created dilemmas. The firms had to balance how much they spent on technology development to have the upper hand versus how much they discounted to remain attractive to shoppers who had access to price-comparison tools and information at their fingertips.

Major Industry Players

The four largest discount brokers (Schwab, TDAmeritrade, Scottrade, and E*Trade) accounted for more than 40 percent of the segment's revenue.[25] However, the industry was easy to enter, and new companies with strong trading platforms specializing in different types of investments entered it regularly. After the great financial meltdown of 2007, confidence in the stock market tanked, and trading volume decreased. Consolidation took place as Ameritrade purchased TD Waterhouse.

Charles Schwab was the largest of the discount brokers. Its financial strength allowed it to cut the rates for online trades in 2010, yet it was not keeping up with the other brokers in the perceived quality of its online platform, nor was it able to keep up with Scottrade's discounting.[26] Unlike the other major discount brokers, Scottrade was a privately held company. It had more leeway in the discounts it could offer and was an aggressive discounter. TD Ameritrade, the second-largest discount broker, had augmented its Internet trading services. Like Charles Schwab, it also had brick-and-mortar branches. Its online applications for the self-directed investor included trademarked in-house products. It had desktop and mobile trading software that provided streaming quotes and gave its clients access to foreign-exchange markets as well as specialized automated online tools for trading equities, futures, options, exchange traded funds (ETFs), and bonds. All the discount brokers regularly upgraded their trading platforms and improved the number of products and services they offered online to give traders enhanced market information and better tracking tools. They made these moves while trying to keep prices as low as possible.

Best Buy's Comeback Plans

In 2012, Brian Dunn had to resign as CEO of Best Buy because of alleged improprieties with a female employee. After a period of time with an interim CEO, Hubert Joly, who had been the CEO of the Carlson Companies, became Best Buy's top executive.[27] Joly's first move was a stopgap measure to try to prevent showrooming. The company guaranteed it would match the price offered by any local retailer and 19 major online retailers, including Amazon, Apple, Dell, HP, Sears, Staples, and Walmart. In 2013, Best Buy spent millions of dollars on a pre-Christmas TV campaign against showrooming that included celebrity storytellers. Joly then introduced a comprehensive plan to turn Best Buy around.

Transforming E-Commerce

Accelerating growth in the online segment was a key priority for Best Buy.[28] It aimed to update its website to make it the equal of Amazon and its other competitors. It had more than one billion annual online visitors, but only one in every 100 visitors made a purchase. Best Buy's goal was to increase both web traffic and web conversion rates. Its online sales, which accounted for approximately 13 percent of its sales in 2014, had grown by more than double digits in the previous three years. However, among brick-and-mortar competitors, its online market share remained low.

Shipping from Stores

Best Buy's analyses showed that that 2–4 percent of its online traffic did not yield a purchase because inventory was not available in its distribution centers. However, 80 percent of the time, the missing items could be found in one or more of its retail stores. These calculations suggested that it made sense to route the shipping of merchandise from its stores. The company's pilot trial of this concept in 50 stores was successful enough to move the ship-from-store concept to virtually all stores. This change made it possible for the company to deliver items two days faster than previously. An important side benefit was that this concept took inefficient slack out of its system and helped to streamline inventory management.

Improving the E-Commerce Platform

Best Buy also attempted to improve its e-commerce platform by introducing new search elements, an optimized search engine, better searching tools, more suitable recommendations to specific classes of customers, and more accurate product price and value comparisons, among other improvements. The aim was to assist customers in more easily locating products they wanted to buy. Other initiatives it took to make the shopping experience on the website better were improved design, a more robust and streamlined wish list, richer visual and editorial content, and enhanced navigation as well as interactive shopping and precise, useful recommendations based on customers' browsing history.

Best Buy was trying to make its product search capabilities not only more navigable, but also more consistent across the different devices a customer might use. The company transferred promotional spending from print and television to online channels. It detected some signs of improvement; in the first quarter of 2015, domestic online revenue grew 29.2 percent.[29]

Reverse Showrooming

Showrooming turned out to not be the threat Best Buy thought because a reverse dynamic was also common among shoppers. Many shoppers consulted online before making in-store purchases. A Harris poll showed that 69 percent of American reverse-showroomed, whereas only 49 percent did the opposite.[30] Millennials, in particular, preferred to research online and then buy electronics, shoes, sports equipment, and cosmetics in a store. Best Buy's challenge lay in how to meld the two tendencies and integrate the online and in-store experiences. A start was a section on its website called Best Buy Outlet, which expanded visibility of products that could be purchased online and picked up in-store. Best Buy was still working on making shopping more attractive and convenient by combining the capabilities of mobile devices with store layout.

Cost Savings and Product Innovation

Best Buy's comeback also relied on many cost-saving initiatives. In 2012 and 2013, earnings were out of balance with revenue, and it began to close underperforming U.S. stores, shut down unprofitable operations in China, Europe, and Canada, shrink the workforce, make efforts to better manage inventory, and introduce supply-chain-efficiency initiatives, among others. By the end of the third quarter in 2014, the company generated cost reductions of $965 million.

Best Buy was heavily dependent on its suppliers to come up with exciting new products that its customers wanted. However, there had been limited innovation in the consumer electronics industry in such products as televisions, computers, and gaming; prices were declining; and customers regularly undertook comparison shopping on the Internet.

Best Buy's revenue mix was composed of six product categories: (i) consumer electronics; (ii) computing and mobile phones; (iii) entertainment; (iv) appliances; (v) services; and (vi) other. The computing and mobile phone category, which included laptops, desktop computers, tablets, mobile phones, and related accessories, was the largest, making up 48 percent of the company's revenues. The consumer electronics category, which included TVs, home theaters, digital cameras, DVD players, MP3 devices, and related accessories, was next, at 30 percent of revenues. Entertainment (video gaming, DVDs, CDs, Blu-ray, and computer software), appliances, services, and other, which included programs for installing home energy-efficiency equipment and devices and musical instruments sold in many of its stores, accounted for the remainder of the company's revenue.

Best Buy had a number of its own in-house brands and labels. They were Insignia for high-end electronics; Dynex, which offered HDTVs, Blu-ray players, and office supplies; Init, which sold furniture and home storage products; and Rocketfish, which was involved in home theater installation and gaming. The profit margins on the in-house brands were high, and Best Buy intended to expand their availability.

Other opportunities existed for innovation in new sets of products, such as these:

- 3D printers
- 4K ultra-high-definition televisions
- Connected thermostats
- Unmanned systems, such as unmanned aerial vehicle and home robots
- IP (Internet protocol) cameras
- Wearables, such as health and fitness devices, smartwatches, and smart eyewear

However, there were risks involved in moving in these directions because, as opposed to staples, almost all of these products were discretionary purchases and were therefore sensitive to changes in the economic cycle.

Best Buy also reserved large sections of its stores for Apple products. It had "stores within stores" for high-end electronics, its Magnolia Design Centers, and appliances, like Pacific Kitchen and Homes. The company had kiosks where it sold phones and phone plans. It aimed to expand the store-within-a-store concept to two of its main suppliers, Samsung and Microsoft, which had virtually no stores of their own. Best Buy partnered with Samsung to open 1,400 Samsung stores-within-a-store called Samsung Experience Shops and reached a similar arrangement with Microsoft to open 400 of these to sell Windows products. These would allow Best Buy's suppliers to interact directly with customers using dedicated in-store sales consultants.

Enhancing the Internet Platform: Charles Schwab

Customers often decided to go with one broker over another based on the features available on their platforms. Charles Schwab had technologies that made it easier and more convenient for investors to manage their accounts, but they did not make the company stand out. Charles Schwab needed a stronger online presence.

Ranking the Platforms

Barron's Magazine annually ranked brokers' platforms, applying criteria like technology usability, research, service, and costs.[31] A broker got a maximum of five points in eight different categories for a total of 40 points. In the 2014 rating, TD Ameritrade (ranking of 34.1) and E*Trade (ranking of 30.8) had better ratings than Charles Schwab (29.6). Charles Schwab did better than Scottrade (26.3). TD Ameritrade rated best in long-term trading. Ameritrade did better than Charles Schwab in frequent trades, E*Trade fared better in international trades, and TD Ameritrade, E*Trade, and Scottrade fared better for novices. Charles Schwab, TD Ameritrade, and Scottrade tied for the best for in-person service.

Barron's highlighted the many strengths of TD Ameritrade's mobile trading platform. It worked seamlessly on multiple devices. Charts were shared across devices. Trading ideas could be tested on any platform. TD Ameritrade's mobile trading platform had powerful tools for options traders who executed bid-ask orders, a special search function, topical organization of educational programs, and a variety of high-quality, well-organized videos. Almost half of TD Ameritrade's new customers had started by downloading the mobile app and then signing up for the desktop application.

The magazine's comments about Charles Schwab were less laudable. Rather than its Internet platform, the magazine emphasized Charles Schwab's pricing policies—its $8.95 flat-rate stock trades, which were less expensive than E*Trade and TD Ameritrade's $9.99, while being more expensive than Scottrade at $7.00. *Barron's* praised the way in which Charles Schwab's platform conducted option trades and priced them. It also gave Charles Schwab high marks for the number and quality of its commission-free ETFs (182 in total). It praised the research that could be done on Charles Schwab's platform. The platform permitted users to access outside analysts (25 of them) as well as Schwab's in-house staff. *Barron's* noted that Charles Schwab was the only broker with its own equity rating system.

In contrast to TD Ameritrade, however, *Barron's* criticized Charles Schwab for not having a seamless mobile and desktop system. *Barron's* held that the mobile system was functional, but that it had few advanced features. In contrast, its desktop system had advanced features but, according to *Barron's*, required substantial learning. *Barron's* noted that although Charles Schwab had started to integrate features from optionsXpress, a company that it had acquired, including an easy-order entry system and a calculator, this process was slow. As a result, the tools on the Charles Schwab platform were not exceptional; they were improving, though.

The Robo-Advisor

Charles Schwab obviously found this evaluation disappointing. It looked to so-called robo-advising to stand out. Robo-advisors, which provided algorithm-based portfolio management methods and sometimes even automatic portfolio rebalancing and tax-loss harvesting and made use of low-cost, passive exchange-traded funds (ETFs), were beginning to attract investor interest even though some critics held that they were no better in helping investors than human advisers.[32] Other brokers as well as a number of start-ups had developed these automated online investment tools. In 2014, they attracted an estimated $20 billion in assets and were projected to attract as much as $450 billion by 2020.[33] Because they relied on algorithms, their cost was less than the cost of human financial advising.

Charles Schwab's robo-adviser was called "Institutional Intelligent Portfolios." It had a number of unique features. The most important was that it was basically a free service (except for small accounts below the free minimum), which meant that investors who used competing products were paying fees for no reason. In addition, other companies that had robo-advisers could not match what Charles Schwab offered because they did not have as complete a set of their own ETFs and had to pay for ETF access. Clients paid an ETF fee and a management fee. Charles Schwab clients did not have to pay either of these fees. These unique features gave its approach to robo-advising the potential to drive other firms out of this business.

Reviewers liked the strengths of the "Institutional Intelligent Portfolios" but pointed to some deficiencies.[34] Its benefits were absence of fees, access to Charles Schwab's ETFs, tax-loss harvesting, and automatic rebalancing. Its disadvantages had to do with the large percentage—anywhere from 6 to 30 percent—of portfolios allocated to cash. Over the long term, this allocation was likely to be a drag on an investor's earnings. Charles Schwab's marketing material claimed that the reason for the high percentage of cash was to help smooth returns, but critics held that it helped Charles Schwab make money.[35] Charles Schwab was a bank and thus made money off the cash either by investing it or lending it and charging interest.

Conclusion

Best Buy and Charles Schwab had to innovate in ways that would allow them to stand out in industries in which they were positioned in the middle. What could they do to distinguish themselves from their peers? Best Buy's challenge was melding brick-and-mortar retail and the Internet. The main issue for Charles Schwab was improving its Internet platform and robo-advisor. With cutthroat competition in retail electronics and Internet brokerages, the two companies had to figure out how to maintain a competitive edge.

Endnotes

1. Kris Hudson, "Wal-Mart Looks to Grab Gains in Gadgets," *The Wall Street Journal*. Aug. 2, 2007. http://www.wsj.com/articles/SB118602013737585673.

2. Stephen P. Bradley and Tom Esperson, "Charles Schwab: A Category of One." Case Study. Boston: Harvard Business Publishing, December 1999. Lynda M. Applegate, F. Warren McFarlan, and Jamie Ladge, "Charles Schwab in 2002," Case Study. Boston: Harvard Business Publishing, November 2002.

3. Alfred Marcus, *Winning Moves*, Lombard, IL: Marsh Press, 2009.

4. Balaji Chakravarthy and V.K. Rangan, "Best Buy." Case Study. Boston: Harvard Business Publishing, October 1997.

5. Marcus, *Winning Moves*.

6. Melissa Levy, "Best Buy CEO Marks End of First Year at Helm," *Star Tribune*. June 24, 2003: B24.; Matthew Boyle, "Best Buy's Transformative CEO." *Fortune*. March 23, 2006. Kris Hudson, "Q&A with Best Buy CEO Brad Anderson," *Fortune*. April 18, 2007.

7. Ranjay Gulati, "Inside Best Buy's Customer-Centric Strategy," *Harvard Business Review*. April 21, 2010. https://hbr.org/2010/04/inside-best-buys-customer-cent/.

8. Ian Kwok, Rhett Dornbach-Bender, and Rebecca Lange, "Strategic Report for Best Buy Co., Inc.," Oasis Consulting. April 20, 2009. http://economics-files.pomona.edu/Jlikens/Seniorseminars/Oasis/Reports/BBY.Pdf.

9. Thomas Lee, "Best Buy Hits Slump." *Star Tribune*. Feb. 15, 2008. http://www.startribune.com/best-buy-hits-slump/15663872/.

10. Kris Hudson, "Circuit City Enters New Turnaround Stage; Retailer's Response to Competition Includes Job Cuts, Store Openings." *The Wall Street Journal*. May 31, 2007. http://www.wsj.com/articles/SB118057649130319525.

11. Thomas Lee, "Best Buy Hits Slump."

12. Louise Lee and Emily Thornton, "Schwab vs. Wall Street," *Business. Week* June 2, 2002. http://www.bloomberg.com/bw/stories/2002-06-02/schwab-vs-dot-wall-street.

13. Laura Mandaro, "The Pitch by Schwab: Advice Free of Conflicts," *American Banker*. May 15, 2002. http://www.americanbanker.com/issues/167_94/-174105-1.html.

14. Lynda M. Applegate, F. Warren McFarlan, and Jamie Ladge, "Charles Schwab in 2002."

15. David M. Darst, Ann K. Rusher, and Catherine M. Conneely, "Morgan Stanley Dean Witter Private Client Services," Case Study. Boston: Harvard Business Publishing, December 1999.

16. Fred Vogelstein and Ellen Florian, "Can Schwab Get Its Mojo Back," *Fortune*. Sept. 17, 2001. http://archive.fortune.com/magazines/fortune/fortune_archive/2001/09/17/310296/index.htm.

17. Stephen P. Bradley and Tom Esperson, "Charles Schwab: A Category of One."

18. Trefis Team, "Wal-Mart Expects 30% Rise in E-Commerce Revenues This Year." *Forbes*. June 9, 2014. http://www.forbes.com/sites/greatspeculations/2014/06/09/wal-mart-expects-30-rise-in-e-commerce-revenues-this-year/.

19. Cooper Smith, "US E-Commerce Growth Is Now Far Outpacing Overall Retail Sales," *Business Insider*. April 2, 2014. http://www.businessinsider.com/us-e-commerce-growth-is-now-far-outpacing-overall-retail-sales-2014-4.

20. Market Line, "Best Buy Co., Inc." MarketLine.com. Feb. 22, 2013.

21. Michael Carney, "Showrooming Is Real, Best Buy Is the Big Loser, and Amazon Is Eating Everyone's Lunch," *Pando*. Dec. 8, 2012. https://pando.com/2012/12/08/showrooming-is-real-best-buy-is-the-big-loser-and-amazon-is-eating-everyones-lunch/.

22. Kim Bhasin, "This Chart Shows Why Best Buy Should Be Particularly Terrified of 'Showrooming,'" *Business Insider*. June 25, 2012. http://www.businessinsider.com/showroomings-consumer-electronics-best-buy-2012-6.

23. "Compare Online Brokers," *The Motley Fool* n.d. http://www.fool.com/how-to-invest/broker/.

24. Theresa W. Carey, "The Best Online Brokers of 2014," *Barron's*. March 15, 2014. http://online.barrons.com/Articles/Sb50001424053111904628504579433251867361162.

25. "The Largest Stock Broker By Market Share: Part 1 – The US," *The International Investor*. July 30, 2011. https://the-international-investor.com/2011/Largest-Stock-Broker-Market-Share.

26. Theresa W. Carey, "The Best Online Brokers of 2014."

27. Kevin Kelleher, "Best Buy: Not Your Standard Corporate Comeback," *Fortune*. June 12, 2013. http://fortune.com/2013/06/12/Best-Buy-Not-Your-Standard-Corporate-Comeback/.

28. Michael Fitzgerald, "Best Buy Battles Back Online," MIT Technology *Review*. Nov. 20, 2013. http://www.technologyreview.com/News/520821/Best-Buy-Battles-Back-Online/.

29. John Kell, "Best Buy and Four Other Blockbuster Corporate Turnarounds," *Fortune*. March 4, 2015. http://fortune.com/2015/03/04/best-buy-turnaround-stories/.

30. Emily Adler, "'Reverse Showrooming': Bricks-and-Mortar Retailers Fight Back," *Business Insider*. July 13, 2014. http://www.businessinsider.com/reverse-showrooming-bricks-and-mortar-retailers-fight-back-2-2014-2.

31. Theresa W. Carey, "The Best Online Brokers of 2014."

32. Liz Moyer, "Putting Robo Advisers to the Test," *The Wall Street Journal*. April 24, 2015. http://www.wsj.com/articles/putting-robo-advisers-to-the-test-1429887456.

33. Ibid.

34. Ibid.

35. Ibid.

13

Content for a New Age: Disney and Time Warner

D isney and Time Warner had similar business models. They combined the distribution of entertainment content by means of cable channels—for example, ESPN, which was part of Disney, and HBO, which was part of Time Warner—and the creation of such content in studios, such as Touchstone and Pixar, which were part of Disney, and New Line and Castle Rock, which were part of Time Warner. Three other large entertainment companies had similar business models:

- NBCUniversal, which was owned by Comcast, had cable channels (such as the USA Network and CNBC) and production studios (like Universal Pictures).

- Twentieth Century Fox, a spin-off of Rupert Murdoch's Newscorp, had the Fox cable networks and the production studio that bore its name.

- Viacom, which had divested CBS, had cable TV channels (such as MTV and Comedy Central) and production studios (like Paramount and DreamWorks).

Although these companies had similar business models, they applied them in different ways.

However, the Internet increasingly was becoming the medium by which people viewed entertainment. Many people had cut their ties with large cable companies like Comcast and Time Warner Cable, which Time Warner divested in 2009, and increasingly obtained content from streaming services like Netflix and Amazon Prime, viewing it on their smartphones, tablets, and other devices.[1] In the fourth quarter of 2015, Netflix added 4.33 million new subscribers worldwide, bringing its total number of subscribers to 57.4 million.[2] The estimates were that a fifth to a quarter of U.S. households subscribed to Amazon Prime and that the number was growing.[3] The cable industry, on the other hand, was no longer growing. The number of cable subscribers had peaked, and cable was starting to lose customers. Facing these circumstances in which people were changing the way they consumed entertainment, Disney, Time Warner, and their rivals had to decide what to do.

These firms also had studios that made movies and TV shows, and they competed fiercely in movie production to win the box office wars. Yet in addition to the shift away from cable, they had to battle the decline of the production studio segment of their businesses because many people simply did not go to the movies anymore, or they went less frequently. The number of tickets sold at movie theatres fell by 11 percent from 2004 to 2013.[4] Revenues were a bit higher, but only because ticket prices had increased. Raising ticket prices, however, was not sustainable because there was too much competition from other forms of entertainment, from live sports events to dining, museums, outdoor recreation, and working out at health and sports centers.

Vertical Integration: Disney

Disney established the model for vertical integration in an entertainment company consisting of many branches of distribution supporting content production (see Exhibit 13.1). It started on this road when it acquired Capital Cities in 1994, a key distribution channel, which it added to existing studios and theme parks.[5] Among the channels held by Capital Cities were ABC, which turned out to be a troubled division that never produced the results Disney expected, and ESPN, the real treasure. In 2015, ESPN provided 56 percent of Disney's profits.[6] In the prior decade, it was responsible for more than 60 percent of Disney's profit growth. For all intents and purposes, ESPN was a monopoly because people with cable company contracts expected that ESPN be part of the bundle of channels these companies offered.

ESPN had a stranglehold over the cable companies and extracted high prices from them to obtain the rights to broadcast its programs. The cable companies paid 10 times more to purchase rights to ESPN's programs in 2015 than to purchase rights to Fox Sports, ESPN's closest competitor. Buying rights to Disney programming was four times more expensive than rights to the TNT programming Time Warner offered. If the cable companies removed ESPN from the package, most people would not buy cable TV. Disney maintained that it had to regularly increase the fees paid by cable companies because of the high prices commanded by professional and college sports leagues. This programming, in turn, attracted substantial advertising revenue, which benefitted Disney and the cable companies.

Thus, led by ESPN, Disney's cable networks supported other Disney divisions. They produced the highest percentage of Disney's revenue and an even higher percentage of its net income (see Exhibit 13.1).

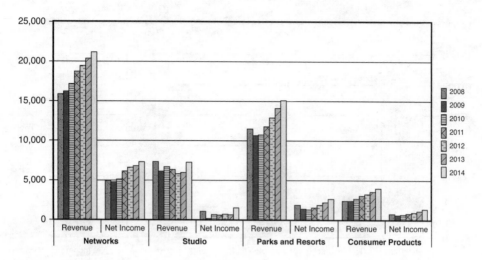

Exhibit 13.1 Disney Revenue and Net Income, 2008–2014 (in millions $)

Data based on Disney Annual Reports

Vertical Integration: Time Warner

Time Warner's vision for uniting distribution and content had been bolder than Disney's.[7] To carry it out, the company allowed AOL to use its late-1990s inflated stock valuation to buy the company. However, with the crash of the dot-com bubble in 2001, the value of Time Warner's stock dropped from $226 billion in 2000 to less than $20 billion in 2001.[8] The company reported a loss of $99 billion in 2002, at the time the largest in corporate history.[9] This turn of events was a great disappointment to Time Warner. When the deal with AOL was announced, the purpose was to tap into AOL's 130 million subscribers and use the company's high-speed cable lines to deliver its content. The content consisted not only of Time Warner's movies and TV shows, but also the magazines, books, and music it held. This content was to be delivered via the Internet to millions of American homes.

In recognizing that the Internet was the ultimate distribution channel for its content, Time Warner was ahead of its time. Distribution of content had evolved through a number of stages. Print was the first, followed by radio, movies, conventional television, and cable. Each of the stages provided people with more choices with regard to what they could watch and read. Like Disney, Time Warner's cable networks were the most profitable part of the company if not yielding the most revenue (see Exhibit 13.2). The ultimate stage in the evolution of distribution was the Internet.

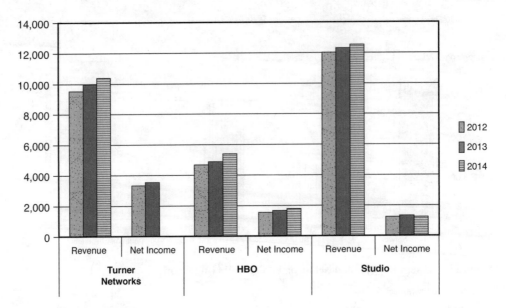

Exhibit 13.2 Time Warner Revenue and Net Income, 2012–2014 (in millions $)

Data based on Time Warner annual reports

Time Warner, however, was unable to deliver on this vision. The first reason was because the technology was not entirely ready. Fast, broadband connections that would make it possible were not universally available. In the decade after the merger, too many people continued to rely on slow dial-up connections. The second reason was internal to Time Warner: AOL's, Time Warner Cable's, and the content divisions' incessant feuding made it difficult to achieve, as these examples show.[10] AOL refused to work with *Sports Illustrated* on a plan for a massive sports site because it believed that *Sports Illustrated* did not understand the Internet. A plan to get AOL to work with *Time* also unraveled because of clashes about who would bear the cost, who would reap the profit, and who would exert control over content. AOL, more over, did not choose *Fortune, Money,* or other Time Warner publications as its partner for financial news and information but CBS Market Watch.

Mergers, Acquisitions, and Divestitures

The industry in which Time Warner and Disney competed was one in which merger, acquisition, and divestiture activity always had played a leading role.[11] In 1988, this industry was fragmented and consisted of many separate companies, including these:

- Warner, which had $3.4 billion in revenues in movies and TV production
- Time, which had $4.2 billion in revenues in publishing and cable

- Disney, which had $2.9 billion in revenues in cartoons and theme parks

- Capital Cities/ABC, which had $4.4 billion in revenues in TV and radio stations and a broadcast network

- Paramount, which had $3.2 billion in revenues in movies and publishing

- Viacom, which had $.6 billion in revenues in TV syndication and cable

- News Corp, which had $3.5 billion in revenues in tabloids and a production studio (20th Century Fox) and was starting to build a TV network (Fox)

Sony bought Columbia Pictures from Coca-Cola in 1989, and many mergers, acquisitions, and divestitures took place:

- Time and Warner merged (1991) into Time Warner, which bought Turner (1995) and was then acquired by AOL (2001).

- Disney bought Capital Cities/ABC (1995); it rebuffed a purchase bid by Comcast (2004).

- Viacom bought Paramount and Blockbuster (1993), acquired CBS (1999), and divested CBS (2007).

- GE (NBC) bought Universal Studios from Vivendi (2003), which had acquired Seagram (2001), owner of Universal (MCA)/Polygram; later it sold NBC Universal to Comcast.

- News Corp built the Fox network, and acquired the *Wall Street Journal* (2007).

With its acquisition of Capital Cities, Disney was the first company to recognize that the convergence of entertainment, computing, telecom, and information industries created a hierarchy with content, the scarcest commodity, lying at the bottom of a pyramid that fed many distribution channels. Each distribution outlet provided the opportunity to serve audiences in different ways. TV networks allowed entertainment companies to attract broad mainstream audiences. Cable channels allowed them to aggregate, bundle, and tailor their offerings to specific groups, such as children, sports enthusiasts, or devotees of travel, home improvement, history, and old movies. This allowed them to cater to even more widespread and fine-grained interests.

With new distribution outlets, the entertainment companies could hone their offerings to different groups of viewers' distinct identities and desires. The technologies of cable, satellite, and the Internet allowed the entertainment companies to meet the specific needs of a fragmented public. Advertisers preferred targeting messages to groups that were sympathetic and receptive to them rather than to indifferent, indistinct people. The national networks, like NBC, CBS, ABC, and Fox, which catered to viewers with common interests and homogenous tastes, receded in importance.

The 21st century saw continued merger-and-acquisition activity in this industry:

- Time Warner divested its music business in 2004, AOL in 2008, and Time Warner Cable in 2009.

- Disney acquired Pixar in 2006.

- News Corp divested 20th Century Fox, and Comcast bought NBCUniversal in 2013.

- Disney acquired Marvel Entertainment and Time Warner bought DC Comics in 2009.

- Disney bought Lucas film in 2012.

- Time Warner spun off its legacy magazines including *Time*, *Fortune*, and *Sports Illustrated* in 2013.

- Disney bought Maker Studios, a YouTube company in 2014.

Disney reaped the benefits of its acquisitions, strengthening its capabilities to make content, whereas Time Warner struggled and did away with many of its distribution assets. The most important asset Disney added was Pixar, which delivered hit after hit to its parent company, culminating in *Toy Story 3*, which had worldwide box office revenues of more than $1 billion (see Exhibit 13.3).[12]

Exhibit 13.3   Pixar's 20-Year String of Hits, 1995–2015

Release Date	Movie	Worldwide Box Office (millions $)
1995	*Toy Story*	364.4
1998	*A Bug's Life*	363.1
1999	*Toy Story 2*	511.3
2001	*Monsters, Inc.*	559.8
2003	*Finding Nemo*	936.4
2004	*The Incredibles*	614.7
2006	*Cars*	461.6
2007	*Ratatouille*	626.5
2008	*WALL-E*	532.6
2009	*Up*	731.5
2010	*Toy Story 3*	1,069.80
2011	*Cars 2*	560.2

Release Date	Movie	Worldwide Box Office (millions $)
2012	*Brave*	554.6
2013	*Monsters University*	743.6
2015	*Insider Out*	363.2

Compiled from data on Box Office Mojo http://www.boxofficemojo.com/

The Disney-Capital Cities Merger

At the time, the 1995 Disney-Capital Cities merger was the largest ever among media companies.[13] Disney paid handsomely for Capital Cities (22 times 1995 estimated earnings), and initially its share prices grew, but Disney earnings dropped. Growth was slow, the company's stock price plunged, and many key executives left. Post-merger culture problems were at the heart of the problem. Capital Cities had been decentralized, whereas Disney was top-down and hierarchical.

Michael Eisner, Disney's CEO and chair of its board, was considered insular and arrogant. His decision making was plodding and not appropriate to the needs of a rapidly changing business environment. He did not delegate well, nor did he grant sufficient autonomy to the company's divisions. A synergy department he created was artificial, and the internal transfer pricing mechanism he institutionalized was cumbersome. Eisner abandoned his "gong-show" method of managing creative people because these people resented having their ideas so heartily dismissed when they were asked to brainstorm for them.

Disney lost 75 of its top-level managers who decided that this environment was not the one in which they wanted to work. The company's president, Frank Wells, on whom Eisner relied, had died in a helicopter crash in 1994. Jeffrey Katzenberg, who had been the head of the animated film division, quarreled with Eisner and left the company for DreamWorks, the independent film production company Steven Spielberg started.

Disney, nonetheless, made a comeback based on movie successes Eisner had between 1985 and 1989. Disney succeeded with films like *Down and Out in Beverly Hills* (1985), *Ruthless People* (1986), *Outrageous Fortune* (1987), and *Pretty Woman* (1990). These were low-cost comedies that relied at the time on less well-known actors, writers, and directors.

Eisner also made deals to show Disney programs on cable. He brought Disney's films to the Showtime Network. Starting with *Who Framed Roger Rabbit* in 1988, Disney's animation studio also had a series of successes, including *The Little Mermaid* (1989), *Beauty and the Beast* (1991), *Aladdin* (1992), and *The Lion King* (1994). The company successfully entered the field of television animation with the well-budgeted and acclaimed series *The Adventures of the Gummi Bears*. In 1993, Disney, under Eisner, broadened its offerings to adult films with the acquisition of Miramax.

ABC

A sore point continued to be the performance of ABC. ABC had been the number-one-ranked network in number of viewers the year Disney acquired it, but after the merger, its results were disappointing. It regularly trailed NBC and CBS in the ratings. Fox supplied Disney and other networks with many of their hits as well as producing shows for its own network. Touchstone, Disney's television studio, was not producing enough good shows. Disney therefore merged Touchstone with ABC in 1999 in the hope that this merger would revive the studio. However, the merger created tension between ABC executives who chose the shows and the Touchstone executives who produced them. The ABC executives did not want to feel obligated to choose Touchstone's products, especially if they were inferior in quality, simply because they were made by a Disney affiliate.

In 1999, ABC experienced a temporary resurgence with the program *Who Wants to Be a Millionaire,* but it soon fell again to third place in the ratings. ABC's disappointing results were a serious problem for Eisner. Longtime board member and Disney family member Roy Disney as well as other prominent board members called for him to step down.

National networks like ABC had been declining for a long time. The combined audience share for their nightly news shows continued to dwindle. The main viewership for the nightly news was people over the age of 65. Cable news channels like CNN, Fox, and MSNBC, unlike the national network news, had been advancing. They offered programming around the clock and catered to different political viewpoints, the more extreme the better.

In 2004, Anne Sweeny took over at ABC. She had a history of turning around weak cable channels and revitalizing them.[14] She had helped build the FX cable channel, with racy shows like *Nip/Tuck*. Her first year at ABC was successful largely because of the popular Sunday night hit *Desperate Housewives* about a mythical suburban cul-de-sac called Wisteria Lane where women killed their husbands and had sex with the gardener, among other provocative plotlines.

In the mid-1990s, Disney switched to high-budget action films, many of which flopped. Eisner's ultimate downfall came about because he was unable to extend Disney's relationship with Pixar; Disney's 12-year contract came to an end in 2004. Pixar's relationship with Eisner was strained because of issues of control and money. Largely because of Eisner's inability to renegotiate this contract, the Board forced Eisner to cede the CEO position to Robert Iger in 2005.

The Iger Era

Because Disney's own animation unit was no match for Pixar's creativity and advanced technology, Iger's first priority was to reestablish Disney's ties to Pixar.[15] To bring Pixar back into the fold, he gave up creative control over the company, something that Eisner had not been willing to cede. Pixar brought with it Steve Jobs, who sat on Disney's Board of Directors as its largest shareholder. In 2006, Iger also broke with Miramax's Bob Weinstein and Harvey Weinstein, allowing them to leave the company and form their own studio. Outside of Disney, they were free to create content of their own choosing, even if it was not family friendly.

Iger's leadership style was very different from Eisner's. He gave more control to Disney's veteran managers and credited the company's successes to teamwork. Managing by consensus, and not by fiat, he reached out to people with whom his predecessor had fought. He agreed to broadcast a *Shrek* special that former studio chief Jeffrey Katzenberg, the head of DreamWorks, had made. He also gave dissident shareholders Stanley Gold and Roy Disney new roles in the company, the former as a consultant and the latter continued as a board member.[16] Other decisions he made showed his willingness to make a deal when it was to the mutual advantage of the parties. He agreed to be part of Hulu in 2007 and to work together with NBCUniversal and 21st Century Fox on a streaming service. Hulu started by offering a selection of TV shows, clips, and movies as a free service, while subscribers who paid for the service could access episodes from ABC, Fox, and NBC the day after they had aired.

The AOL-Time Warner Merger

After the 2000 merger, Time Warner had a market value of $290 billion. The company's 1999 earnings of $2.7 billion, including large gains on asset sales, could not support this valuation.[17] Time Warner was under pressure to quickly achieve benefits from its complementary assets. Tactical synergies, such as reduced operating expenses from sharing assets and activities like marketing and IT, were relatively easy. Strategic synergies were hard to generate. The routes to achieving these synergies included these:

- Selling additional products and services to subscribers of the company's magazines, cable networks, and Internet services

- Raising advertising prices after increasing the subscription base

- Promoting creative productions across channels such as print, cable networks, and the Internet

- Delivering content on the Internet in personalized ways

To realize these gains, there had to be cooperation and coordination across the company's many independent business units.

However, a dual reporting structure existed after the acquisition. Jerry Levin from Time Warner was CEO, and Steve Case from AOL was chair. Robert Pittman from AOL was responsible for the networks, cable, magazines, and online delivery and controlled 65 percent of the firm's revenue. Dick Parsons from Time Warner was responsible for TV, movies, and music production and controlled 35 percent of the firm's revenue. In the background was Ted Turner, who was still a board member. The internal struggles among Levin, Pittman, and Turner were fierce, and they soon left the scene or were forced out. Parsons, a lawyer known for his negotiating skills, became CEO.

Parsons did not have the will or the desire to impose a common vision.[18] Time Warner remained a loosely organized coalition. This result was not what Case or Levin had envisioned when they announced the merger. The company had the assets it needed to capitalize on Internet convergence, but it was not able to put them together for increased consumer empowerment and choice. Cross-promotion collided with the need of each of the company's units to generate its own revenue. The individual pieces of the merged company faced their own challenges. Among 25-to-54-year-olds, CNN's audience share was down as much as 40 percent. It was viewed as having second-rate programming, production, and talent in comparison to Fox News.

Time Warner had a history of being contentious and slow moving. AOL added to the problems. Time Warner paid cash bonuses based on the performance of individual business units, whereas AOL's compensation was based on the stock gains of the whole company. Power and status was in the hands of individual units with strong brands. The top management team could ill afford to antagonize the diffuse talent in the ranks because talent was the company's most valuable asset. The CEO and top management team coaxed, urged, and tried to persuade the units they led to change. The challenge was to get these many moving parts to work together. Parsons, a consummate negotiator, was reluctant to directly tell Time Warner's divisions what to do.

Trying to Revive AOL

AOL was the weakest link in Time Warner. Efforts were taken to revive it in the face of the downward spiral in which it was moving. Revenue and profits were declining with the rise of cable Internet. Although AOL was a top U.S. Internet service provider (ISP), it was losing subscriptions to cheaper alternatives, some of which provided basic dial-up service for free. AOL's market share was the largest in the dial-up Internet world, but what value did this hold when the world was moving to broadband cable? AOL also was under investigation by the Securities and Exchange Commission (SEC) for puffing up 2001 and 2002 subscriber numbers. Apparently it did not regularly remove the nonpaying subscribers from its subscription rolls. When it admitted to the problem, its advertising and e-commerce revenues fell.

AOL tried to obtain more revenue per subscriber, introducing a complex fee structure meant to transform itself from a provider of online access to a one-stop shop for movies, music, interactive videogames, phone service, Internet shopping, and more. However, the bundle of services it offered was not attractive to customers. In addition to being hard to sell, it generated billing problems and had technological difficulties.

Time Warner investors wanted the company to divest AOL. As a sop to the critics, the company dropped AOL from its name, calling itself Time Warner only. Steve Case, AOL's founder, remained a board member. He argued that the movement toward a more-connected society could not be halted and that AOL was in a great position to exploit it. People's use of the Internet would keep growing, and AOL was well situated to connect the dots. Advertisers preferred to deal with a single entity, and AOL could lead the charge. However, the cross-divisional coordination and innovation needed to make this vision a reality was not forthcoming.

Although Time Warner had a cable division, broadband was not the same kind of high-margin business as narrowband. The equipment was expensive to install. The monthly charge had to be low enough to attract early adopters. AOL did not have phone lines or cable running into its customers' homes, and Time Warner Cable refused to subsidize AOL relationships with other cable providers, which would have smoothed transition from dial-up Internet provider to high-speed Internet coordinator.

Slimming Down

In 2005, Viacom split into separate units: CBS and Viacom.[19] The broadcasting network CBS was meant for risk-averse investors mainly interested in dividends, whereas the film studio Viacom was for risk-taking investors interested in growth. For customers, the break-up had little meaning other than that each unit could go its own way. At the time, the company's CEO Sumner Redstone declared that the age of media conglomerates was over. Corporate raider Carl Icahn used this reasoning in an attempt to take over Time Warner.[20] The rationale Time Warner provided for its merger with AOL was that it could make the disparate pieces in its business portfolio work together as one company. Books, magazine, movie, and music content would feed television, movie, and Internet distribution outlets. These gains, Icahn maintained, had not been achieved. It was time to split up Time Warner. Icahn, who owned 1.3 percent of the firm's stock, claimed that the separate pieces were worth more than the sum of the parts. An aggressive breakup should be completed as soon as possible.

Time Warner executives continued to defend themselves by referring to the advantages of adjacencies now that it was clear that the strategic synergies for which they had aimed had not been achieved. In 2004, they divested Time Warner's ailing music business. Yet, they admitted openness to options not previously considered, such as selling all or part of AOL or the firm's iconic magazines such as *Time, Sports Illustrated,* and *People,* which had limited growth potential. Parsons, who had the last say, resisted a further breakup, maintaining that the company was stable and durable precisely because of its size. The 87,000 employees that Time Warner had then and its $44 billion in revenues, according to Parsons, provided clout and protection.

Parsons beat back Icahn's challenge, despite support from 6 percent of the company's shareholders for the initiative. By increasing its share buy-back program, the company boosted its market value by about $40 billion or nearly 50 percent, enriching Icahn.[21] When asked about the company, Parsons continued to maintain that vertical integration was an advantage: for example, Warner Bros. made movies, the cable channels acted as wholesalers of content aggregating it in bundles for particular groups of viewers, and cable delivered the product directly to end users.

This theory, to which Parsons was committed, did not prevail under his handpicked successor, Jeff Bewkes, who took over in 2008. Bewkes agreed to AOL's divestiture in 2008, the Time Warner Cable divestiture in 2009, and the divestiture of the legacy magazines including *Time, Fortune,* and *Sports Illustrated* in 2013.

HBO's Edginess and Success

Time Warner's biggest success was HBO, which transformed itself into a premium cable channel and streaming service by producing edgy drama and comedies like *The Sopranos, Sex and the City, The Wire, Entourage, Six Feet Under, Boardwalk Empire, Game of Thrones,* and *True Blood.* Its shows were highly acclaimed and popular. Bewkes had been the division's head and was credited with these successes.

The Sopranos premiered in 1999. With this series, Time Warner first achieved mass critical acclaim. It was the recipient of 111 Emmy nominations during its six-season run. The 12-part miniseries *From the Earth to the Moon* also came out in 1998. Produced by Tom Hanks among others, the show depicted the history of the U.S. space program and won an Emmy for Outstanding Miniseries. HBO followed up with other popular and critically praised miniseries based on historical events. The year 1999 also saw the debut of *Sex and the City* based on the book by Candace Bushnell, which, over its six-season run, broke many TV taboos.

In response to the success of HBO, ESPN, too, was on the lookout for new programming.[22] Two of its original movies did well: *A Season on the Brink*, about college basketball coach Bobby Knight, and *The Junction Boys*, about Alabama football coach Bear Bryant. It then developed a series called *Playmakers*, a drama that included stories about a football player in a crack house, a team doctor who gave shots to players who clearly should not be going back on the field, and players who, when pulled over by police, quickly hid cocaine in the glove compartment. The NFL was upset about the negative impact the show would have on the league's image and threatened that ESPN might not be the winning bidder to carry football the next time around. Likewise, NBA officials were concerned that ESPN was considering a reality show with former basketball player Dennis Rodman, tentatively called "Rodman on the Rebound." Under pressure from the professional sports leagues, ESPN backed down from pursuing the edginess that had resulted in HBO's successes. The two companies pursued different paths and different audiences.

Disney's Dominance

By 2015, Time Warner was a much smaller company than Disney. In most areas, its financial performance also trailed Disney. For example, in the second quarter of 2015, it was behind Disney in quarterly revenue growth, gross margins, and net income (see Exhibit 13.4). That Disney's gross margins were lower than Time Warner's was surprising given that Disney had a labor-intensive and asset-heavy theme parks and resorts division. The competition between Disney and Time Warner was mainly in two areas: cable channels and studio production.

Exhibit 13.4   Disney and Time Warner Financial Performance, 2nd Quarter 2015

	Disney	Time Warner
Market Cap (billions $)	201.96	75.14
Employees	180,000	25,600
Quarterly Revenue Growth (%)	0.07	0.05
Revenue (billions $)	50.71	27.68
Gross Margins (%)	0.45	0.44
Operating Margin (%)	0.24	0.25
Net Income (billions $)	8.03	3.45

Data based on quarterly financial reports

Cable Channels

Time Warner's holdings included HBO, TNT, CNN, and TB, whereas Disney's included ESPN and ABC. In 2015, Disney's market share was 21.3 percent, whereas Time Warner's was 14.3 percent). Although Time Warner's market share was second in the industry to Disney, it had the lowest average annual 2009–2015 revenue growth rate among the major cable channel companies. Like Disney, Time Warner was heavily dependent on cable channels for its profits, yet here too it trailed Disney and the other cable companies in profit growth. Viacom was the leader with a 16.10 percent average annual increase in operating income from 2009–2015, and 21st Century Fox's was second at 14.15 percent.

Neither Time Warner nor Disney was winning the cable wars. Cable industry revenues ($71.5 billion) at best had been stable for the prior half-decade.[23] The segment was mature. Growth had peaked and was projected to decline. Whereas consumers were paying more for upgrades, new channels, and specialized services, advertisers, who were a large source of the segment's revenues, were starting to leave cable for other advertising venues, in particular the Internet. They were leaving because the cable companies were losing subscribers.

Although the losses affected all the cable channels, they were especially great at ESPN.[24] From 2011–2015, ESPN lost 7.2 percent of its subscribers. Only The Weather Channel had more desertions, losing 11.2 percent of its subscribers. Nickelodeon, owned by Viacom, lost 6.1 percent of its subscribers and TNT, TBS, and CNN, owned by Time Warner, lost 6.1 percent, 5.7 percent, and 5.0 percent, respectively. This loss in subscribers led to ESPN cutting costs by letting go of controversial yet high-priced talent like Keith Olbermann, Bill Simmons, and Colin Cowherd.

The Studios

The decline of cable was a blow to Disney, Time Warner, and the other entertainment companies because they depended so much on cable for their growth and profitability. The dependable financial rewards of this outlet allowed them to invest in the risky projects that their movie studios undertook. The business of movie and television program production was very competitive. Returns from movie production, although they could be high, were hard to predict. Diversification into the less risky cable business had been a way for entertainment companies to manage this risk.

With the cable business slowing down, the studios were even more important to Disney and Time Warner. Movies, however, also were a mature to declining industry. The Internet was just the latest factor driving people away from theaters. The trend of declining U.S. movie ticket sales continued in 2014.[25] In that year, they were down 6 percent compared to the previous year. Revenues gained from DVD and media sales also declined, as people increasingly turned to streaming. The margins the studios earned on a streamed movie or TV show were far less than those they earned when people watched a movie in a theater or purchased a DVD.

Technology and marketing costs added to the expense of making movies, while revenues were diminishing. Blockbusters were the key to boosting revenues, but making a blockbuster was very uncertain. Predicting which movies would achieve this status was not a science even with the experience the studios had and the data they collected. Without global sales, it was not possible to justify the costs of making most films. Almost 44 percent of the studios' estimated $31 billion in revenues in 2015 was earned abroad, where people still went to movies.[26]

The studios grappled with mounting production costs and the simultaneous dwindling theater attendance. Their mainstay was action and adventure films, which constituted 46.7 percent of the U.S. market for movies in 2015.[27] Comedies had the second-largest market share at 21.9 percent, and thrillers and suspense films were third at 14.5 percent. Dramas and miscellaneous were the remaining categories of importance. The industry-market-share leader in 2014 was Disney with 21.3 percent of the U.S. market. It was followed by 21st Century Fox with 18.9 percent, NBCUniversal with 14.9 percent, Time Warner with 14.3 percent, and Viacom with 11.6 percent, but these numbers were volatile and changed from year to year.

Internet Initiatives and Cable's Abandonment

Disney and Time Warner developed Internet platforms of their own in response to the movement away from cable and the weakness of their studios: in Disney's case it was Hulu, the partnership with 21st Century Fox and NBCUniversal, which had a subscription price of $7.99 a month. In Time Warner's case the platform was HBO NOW, which had a subscription price of $14.99 a month.

HBO NOW did not require that a customer pay for a traditional connection with a cable company. Previously it had streamed its programming through a service called HBO Go, but access to this service required a traditional, paid TV provider subscription. HBO NOW opened up the same programming to people without cable or satellite TV. HBO and ESPN viewers as well could obtain viewing rights as part of a $20-a-month package from Sling TV. Sling TV provided 20 live cable channels, including HBO, ESPN, AMC, and the Food Network. In comparison to these services, Netflix cost subscribers $8.99 a month and Amazon Prime cost $8.25 a month. Time Warner's CEO Jeffrey Bewkes asserted that the success of HBO NOW was critical and that it would create a blueprint for all companies.[28] All of them would make their programming available on demand with a seamless search interface for viewing on mobile devices. The problem with Bewkes' statement was that it risked prodding even more cable subscribers to cancel their contracts. If traditional cable contracts were considered costly and more consumers were not willing to pay for channels they rarely if ever watched, then Time Warner and Disney would lose revenue.

The viewpoint of Disney CEO Bob Iger therefore seemed to be that the growing preference of viewers seeking greater control over media consumption via digital online platforms was not in the interests of the cable channel companies.[29] In contrast to Bewkes, he defended the role the cable companies played (see Exhibit 13.5). He spoke out against the growing number of consumers who wanted to watch programs on demand via their mobile devices. He asserted that the distributors, whether cable or satellite, were critical in creating value by investing in expensive infrastructure and developing methods for effectively managing necessary customer transactions, such as billing. Iger admitted that without the cable companies, entertainment companies like Disney would have great difficulty in acquiring and maintaining their customers.

Exhibit 13.5 Dollar Value of the Subscriptions of the Major Cable Companies, 2015

Provider	Total Subscriptions (in Millions $)
Comcast	22.38
DirecTV	20.35
DISH Network	13.98
Time Warner Cable	10.79
AT&T	5.94
Verizon	5.65
Charter Communications	4.17
Cablevision	3.12
Suddenlink Communications	1.14
Frontier Communications	0.59
CenturyLink	0.24

Compiled from FCC 14th Video Competition Report. Federal Communications Commission. Jul 20, 2012.

Losing Young People

The cable industry was losing its most valuable customers: young people. More than 21 percent of cable customers were age 65 or older, whereas fewer than 11 percent were in the 18-to-24-year-old age range.[30] Millennials (the 14-to-31-year-old category) were far less attracted to cable than their parents. According to a Deloitte survey, younger millennials (14–25 years old) valued cable less than older millennials (26–31 years old). Many younger millennials had never paid for cable and said that they would refuse to pay for it even when they set up permanent households. These people were called "cord nevers," who ranked broadband Internet service as important, but not cable TV.

There were also the potential "cord cutters." They had cable TV but were dissatisfied and planned to leave cable in favor of the streaming services. Conventional TV viewing, Nielsen found, was declining at a rate of about 10 percent per year.[31] Many viewers wanted slim channel bundles they streamed rather than thick bundles they watched on TV. Many young people did not watch TV at all; rather, they viewed movies or shows on their PCs, tablets, and smartphones.

The typical cable TV viewer watched only 10 or 20 channels. The cost of cable had skyrocketed. People's budgets were stretched because of the slowness of the economic recovery. Cable was a discretionary expenditure. It was not surprising that people dropped or were thinking of dropping their subscriptions. Internet plus cable without streaming generally cost more than $1,000 a year, yet people could get an Internet connection plus a selection of streaming services they most wanted for less money (see Exhibit 13.6).

Exhibit 13.6 Streaming Services and Their 2015 Prices

Streaming Services	2015 Price ($s)
Amazon Prime—TV shows, movies, and original series like Transparent, Alpha House, and Mozart in the Jungle.	99.00
Hulu Plus—TV shows, movies, and original series like A Day in the Life and The Awesomes.	95.88
Netflix—TV shows, movies, and original series like House of Cards, Orange Is the New Black, and BoJack Horseman.	107.88
Sling TV—Live streaming of ESPN, ESPN2, TNT, TBS, the Food Network, HGTV, Travel Channel, Cartoon Network, Adult Swim, Disney Channel, ABC Family, and CNN.	240.00
HBO NOW—Streaming of HBO series.	180.00
PlayStation Vue—Live streaming and playback of local affiliates and cable channels with a basic plan of 50 cable channels, including AMC, CNN, and MTV. Available in select markets.	599.88
CBS All Access—Live and on-demand streaming of CBS shows.	71.88
NFL Game Rewind—Replays of NFL games.	69.99
Choice NBA League Pass—Live streaming of NBA games for five teams.	125.00
MLB.tv—Live streaming and replays of MLB games.	109.99
NHL GameCenter Live—Live streaming and replays of out-of-market NHL games.	99.95

Compiled from Internet websites

Conclusion

People were moving away from cable, the most profitable parts of Disney and Time Warner, and increasingly they expected to obtain their entertainment online. Disney had to connect better with young audiences in households without children that did not want old-fashioned family fare. Time Warner had edgy programming that had the potential to appeal to a young audience, but Netflix and Amazon Prime had the lead in this area, and neither Disney nor Time Warner were first movers. Google and Apple had plans to serve this market. Even if Disney and Time Warner decided to move aggressively, would they be able to catch up?

Endnotes

1. Jim Edwards, "Goodbye, Cable TV: 2.3 Million Americans Have Pulled the Plug Since 2010," *Business Insider.* Feb. 28, 2012. http://www.businessinsider.com/goodbye-cable-tv-23-million-americans-have-pulled-the-plug-since-2010-2012-2.

2. Lauren Gensler, "Netflix Soars on Subscriber Growth," *Forbe.* Jan. 20, 2015. http://www.forbes.com/sites/laurengensler/2015/01/20/netflix-soars-on-subscriber-growth/.

3. Dan Frommer, "Half of US Households Could Have Amazon Prime by 2020," *Quartz.* Feb. 26, 2015. http://qz.com/351726/half-of-us-households-could-have-amazon-prime-by-2020/.

4. Erich Schwartzel and Ben Fritz, "Fewer Americans Go to the Movies," *The Wall Street Journal.* March 25, 2014. http://www.wsj.com/articles/SB10001424052702303949704579461813982237426.

5. Geraldine Fabrikant, "Walt Disney to Acquire ABC in $19 Billion Deal to Build a Giant for Entertainment," *The New York Times.* Aug. 1, 1995. http://www.nytimes.com/1995/08/01/business/media-business-merger-walt-disney-acquire-abc-19-billion-deal-build-giant-for.html; Michael G. Rukstad, David J. Collis, and Tyrell Levine. "Walt Disney Company, The: The Entertainment King." Harvard Business School Case 701-035, March 2001. (Revised January 2009.)

6. Shirley Pelts, "Disney's Cable Networks: Driven by ESPN," *Market Realist.* July 24, 2015. http://marketrealist.com/2015/07/Disneys-Cable-Networks-Driven-Espn/.

7. Mary Barth and Hilary Stockton, "AOL Time Warner." Stanford Graduate School of Business Case A171, February 2000. Stephen P. Bradley and Erin Sullivan. "AOL Time Warner, Inc." Harvard Business School Case 702-421, March 2002. (Revised June 2005.)

8. Carol Loomis, "AOL Time Warner's New Math." *Fortune.* Feb. 4, 2002. http://archive.fortune.com/magazines/fortune/fortune_archive/2002/02/04/317481/index.htm.

9. Marc Gunther and Stephanie N. Mehta, "The Mess at AOL Time Warner." *Fortune.* May 13, 2002. http://archive.fortune.com/magazines/fortune/fortune_archive/2002/05/13/322863/index.htm.

10. Tom Lowry, Ronald Grover, and Catherine Yang. "Dashed Digital Dreams," *Business Week*. July 15, 2002. http://www.bloomberg.com/bw/stories/2002-07-14/dashed-digital-dreams.

11. See Rukstad, Collis and Levine, "The Walt Disney Corporation: The Entertainment King"; Barth and Stockton, "AOL Time Warner"; Bradley and Sullivan, "AOL Time Warner, Inc."

12. Bruce Orwall, "Disney Decides It Must Draw Artists into Computer Age." *The Wall Street Journal*. Oct. 23, 2003. http://www.wsj.com/articles/SB106686389992986500.

13. Marc Gunther, "Has Eisner Lost the Disney Magic?" *Fortune*. Jan. 7, 2002. http://archive.fortune.com/magazines/fortune/fortune_archive/2002/01/07/316039/index.htm; Marc Gunther, "The Wary World of Disney." *Fortune*. Oct. 15, 2001. http://Archive.Fortune.Com/Magazines/Fortune/Fortune_Archive/2001/10/15/311520/Index.Htm.

14. Chuck Salter, "Disney-ABC's: Anne Sweeney Does Her Own Market Research. Really," *Fast Company*. June 6, 2007. http://www.fastcompany.com/678901/disney-abcs-anne-sweeney-does-her-own-market-research-really.

15. Ronald Grover, "How Bob Iger Unchained Disney," *Business Week*. Feb. 5, 2007. http://www.bloomberg.com/bw/stories/2007-02-04/how-bob-iger-unchained-disney; Marc Gunther and Corey Hajim, "The Iger Sanction," Fortune. Jan. 23, 2006. Http://Archive.Fortune.Com/Magazines/Fortune/Fortune_Archive/2006/01/23/8366987/Index.Htm.

16. Bruce Orwall, "Roy Disney Quits Company Board and Calls on Eisner to Resign, Too," *The Wall Street Journal*. Dec. 1, 2003. http://www.wsj.com/articles/SB107022298535883000.

17. Stephanie N. Mehta and Marc Gunther, "Dick Parsons' Make or Break Year," *Fortune*. Feb. 3, 2003. http://archive.fortune.com/magazines/fortune/fortune_archive/2003/02/03/336457/index.htm; Martin Peers, "Time Warner's Quarterly New Jumps," *The Wall Street Journal*. Oct. 23, 2003. http://www.wsj.com/articles/SB106667894539321400.

18. Matthew Karnitschnig, "Defending Time Warner," *The Wall Street Journal*. Feb. 17, 2006. http://www.wsj.com/articles/SB114014362463776608.

19. Joe Flint, "Viacom to Split, Create 2 Companies," *The Wall Street Journal*. June 15, 2005. http://www.wsj.com/articles/SB111877911609259421.

20. Matthew Karnitschnig, "Icahn Report Makes His Case for Breaking Up Time Warner," *The Wall Street Journal*. Feb. 9, 2006: 19.

21. Matthew Karnitschnig, "Icahn Ends Effort to Take Control of Time Warner," The *Wall Street Journal*. Feb. 17, 2006. http://www.wsj.com/articles/SB114010945965176010.

22. Joe Flint, "ESPN's Risky New Game Plan: Relying Less on Pro Sports," *The Wall Street Journal*. Oct. 24, 2003. http://www.wsj.com/articles/SB106694517446756600.

23. Amadou Diallo, "Cable TV Model Not Just Unpopular But Unsustainable," *Forbes*. Oct. 14, 2013. http://www.forbes.com/sites/amadoudiallo/2013/10/14/cable-tv-price-hikes-unsustainable/.

24. Shalini Ramachandran and Joe Flint, "ESPN Tightens Its Belt As Pressure on It Mounts," *The Wall Street Journal*. July 9, 2015. http://www.wsj.com/articles/espn-tightens-its-belt-as-pressure-on-it-mounts-1436485852.

25. Anthony D'Alessandro, "2014 Box Office Final: Admissions Lowest Since 1995; Studio Marketshare," *Deadline Hollywood*. Jan. 5, 2015. http://deadline.com/2015/01/2014-box-office-hollywood-studios-20th-century-fox-admissions-1201338183/.

26. Nick Petrillo, "Movie & Video Production in the US—Industry Market Research Report," Ibisworld Industry Report 51211a, March 2015.

27. Ibid.

28. Keach Hagey, "Behind Time Warner Chief's 'Cord-Cutter' Pitch," *The Wall Street Journal*. April 12, 2015. http://www.wsj.com/articles/behind-time-warner-ceo-jeff-bewkess-cord-cutter-pitch-1428870356.

29. Emily Steel and Sydney Ember, "Networks Fret as Ad Dollars Flow to Digital Media," *The New York Times*. May 10, 2015. http://www.nytimes.com/2015/05/11/business/media/networks-fret-as-ad-dollars-flow-to-digital-media.html.

30. "Survey Shows That Cable May Be Dying a Slow Death," *The Motley Fool* n.d. http://www.fool.com/investing/general/2015/05/09/survey-shows-that-cable-may-be-dying-a-slow-death.aspx?source=iedfolrf0000001.

31. Victor Luckerson, "Fewer People Than Ever Are Watching TV," *Time*. Dec. 3, 2014. http://time.com/3615387/tv-viewership-declining-nielsen/.

Final Thoughts

The Future of Technology Management and the Business Environment: Lessons on Innovation, Disruption, and Strategy Execution

This book has explored the potential of information technology (IT), medical technologies, genetics, alternative energy, and other technologies as engines of growth and fulfilling employment. It has explored the potential of these technologies as well as the routes to their implementation. It has revealed obstacles to commercialization these innovations face that must be managed by business firms, other organizations, and society.

From a commercial point of view, let alone a scientific and technical point of view, the success of innovations, no matter how promising, is not guaranteed. Their introduction involves risky and uncertain decision making. As an unintended by-product of their introduction, these technologies can and do create harm as well as good. This harm must be anticipated and prevented to the degree possible without compromising society's willingness to take risks and make progress.

New technologies offer tremendous potential for dealing with the most important societal challenges of this era. This era is characterized by divisions between young and old, between rich and poor, and between energy scarcity and abundance. Technologies can address these issues constructively. They can play a role in easing these tensions, but they also can exacerbate them.

This book has revealed the foresight and strategic actions that are needed for technologies to play a positive rather than a negative role. It has covered the pathways that have been taken to commercialize some of these technologies, how some of these pathways have been blocked, and how some of them have been opened. It has discussed the disruptions that organizations have faced as a result of technological innovations they did not expect and how they have dealt with these disruptions by altering their business strategies and executing novel approaches.

This book has depicted the stories of many companies and how they have confronted these issues. The purpose has been to learn lessons from these companies' experiences. The juxtaposition of the material found in this book has been designed to generate new insights. Reflection on the material will yield you takeaway lessons on innovation, disruption, strategy execution, technology management, and the business environment.

Index